OTHER VOICES of GNOSTICISM

Also Available from Bardic Press

Voices of Gnosticism
Miguel Conner

*The Gnostic: A Journal of Gnosticism, Western Esotericism
and Spirituality 1 – 6*

Spirit Possession and the Origins of Christianity
Stevan Davies

Revolt of the Widows
Stevan Davies

The Gospel of Thomas and Christian Wisdom
Stevan Davies

My Dear Father Gurdjieff
Nikolai de Stjernvall

New Nightingale, New Rose: Poems From the Divan of Hafiz
Richard Le Gallienne

*The Quatrains of Omar Khayyam:
Three Translations of the Rubaiyat*
Edward Fitzgerald, Justin McCarthy and Richard Le Gallienne

Door of the Beloved: Ghazals of Hafiz
Justin McCarthy

The Four Branches of the Mabinogi
Will Parker

Songs of Sorrow and Joy
Lala Ashford-Brown

Visit our website at www.bardicpress.com
email us at andrew@bardicpress.com

OTHER VOICES of GNOSTICISM

Miguel Conner

interviewing

Tobias Churton • Nicola Denzey-Lewis
Richard Smoley • Gary Lachman
Stephan Hoeller • David Brakke
Robert Price • Eric G. Wilson
Nathaniel Deutsch • Sean Martin
Erik Davis • Daniel C. Matt
Willis Barnstone • Ismo Dunderberg

Foreword by Andrew Phillip Smith

Bardic Press
Dublin

Cover image Abraxas by Tessa Finn
Printed on acid-free paper

Published by Bardic Press
71 Kenilworth Road
Dublin 6W
Ireland

http://www.bardicpress.com
info@bardicpress.com

ISBN 978-1-906834-30-2

CONTENTS

Other voices have whispered to us in the place where echoes meet.

Anonymous

Dedicated to my brother. When this book was first conceived, he departed this world. Both are now eternal. You will never fade for me, Sean.

As with the first book, *Voices of Gnosticism*, I am extremely grateful to all the guests who contributed their wisdom and time to appear on *Aeon Byte Gnostic Radio*. In fact, I would like to thank every guest of every show ever produced, and every content creator in the fields of Western Esotericism. It's hard work that you do, often thankless in world still ruled by orthodoxy. There are many, though, who are waking due to your Gnosis.

Also, much appreciation to Andrew Phillip Smith, who resurrected this book when it was floundering in the sublunar realms of "I'll get to it," and, as with the first book, breathed so much Spirit into it.

Lastly, I would like to thank my family for their continued patience—as well as those who assisted in transcribing interviews and supported this book via our Indiegogo campaign. Like Iscariot in the *Gospel of Judas*, you are stars (but in higher Aeons).

Patrons:

Erik Davis
Spence Fothergill
Ricardo Bianca de Mello
Rebecca Barham
Sid Sowers
Agustin Reyes
Rhea L. Sewell
Myles Gisel
Rane Bowen
Paul Hillman
E. Carlson
Richard Spelker
Glenn Ball

Frances Prevas
Raymond McKenzie
Zoei Ingersoll
Leslie Russo
Lance Leeson
Steven Ellis
Christopher Lyons
Andrea Ilytch
Tammy Ornelas
Michael Hagan
Samuel Newman
Mary Pauli
Amber Geislinger

Transcribers:

Chris Henley

FOREWORD

Voices of Gnosticism presented a wide range of scholars' viewpoints in an informal accessible mode. Every interviewee in the first volume was an academic expert in Gnosticism, early Christianity or a related field. The decision to only include academic scholars was my contribution as editor to the shape of the book. Miguel's shockjock gnosis and caffeinated style combined with his deep understanding and careful examination of the material to produce a uniquely approachable presentation of up to date scholarship.

My own definition of Gnosticism is a jokey "Stuff like what the ancient Gnostics used to do." Few of the scholars and experts here are inclined to come up with some arbitrary definition, I suspect. The Gnosticism of *Other Voices* is a broad canon that incorporates the Nag Hammadi library, Hermetism, the Cathars, the Mandaeans, Blake, Jung and Dick and more besides.

However, some felt that the focus of the first volume was too limited. Miguel Conner has interviewed a very wide range of people over the years of his podcast *Aeon Byte* and its predecessor, *Coffee, Cigarettes and Gnosis*. Not everyone who is interested in Gnosticism has a deep concern with historical-critical matters.

Thus in *Other Voices of Gnosticism* we have a much broader mix of scholars and writers of Gnosticism. To be sure, the academics are still present, yet the center of gravity has shifted. Of those who are included here, Nicola Denzey-Lewis is an excellent case in point: she is very much an academic scholar, yet her sympathy to modern spirituality and her love of the material offer a doorway to those who would approach Gnosticism from a more personal point of view. Likewise we have interviewees such as Richard Smoley or Gary Lachman or Sean Martin, who are primarily writers and not academics but who accurately represent historical issues or, we have in Tobias Churton a writer who has also lectured on esotericism at the University of Exeter and in Robert M. Price another figure who straddles the boundaries of the academic and the creative. In others we see an enthusiasm or sympathy for a particular subject, or an approach to the subject, such as Erik G. Wilson's examination of William Blake and creativity, that takes us beyond the narrower bands of traditional academic work. With Willis Barnstone we come at Gnosticism from the perspective of a genuine litterateur. Stephan Hoeller is a bona fide Gnostic bishop who has also lectured extensively and knew well many of the prominent scholars involved with the resurgence of academic study on the subject. For some Gnosticism is a coherent field of study, for others a category that is outmoded or which requires a new approach; other prefer to speak of a Gnostic legacy or a Gnostic philosophy. My own view of Gnosticism has benefited from my time spent with each of these interviews.

All of the above makes the book sound like a very deliberate and methodical selection by commitee, but in truth this volume is very much based on Miguel's own intuitive understanding of knowing which faces fit. There were many additional interviews that had to be excluded due to length or not quite blending with the themes in the book.

Although this volume is characterized by its wide variety of topics and experts, the "other voice" in a further sense is Miguel's own bass rumble. His immersion in both the scholarship and the Gnostic worldview is what allows the interviewees to speak. His language may be spiced with impromptu metaphors and peppered with pop culture allusions, but it is the unobtrusive deftness of his questions that brings out the best in these scholars and writers.

The themes that emerge here are of the value of scholarship in orienting oneself in a personal investigation of our Gnostic heritage; of a wider view of Gnosticism than that of just the ancient Gnostics and the Nag Hammadi library; of the connection of Gnosticism with a broader category of esotericism; of a pushing forward and exploration while remaining within a tradition. I hope that seekers and students alike will benefit from hearing these Other Voices of Gnosticism.

INTRODUCTION

Mark Twain is alleged to have said, "History doesn't repeat itself but it often rhymes."

One could make a strong case that the history of orthodoxy—the mainstream victor chiseling the hard stone tablets of cultural norms—is repetitive. Painfully repetitive. Yet one could also say that the history of the western esoteric tradition, specifically the Gnostic impulse, is a fluid and dynamic rhyme, an echoing melody that has deeply informed both artist and mystic for almost 2000 years.

This alternative history is what *Other Voices of Gnosticism* seeks to present. *Voices of Gnosticism* focused on the muffled explosion of the Gnostics during early Christian times. The sequel expands its voice outward and forward into European chronicles.

It is my hope that you, adventurous reader, will find a deeper understanding of the poetry of this ancient heresy known as Gnosticism. The pages here, transcriptions from years of interviews, first provide a summary of the ancient Gnostics. They also cover movements overlooked in the first book such as the Mandaeans, the last remaining Gnostic sect from antiquity that are today sadly facing extinction because of repeated war. Unlike the first book, attention will be given to Gnostic exemplars like Paul of Tarsus, Hermes Trismegistus and John the Baptist—in all their fiction and fact. Yet as with the first book, in the hope of drawing a more complete picture (if not song), we will involve traditions that are parallel but just as incendiary like Hermeticism and Kabbalah.

Further along this historical journey, this choir of the voices of Gnosticism will aver how the underground stream of the Gnostics flowed across the Common Era—from the rise and fall of the Cathars to the visionary cosmologies of William Blake, from the machinations of the serpent Sethians to the popcorn apocalypses of Philip K. Dick. And more.

As with the first book, *Other Voices of Gnosticism* provides the keen insights of acclaimed academics deeply involved in Gnostic history. Some of these include David Brakke, Robert M. Price and Nicola Denzey Lewis (whose alternative theory on the why the Nag Hammadi library was buried caused quite a stir).

The main difference in this work, though, is that you will find the views of nonacademic but lauded researchers—many who have spent their lives mining the Gnostic ethos for a modern meaning; some of these have looked beyond the printed word towards film. You could call it an esoteric British invasion that includes Tobias Churton, Sean Martin, and even Gary Lachman (who these days makes his home in London and is an acolyte of Colin Wilson) and Sean Martin. Some of the guests are just as scholarly as the academics in the first book, even those who translated the Nag Hammadi library, inasmuch as their contribution to Gnostic research. Two chief examples would be Erik Davis, an editor of Philip K. Dick's *Exegesis* and Stephan Hoeller, a force in the publication of Carl Jung's *The Red Book*.

The range of guests presented in this work are, in my view, ideal in this next stage of deciphering the voices of the Gnostics. I feel you will find a coherent flow of data from a movement never truly allowed to evolve beyond secret societies, heresy hunter meltdowns, or from being attached like a lamprey to the underside of mainstream religions. The great Theosophist G. R. S. Mead in the 20th century summarized the Gnostics appropriately by the title of his book on them, *Fragments of a Faith Forgotten*. That is no longer the case, thanks in part to the work of the guests from both *Voices of Gnosticism* books.

The feedback from *Voices of Gnosticism* has been generally very positive. Many said the book presented a coherent understanding the Gnostics, as well as their relation to early Christianity, Classic Judaism and late Greco-Roman cults. In my view, the purpose of the book pairs well with what William T. Vollman wrote in a piece in *The New York Times*:

"As a corpus, the scriptures are nearly incoherent, like a crowd of sages, mystics and madmen all speaking at once. But they always call upon us to know ourselves."

If I get my wish, *Other Voices of Gnosticism* will inch you closer to knowing yourself. If anything, it will at least grant you a clearer historical picture of the Gnostics and other western esoteric traditions. They may have not been allowed to write history but at least left a helluva note, if you listen carefully.

Will there be a third *Voices of Gnosticism*? Perhaps. However, it's obvious what the theme will be when and if it is published: We live in Gnostic times. Alternatively, as English science fiction novelist, Michael Moorcock said: "We live in a Philip K. Dick world."

I'm getting ahead of myself, though.

THE QUEST
FOR THE HISTORICAL
GNOSTICS

NICOLA DENZEY LEWIS

Nicola Denzey Lewis is Professor of Religious Studies at Brown University, as well as author of *Introduction to "Gnosticism": Ancient Voices, Christian Worlds*.

Nicola Denzey Lewis is part of the new generation of groundbreaking American Gnostic scholars, along with David Brakke, Dylan Burns, and April DeConick. They may have not participated in the translating of the Nag Hammadi library in the 70s, but they are finding deeper strata of Gnostic theology and philosophy. Nicola studied under Elaine Pagels at Yale, so it seems any torch that may have been passed is in good hands.

The interview centered on her book, *Introduction to "Gnosticism": Ancient Voices, Christian Worlds*. The work is basically a textbook, replete with comparison charts on Gnostic history and their texts that simplify the often confusing and overlapping Nag Hammadi corpus. In addition, her book provides the latest theories on the classic Gnostics—such as an alternative reason the Nag Hammadi library was buried, or the political anarchism of groups like the Sethians. Nicola's expertize (and passion) is in ancient Roman culture, therefore granting her the ability to place the classic Gnostic culture within the context of the surrounding, visceral world—in a way that could perhaps make Hans Jonas or Edward Gibbon slightly envious.

As with the interview with David Brakke, we dealt with somewhat controversial notion of Gnosticism as a viable term. Since Nicola placed the word Gnosticism in parenthesis in her book, one wonders if the term has a place in future generations of Gnostic scholars.

MC: As you mention in your book, Gnosticism is a movement that people might find interesting, exposed to it perhaps through pop culture, literature, or education; yet when they finally open these so-called Gnostic texts they're often perplexed at the seeming weirdness. What approaches did you take in your book, or in your classes, to make Gnosticism more approachable and less like a sixties psychedelic sci-fi movie?

NDL: I think that's a great and hilarious question because I happen to be really partial to sixties psychedelic sci-fi movies. I think the weirdness, the strangeness, of those texts is part of their beauty. I think it makes them more compelling and you can use it to spark students' curiosity. Find the part in us that's curious, that wants to know how, then you're already part of the way there to engaging them. I'm a scholar of religious studies and one of the dictums that we use in Religious Studies is to make the familiar strange and the strange familiar. I take that seriously, when I'm planning out courses in Gnosticism, to try to see how I can do that. How can I make these strange texts familiar to them, but how can I also start with what's familiar to the already, and make that strange, to lessen the distance between them. In my experience the stuff that people now, that's familiar, tends to be either pop culture or the Bible, or if you're lucky both. So let's say in the case of the Bible, before we try to make sense of the Gnostic texts like *Hypostasis of the Archons*, we go back to Genesis.

Actually, we did this in my class yesterday. And we read Genesis 1, and we go all the way through from the stories of the creation right up to Cain and Abel. And we take turns reading it aloud and after we've done that, for what is a familiar text to people in the class to varying degrees, we go back and I ask them questions about it, and interrogate the text a little bit differently than they're accustomed to. I ask them to find places in Genesis 1 and 2 which don't really make sense. And we can actually do this pretty easily. So there are questions like, why are there two different accounts of the creation of humankind? Or, why doesn't God know where Adam is in the garden? He's omnipotent and omniscient, so why can't hear Adam walking round in the garden, and he calls, "Adam? Where are you?"

Or the more troubling questions, such as, did God set up Adam? Or why does he create this tree and tell them they can't eat of this fruit of the tree, when presumably we know that they're going to do that. Why does God lie? He says on the day they eat that fruit they will die, but they don't die on that day. And the serpent is the one who tells the truth and points this out. So there are a lot of troubling questions that come out of Genesis which, even though it's a familiar text, they start thinking that way, they start thinking that this familiar thing is really very strange. Once we're there we can go back to *Hypostasis of the Archons* and say, this text was motivated by people reading Genesis and asking the exact same questions. Why does God say, "Let us create humankind in our image"? Why does he use the plural? And a text like that looks so strange because it's really a very earnest, intellectual attempt to give a sense of the strangeness of the sacred text. So we can bridge the divide in trying to make the familiar strange and the strange familiar.

MC: You mention pop culture and art. What references do you give your students to give a better perspective on Gnosticism?

NDL: I use movies all the time, from *The Matrix* to *Inception* to *Stigmata*. I show these in the very first class when I talk about the Gnostic myth (according to Hans Jonas). It's in the book as well. I go through that material, what that Gnostic myth looks like, and when we've gotten just a bit of the way through it, generally people say, "Hey! *The Matrix*! That sounds like *The Matrix*!" It happens invariably. It's a great pop culture reference. Everyone's seen this movie and is familiar with it. All of a sudden they realise that they know this story. They've heard this story before. *The Matrix* comes up a lot. Movies are still being turned out all the time that have Gnostic themes in them, and the students are much more likely to be familiar with a film like *Inception* or *Shutter Island*, or something like, that than they are with the texts. So we use that a lot. Movies like *Stigmata* are actually quoting the texts. I use the *Gospel of Thomas* a fair bit. I use music. I played Current 93's *Thunder Perfect Mind* yesterday. David Tibet is a very learned Coptologist. Stephen Emmel who is a very respected scholar of Gnosticism, played guitar with Current 93. So there we are right in the interstitial world between academia and music and they're producing all kinds of amazing sound poems. There's Jordan Scott's *Thunder Perfect Mind* Prada commercial. Anything we can find out there that has tie-ins is very useful.

MC: Didn't Tori Amos actually write music based on the *Apocryphon of John*?

NDL: Yes, exactly. *Thunder Perfect Mind* has been particularly inspiring to people because it's such an extraordinary poem.

MC: For example, if you're talking about the *Gospel of Judas* it's always very easy to lean back on *The Last Temptation of Christ*. That story is already there.

NDL: *Godspell* a little bit, *Jesus Christ Superstar*, really play with the figure of Judas. *The Last Temptation of Christ* is fabulous for that.

MC: Central to Gnosticism is Gnosis. How do you describe this experience to your students and other people.

NDL: That's a great question too. I can't teach Gnosis. I can teach Gnosticism, teach about this historical movement. I have to really teach around Gnosis as something which is an experience they may or may not be able to understand or identify with. We talk about different types of spiritual experience and enlightenment: what that looks like in other religious traditions. Again, I can't attack that directly. I can't teach that. But, again, as in *The Matrix*, what does it mean to have knowledge that profoundly changes your understanding of who you are, and what your role is in this world. Some students get it on an intuitive level and other students don't, but they do understand it intellectually. I think it's fundamental to human experience.

I do a lot of yoga these days and my yoga teacher at the end of class always turns around and says, "The light inside me honors and recognises the light in each and every one of you." It's a standard yoga thing and I remember it from my studies on Hinduism. It's this idea that everyone has within them an inner light, and you can recognise that. It makes me think that years ago I was actually in a Hare Krishna temple and interviewing a devotee and he turned around and said this very thing to me, "The Krishna inside me sees and honors the Krishna inside you," and I remember just being very struck at that moment not only by his sincerity but by the way in which his sincerity ignited something in me. It was like he really recognised this inner light in me and I thought for a moment, I'm there, and I see that and acknowledge that in that person. I was surprised by that encounter and struck by it. It's little moments like that, something very small, where students have their own experiences, and they can think, "Oh, that's a part of what this Gnosis thing seems to be about."

MC: I think Elaine Pagels often called it an "aha" moment, when you have an insight into yourself and the world. Nothing like the road to Damascus or Buddha and the tree. It's more of a process.

NDL: And it can be small and half profound consequences, or it doesn't have to have profound consequences to affect something, to change that experience of that hour or that day.

MC: And do you find Gnosis, versus other traditions like enlightenment or salvation or satori, to be a little bit more intellectual, where you have this moment and you have to philosophise, in the ancient context, to understand the world? Like Neo in *The Matrix*, he had to go out there and see the world and gain as much mental knowledge as he could.

NDL: No, I don't actually see it as connected very much to any kind of intellectual systems, and so on. I think that, as I understand it anyway, that moment of Gnosis is transcendent and doesn't need to be the product of the intellect. Certainly not in the tradition of Socrates, because we only have certain tools and faculties for being able to articulate that experience, to teach it and speak about it we have to use words, we have to use systems and analogies and so on. I think that's where it comes in, in this second order work that we do to process something which is not inherently that.

MC: Nicola, the term Gnosticism itself has been questioned in the last few decades by such scholars as Michael Williams and Karen King, even to the point of proposing that the term be discarded. But other scholars, including Birger Pearson and Marvin Meyer, contend it is a valid and useful term. What position do you take, or how do you approach this, being stuck on one side or the other or the middle?

NDL: I think my sympathies are pretty squarely aligned with Michael Williams and Karen King on this. I consider them senior colleagues and friends and people from whom I've learned a great deal. As I understand it, in the school in which I've been trained, I really think of Gnosticism as something we have to be very careful with as a term. Which is why, after much humming and hahing, we put Gnosticism in scare quotes for the title of this book. I didn't want to have Gnosticism on there at all, I just wanted to say something about Nag Hammadi. Because I don't treat every so-called Gnostic text, I'm really looking specifically at the Nag Hammadi corpus, because no other book does that. It's such a complex world, I think that's where people need the most help. But my editor said no, we really need to put Gnosticism in there so that people will no what it is because most people don't know what Nag Hammadi is, so let's throw in Gnosticism. That is true to how I think about what this thing we call Gnosticism looks like in the ancient world. Way back when I was writing my dissertation under Elaine Pagels she challenged me to write my dissertation, which was on Gnosticism, without using the word Gnosticism. She did not allow me to use it. It was very challenging. I asked her, "If I don't say 'this Gnostic movement', what can I say?" And she said, "Well, was this person Christian?" "Well, yes, it appears so." "Well then, call them Christian. Call her a Christian. Don't call them Gnostic." Then it was a great exercise. It was very frustrating, but an important one, I think, to sit there and go over the texts and say, is this term one we are using for convenience, or really accurate and representative, and what are we doing when we insist on calling Valentinus a Christian instead of a Gnostic, or even a Gnostic Christian?

I think the problem of Gnosticism is that as a term it artificially unites things, but also divides it. It unites things artificially by calling various movements, inclinations, texts, experiences, myths all the same thing. It puts them all in the same rubric. And it divides by separating them from Christianity. And I do think that if we had asked Valentinus he would have called himself a Christian. If he had called himself a Gnostic, as some Christians did, for instance Clement of Alexandria, I don't think he would have seen that as being a separate thing from being Christian. Part of the consequences of that too is that we end of with Christianity as something looking more orthodox than it really actually was. It keeps it as a movement that looks a lot more like modern Christianity, maybe, or more like something that many Christians would like to see it removed from, separate from the taint of Gnosticism. I'm an historian of the ancient world.

MC: Certainly, Morton Smith said in a lecture that Gnosticism wasn't a good term, but we're stuck with it. You were sort of stuck with it in the book. You've just got to use it or else nobody will have noticed.

NDL: It is very tricky, and it's really hard to go without it. I slip up all the time, because it's useful. But I have less of a problem talking about Gnostics than Gnosticism. When push comes to shove I would say that no such thing as Christianity existed in the first four centuries, maybe even five centuries. It's not that you can say that Gnosticism didn't exist but Christianity did. It can keep us from seeing the tremendous diversity of religious experience in the ancient world.

MC: Would you agree with Bentley Layton and David Brakke that it is at least sensible to say that the Sethians were the Gnostics? The artists formerly known as the Gnostics as we call them?

NDL: I haven't been completely sold over. I think tremendously highly of both those scholars. I use them both in teaching. David Brakke's book is something I have students read as well. There appear to have been Sethians running around and no, they weren't calling themselves Sethians and we don't have any indication that they were. I'm not sure whether they called themselves Gnostics but they are a cohesive group with a cohesive doctrine unlike, say, the Valentinians who had a group identity instead of texts. So if you want to call them Gnostics, I'm good with that, I'm comfortable with that.

MC: On a side note, even the Manichaeans called themselves Christians for the most part. That's a term that was given to them, like Valentinians and all the others. They might be going, "What are you calling me?"

NDL: We put a lot of time and energy into categorisation. We have to realise that we are the ones who create these categories. They may or may not work for us. We see that very clearly in the study of Gnosticism where not only do we have this thing called Gnosticism, but we have these groups that we have more or less created like Sethianism or Valentinianism, and we don't know what to do when the texts we use don't sit very nicely into those rubrics. And that happens all the time. It should really lead us to question our categories, and sometimes it does and sometimes it doesn't.

MC: Another roadblock to "Gnosticism", and you do address this in your book, is that on the surface many of the texts seem downright hostile to Jewish scripture. Some have even called them anti-Semitic. I'm sure some of your students when they're reading them, their faces must light up or cringe in terror. How do you deal with this issue?

NDL: I actually wish that more students would be horrified by these aspects of the text. In general I'll have one or two who will go, "Hey, this is terrible!" and that's a good thing. I don't feel that I have to be an apologist for these texts. They are what they are. They are ancient texts. They don't come out of our culture. They have very different sensibilities. They have very different ways of thinking about rape, about whoredom, all these terms that are very loaded for us. They had social systems that were heavily dependent on slavery. And these are there in some of the texts, in a way that should trouble us contemporary modern readers, but also in a way that we understand that that was what the ancient world was like. And these were times where tempers were running high, or fevers were running high, where people were engaged in very protracted battles about identity, and what it meant to be part of a community that pitches itself against another community. We can't even get a sense of what was at stake with some of those things. But it's there.

One of the only things I can do with, say, the anti-Semitism of those texts is to go back to the writings of the New Testament. I'm teaching another class with the contextual history and we get to look at a lot of those texts, which led to a lot of the the anti-Semitic productions of the last 2000 years. Let's call it a tradition. There is a lot of anti-Semitism in the Gospel of John. It saturates it. There's not a lot of anti-Semitism in the Gospel of Matthew but in the one line, in the blood libel line towards the end of the passion, when the Jews say that they're going to take on the guilt of putting Jesus to death, not just for themselves but for their children. Those are blood-curdling moments. Those are terrible moments when Jesus turns and tells the Jews that Satan is their father. Awful! And they're central to the New Testament and formative Christianity. So we have to deal with these painful moments in the New Testament as much as we do in Gnosticism.

MC: Even Paul talks about how angels brought the Torah to Moses and there was a veil over his eyes. Don't you think the Gnostics, like Paul might have been, were trying to make sense of these Jewish scripture, reinterpreting them or, as you say, when you were trying to make your students read Genesis they were filling in the gaps?

NDL: I think they were definitely trying to fill in the gaps. When they're exegeting Genesis I don't see it as protest exegesis. I don't see it as simply inverting the values of the Hebrew Bible and making Yahweh into nothing but an evil demon. I don't really read it that way. I read it as people who have a very deep Greco-Roman education. They know their Plato and what Plato says about happening at the very beginning of creation is very different to what Genesis talks about, then they're trying to reconcile these pictures. As they understand it God has to be only good, so he's behaving in a way that seems not to be good, then the only solution can be that that's not God. So there has to be another God. And I don't think it's so much a castigation of Judaism, but as a way of preserving Genesis as a text which is sacred, which is true. It's only true if you read it in a certain way. I don't see that as inherently against anything.

MC: It's a fact that, as you said, by the time Jews became Hellenized, it was very common to break up god into different things and make his underlings do all the work, and God just stood there and let Metatron or Michael do all the dirty work.

NDL: A lot of work has been done in theology to do with encounters of Greek ideas of divinity. You find that God becomes a more and more distant, abstract figure. That is a very authentic, a very Jewish way of understanding God, not just Yahweh who walks around in the garden but also that Yahweh couldn't possibly walk around in the garden. They're both Jewish ideas.

MC: There was a book that came out on *Thunder Perfect Mind*, written by several different scholars. They talked about how the Gnostics really enjoyed parody and satire, and in your book you show that most ancient writers really loved puns. Do you see the Gnostics using satire at all in their work, or do you think they were taking it really seriously?

NDL: That's a great question. They're definitely using puns. One of the things that has fascinated me in the ancient world is can you detect humour in a text that doesn't seem to be funny? I don't know. What we were reading in class yesterday, *Hypostasis of the Archons*, one of my students is a religious studies major but also he does a lot of dramatic art things, he came in so excited, and he said, "I am going to do a puppet show." So he's off working on his puppet show now and what he said that really inspired him was that scene with the archons huffing and puffing and blowing at Adam and Adam just lies there. Karen King has a wonderful article where she talks about ideas of masculinity and caricature and so on in this text. She points out how funny this is to readers, to have these archons huffing and puffing in a way that's futile. So my student is actually acting this out with the puppets huffing and puffing, but Adam is a real human being in the puppet show. So he just felt that the idea of the puppets trying to blow the breath that puppets don't have into a real living human being who is lying there on the ground is so funny and ironic. So, I think that there are moments there that are very wry.

MC: As you mention in your book, some of it might be horrific to us, like the archons having such a high libido even though they're androgynous, that they go around raping people, but like you said, in the

Roman Empire that was so commonplace, it was something they had to deal with.

NDL: In the stories from Greek mythology gods were coming down and having sex with human women and creating these demi-gods; and the women don't really have much of a choice in it. It was very much part of the landscape for them.

MC: What about the origins of Gnosticism, which has been debated since early Christian times. What do you think are the origins, or what are the more sensible theories out there? It seems you like to take the John turner model of the dissatisfied Jews who went Christian and then later got kicked out of church and became sort of neoplatonic Gnostics.

NDL: I think I'm with John Turner on this. I think he possibly really is correct in this reconstruction. I'm a historian. I look at these texts within the broad context of the Roman Empire, and it seems to me any kind of search for Gnosticism's origins earlier than the second century doesn't make an awful lot of sense to me. I really see the majority of the texts we have as very second century texts. I think the second century of the Roman Empire is a kind of time of religious innovation where people become very interested in individual religious movements and individual salvation, and independent religious entrepreneurs who come passing through the countryside peddling various religious commodities: different groups, different cults, things that people could join in and participate. And that's a very different landscape to first century Rome, which was more focused around a specific cult. So in the second century people are interested in all these things, it's a wave of orientalizing, interest in esoteric traditions of the East, Mithras and Osiris and Isis and Serapis, interest in mystery religions and mystery cults, and I think in that environment, cities like Rome, Edessa, and Alexandria were a crucible for a whole range of religious speculation; and I see those texts as coming out of moments like that when people are free to be experimental, because there are no laws out there on what it looks like to be Christian, what Christianity is, even what Judaism is—we used to think we had a much better idea of what Judaism was than we're prepared to admit now—it looked different in different places at different times.

There really was no normative Judaism, there wasn't a normative Christianity, in the second century. So people are picking and choosing and they're running these experiments, how to conduct ritual and when and where.

It's all very up in the air, and that's why I'm fascinated with that century. I've done an awful lot of work on it and it took a couple of hundred of years for people to work through that, and I think what we do see is these Gnostic groups situating themselves within these different Christian communities and at some point no longer being either welcome there, or finding themselves sympathetic to the way certain Christian groups turned. And I think this can happen even within the so-called Gnostic Christian groups as well. The people who Plotinus knows, these ones we may call Sethians, or we maybe called them Gnostics, I don't think they see themselves as Christians. They do see themselves as Platonists. They're more or less free-floating, they've moved in that direction as a group. I think whoever wrote the *Gospel of Judas*, which is such a bizarre text, my pet theory on that is that it's by somebody who was in a Sethian group and then figured that the Sethians had gotten it wrong and broke away from Sethianism. So not only is it not as simple as the Sethians having broken away from Christianity, but someone has broken away from what was already a splinter movement.

MC: And as you point out in your book, and this might surprise a lot of people, the *Gospel of Judas* has not been fully reconstructed yet. So there's still a lot to be left in the debate of whether Judas was a villain as per April DeConick, or whether Judas was a hero, with Marvin Meyer, and then everybody trying to figure out who Judas was.

NDL: That was a great moment. That was funny. It's such a great example of scholarly hubris in a way, because everybody was so excited that we'd gotten this text, so we've got it, let's go at it and publish critical editions and put it out there, and we had it really incomplete. An I think what happened is we're used to having incomplete fragments and it doesn't throw us too much. But I think it will be very interesting when the whole thing is reconstructed and we'll see if we have an answer to these questions that we've guessed at, and we've guessed differently according to our understandings of the background context.

MC: As you point out in your book, speaking of the *Gospel of Judas* versus the rest of the Gnostic corpus, the Gnostics are always being accused of being like the Emos or Goths of the ancient world, just dour and so forth, but you point out that the endings of their texts are very positive. They basically say that everything's going to be okay, it'll be fine in the end.

NDL: I have a whole book on this, on cosmology and Platonism and on the second century in general. I'm really looking at the ideas that the Gnostics were pessimists and the world has gone to hell in a hand-basket, and it was a very bleak and nihilistic understanding. And Hans Jonas studied nihilism and he studied existentialism before he was reading Nag Hammadi. There are a lot of bleak moments out there in the canonical Christian writings. I find them tremendously helpful, hopeful texts. There are moments of transcendence at the end of many of them. It's really extraordinary. So I don't see them as pessimistic at all. Again, the *Gospel of Judas* is different. And we'll see where it goes. It's not that it's moving towards possible resolutions to be good or bad, and we just don't have the end. To me the entire worldview is cynical in a way I haven't seen in any other texts from the same period.

MC: Your book has many fascinating insights, even for those versed in Gnostic scholarship. One is that you propose that the Nag Hammadi library wasn't buried by monks to safeguard their existence from censorship, but it has to do with an Egyptian custom. Could you tell us about it?

NDL: Yes, this came from some work I was doing with a very talented undergraduate called Justine Ariel, who has now finished her masters degree, but at the time she was a senior at Brown and double concentrating in religious studies and Egyptology. And this is fabulous, because one of the things we are really not good at in Gnosticism is knowing enough about Egyptology or Egyptian religion. It's just not part of our skill set: most of us come from biblical studies. And it's really chastening to think that there's a whole lot out there in Egyptology that could be useful to us. But Justine has been doing this work exploring the idea that these could be Gnostic Christian books of the dead. Not just the Nag Hammadi codices but the other codices we have as well. And while she was working on that, simultaneously I was working on this introduction to Gnosticism text book, and I started to write out the story, the famous find story with Muhammad and Ali al-Samman out there, and they're digging for manure.

And as I started working through that text I realised that there were in fact a lot of discrepancies, lots of things that change from one version to the other. And so I probed that a little more deeply all the way through from the beginning of the story with Muhammad Ali looking for something, all the way through to the end point of the story, which is generally that somebody must have buried these books maybe as a reaction to Athanasius of Alexandria's *Festal Letter* of 367 that says which books should be read and should not be read. So monks had gone out into the desert and deposited these books for posterity. I thought the story was true for a very long time. The more I started doing research and the more I started looking at pathological stuff. Pathological pachological texts were making their way through the social history, going down to Egypt, I though, oh my gosh, if this were the case it would be our only example of Egyptian monks deliberately hiding books for posterity. I thought, okay, so what about the Pachomian theory? There's not a shred of evidence to connect the Nag Hammadi codices with Pachomian monasticism. We don't have that jar even. The lid we have that was supposedly from that jar is a very common piece of red earthware from fifth century Egypt and we don't have anything to connect with that. We don't have the jar, the jar is missing. So we just don't have anything to say these books have anything to do with Pachomian monks. So I thought, okay, if they weren't buried for posterity, what might they have been buried for?

And as it turns out, Egypt has a very, very long history of depositing books in tombs as guides for the afterlife. So I suddenly became intrigued with this idea: could the Nag Hammadi codices have been intended to have been tomb deposits? And all the pieces started to fall in place. It was quite extraordinary, based on the research that Justine did and the research that I did. There's evidence of other tomb robbings that produced books at the time. There's archaeological evidence of books that came out of tombs. We have multiple instances of books put in tombs really very late, all the way through Egyptian history, but not one example of monks burying a book for posterity. So that's my new theory, and I think I'm right. I think these books were deliberately produced volumes with esoteric, eschatological leanings and insights that were compiled as luxury objects that were given to citizens, people with money, to be buried in their tombs with them as guides to the afterlife.

MC: Nicola, when Gnosticism really surfaced in our culture, many scholars, including Elaine Pagels, contended the Gnostics were egalitarian to the point where they flirted with feminism. This trend was reversed, by Ioan Culianu, for example. But this trend seems to be coming around again, especially with the work of April DeConick. Where do you stand on how progressive the Gnostics were?

NDL: Again, this is when the term Gnosticism doesn't get us very far. I think if you look at the range of writings we have at Nag Hammadi we find ones that are astonishingly bigoted and sexist, it seems to me. So there's a lot of diversity, a lot of variations there in the way that women were regarded, apparently. On the one hand you have a text like *Thunder Perfect Mind*, which is really extraordinary in its subaltern voice. You can call it a divine feminine voice, but it's also the voice of a woman who has been just about broken. Someone who has, in a sense, a very small voice, and has been violated. Somebody who has lost a great deal, somebody who has been despised. To have any ancient writing from the perspective of either a divine female or a completely subjugated female is extraordinary and mind-blowing. It's hard to wrap your mind around. Even when you try to make sense of it by going to Jewish wisdom writings, things like Proverbs 8, which has a female wisdom figure speaking, it's still extraordinary that she is there.

Hypostasis of the Archons, the role of women in that text, and Noraea as this savior figure is remarkable. Unparalleled. We just don't see it before this. It jumps out. We were talking in my class yesterday about the account of the archons raping Eve, and the passage that has that spiritual essence going out of her, and going into a tree so that it was only her body that was defiled. And that this was both a very horrifying image, to think that people could be spiritually empty in that same way, but also very modern, when we compare that to modern accounts of women's rapes when women dissociate themselves and say, well, he might have defiled my body, but he can't hurt the inner, pure part of me. And that comes out in some victims' testimonies. Again, it's jarring. Who could have put that there, who would have known about that? It's really hard to say.

On the Origin of the World is another one where the first being created, the first spiritual being, is a female being. And it's sort of mind-blowing. Eve was first, not Adam. Really a thing that seems not just progressive. I think of Paul, in his letter to the Corinthians, when he's talking about sexual roles, that's progressive. Because he says that men and women should honor one another, and their sexual needs, that's progressive, but this is a whole other order.

On the other hand, you have texts like the *Gospel of Thomas* logion 114, where you have Peter saying, "Let Mary go from us because women are not worthy of life," and Jesus talks him down a bit, but maybe not as much as you'd like. Bring her to me so I may make her more male and she can enter the kingdom of heaven, which certainly women in my class aren't very comforted by. Or books like *Thomas the Contender* that aren't very open towards women. It's a mixed bag of a community. But the Roman Empire was, roughly speaking, fairly good about women. You could have women teaching, you could have women who were held in respect, and I don't think the women teachers who were out and running around were deeply shocking to many people. But they were there.

MC: What are some of the so-called Gnostic texts that you find really speak to your students, that maybe surprise you?

NDL: You know, one thing that surprised me—it's not in the text book because it's not a Nag Hammadi text—is Ptolemy's *Letter to Flora*. It's very clear. Here's Ptolemy, a second century Valentinian writing to a female disciple and laying things out for her. I think they like the clarity of it. Especially when we did it very late, after our march through the *Gospel of the Egyptians*, which they find really inscrutable, but they tend to like that. And maybe again because it's grounded in a particular place and time that's more secure, and often with these texts the students have a rough time of it. How can we know when it was written, they say? The other one they tend to like is the *Gospel of Truth*. They really like that, it's usually their favorite.

MC: It's a beautiful gospel from beginning to end.

NDL: It is, it really is a beautiful gospel, and I think they really like the exhortation of going to take care of the sick, minister to the poor, and all that stuff. It looks like a sympathetic and caring one that they like. They do good work, and they're caring for one another, and I recognize this from church. Or they're not awful elitists. They like that human side that they suddenly coming up in the texts.

MC: Is there any text you personally really like, or body of texts that you like?

NDL: I like so many of these texts, and it moves around. From time to time I'll get deeply nestled into one of them and sit there for a while and think, this is really great, and sort of work my way out. I think perennial ones that still come back to me. I think that the Gospel of Thomas is a really extraordinary text just because of its soundbites. You can take little munches out of it, and some of those sayings are just tremendously powerful. I like the tightness of it. The sayings have a logic that is kind of hard to get, but it tends to be pretty associative, and almost intuitive, and I like that, but I think the sayings themselves are so great. Probably one of the early ones that spoke to me was logion 50, where you have the questions in there, "If they take you what shall you say to them? Say to them that we are children of the living father, and we come from the light, and return to the light." I find this one really very moving, and I don't know why. I think it's a beautiful image, and I see those sorts of words percolate through so many religious texts of antiquity. I find something about that very moving, those exact words showing up in other texts, but beyond that you also see very similar articulations showing up in non-Gnostic texts. So that's one that particularly moves me.

MC: And to end, Nicola, what do you tell your students or think is the legacy the Gnostics had on the ancient and modern world?

NDL: Such a hard question, and I don't know that I have any kind of a brilliant answer, or even a good answer. I think, to take us back to the pop culture stuff and the popularity of a movie like *The Matrix*, it's a great testimony to Gnosticism that an ancient set of ideas are still with us today as things people can find inspiration in. Not everybody can read these texts and go and join a Gnostic community—some will, most won't. But I think a lot of people can read these texts and recognize in them themes of alienation and belonging, themes of spiritual return, that are a very powerful reminders for a lot of people

MC: I think that's all the time we have today, Nicola. I'd like to thank you very much for coming on Aeon Byte and discussing your wonderful book *Introduction to "Gnosticism" Ancient Voices and Christian Worlds.*

NDL: Well, it was a great pleasure to be here. Thank you very much.

RICHARD SMOLEY

Richard Smoley is an author and philosopher focusing on the world's mystical and esoteric teachings, particularly those of Western civilization. He is the author of several books including *Inner Christianity*, *Forbidden Faith*, *Conscious Love* and *How God Became God*.

Richard Smoley has been a tireless explorer of esoteric terrain for decades. His research ranges from Theosophy to ancient alternative Christianity, and everything in between. He has graced Aeon Byte Gnostic Radio several times. Like his books, Richard's vision is always spanning across history and geography. Few thinkers I know can cross-reference religious thought better than Richard, connecting the dots of religious movements even to their Asian or antediluvian counterparts.

In this interview, Richard discussed his book, *Forbidden Faith*, a work that not only provides a historical view of Gnosticism in western history, but also of the concept of Gnosis. In other words, he presents those famous and infamous individuals who experienced a direct contact with higher forms of being and granted humanity expanded consciousness in the form of poetry, art, literature and, yes, the echoes of that forbidden faith known as Gnosticism.

MC: What I really liked about your book is that it is kind of the "God of the gaps" of Gnostic books. You plug in a lot of holes that the huge majority of Gnostic books have missed, and you do it very well. At the same time your book is very approachable for a layperson who's trying to understand Gnosticism. So in that sense I really enjoyed your book.

RS: Thank you.

MC: What exactly led you to write such an erudite book?

RS: Well, it was a combination of things. There's certainly a widespread interest in the Gnostic legacy and it was kind of a dialogue between my agent and HarperSanFrancisco, back in 2004. they were looking for something that was a history of Gnosticism, or what I call the Gnostic legacy from the beginnings to the present. There are a lot of different threads to follow, and various interconnections and strands that fuse in with each other. So it was a very interesting idea and I was very excited to do it.

MC: Yeah you actually include a comprehensive chart that shows how everything branches out from the beginning of the Sumerians to the *Da Vinci Code* or *The Matrix*, so that was interesting.

RS: Well, that idea was the publisher's and someone there said, wouldn't it be interesting to have a chart of how all these things connect. So I drew one up, and at first I was taken aback by it, because it looks like a map of urban sprawl, and I wrote back an email and said, Well, the map of the Gnostic legacy is not like a map of urban sprawl, it's far more intricate and confusing. Even that chart is to some extent simplified, because you start having things all over the place, and it starts looking like the ravings of a conspiracy theorist or something like that. It was an attempt to follow some of these threads through like, to take one random example, the greatest scholar of Jewish mysticism in the twentieth century was Gershem Scholem, and Scholem basically said, almost in so many words, that the Kabbalah, the central leg of the Jewish mystical tradition, was taken over from Gnosticism, which is really quite a remarkable thing coming from a scholar of that magnitude and repute, it has a lot of weight. Certain scholars have attempted to challenge it, but those seem rather weak to me. So that's just one thread that we can follow Gnosticism and it looks like you can follow it through from the Kabbalah and it looks quite different in many ways from the classic Gnostic system.

MC: We'll get back to the Kabbalah, but could you tell me what the Gnostic spark that began the Renaissance movement was?

RS: You can see it in a number of ways. A key fact was the fall of Constantinople to the Turks in 1453. A lot of Greek scholars fled to Italy and although the Italians were Catholic and they were orthodox, it was still a Christian world. And a lot of these manuscripts found their way west. Moreover, another key thing happened, which was suddenly the West had a number of people who were able to read Greek and to teach people Greek. So these texts which had only been known in Latin translation if at all, by the educated world in the west, suddenly became more available and accessible.

Certainly one of the key texts was called the Corpus Hermeticum, which is a collection of Greek texts that are now dated to probably within the first to third centuries c.e. But at that time they were believed to have been written by Hermes Trismegistus, a semi-mythical figure who is sometimes associated with the patriarch Enoch, sometimes with the God Thoth of Egyptian mythology, sometimes with Hermes in Greek myth. He was like a founder figure, a fountainhead of original knowledge. And the texts were attributed to him. It was believed that he lived at the time of Moses and may have even been a teacher of Moses. There is a famous inlay from the cathedral of Siena in Italy, dating from around the period which has, in translation from the Latin, Hermes Trismegistus, contemporary of Moses. So the idea that this knowledge is as old as the bible, which of course was considered to be the great sacred text, was mindblowing.

Now, later on, scholars discovered that the text itself was not that old, but the knowledge itself may very well be that old. There are certainly allusions in these texts that suggest that they were an attempt to codify the esoteric wisdom of the Egyptians into the language of the Greek Hellenistic world. Because the knowledge of the Egyptians, the Egyptian tradition, was dying. There's a very poignant passage in one of the Hermetic texts that says, "O Egypt, Egypt, soon all your good works will have vanished and all your worship will have perished." So they knew that that tradition was at its last and they were trying to present it in some kind of form that could pass over into the new world of Greek thought and, eventually, Christianity. And those texts when they were rediscovered in the 15th century by the western world, certainly constituted one of those sparks and launched much of the interest in the Renaissance.

Now, I've already mentioned the Kabbalah, but another around this time, and I'm talking about the mid to late 15th century, that the Christian world started to become aware of the Kabbalah and the riches of Jewish mysticism and the first person who really brought this to the fore was an Italian nobleman named Pico della Mirandola. He edited a number of works. He was studying Kabbalistic texts on his own, trying to present in the philosophical language of his time, and even went so far as to say that Kabbalah itself at its core proved the truth of Christianity. Whether that's so or not, it's certainly the case that that interest in the Kabbalah, in those scholars in the Renaissance, was another one of those sparks.

And the Kabbalah and these Hermetic ideas were very much part of the intellectual current of 15th and 16th and 17th centuries, People were aware of them, much in the way that a modern intellectual might be aware of something like Zen. People didn't know an awful lot about it. They knew it was there are had some general concept of what it was and it was part of that reawakening of the intellectual culture of the west which at that point had begin again. It had been a very frozen, very stiff medieval scholastic philosophy dominated by the Catholic church and the philosophy of Aristotle and Aquinas.

MC: I guess one of the mistakes people made, didn't they believe that the Hermetic philosophy was actually the Egyptian religion complete? I guess until later on when archaeology and so forth discovered it wasn't so?

RS: Well, the relation between the Hermetic texts and Egyptian religion is interesting. And this is a question that I don't really feel has been adequately answered by scholarship. If you look at the oldest evidence from the Greeks of Egyptian religion there seem to be indications of doctrines that resemble reincarnation that don't seem to appear in Egyptian religion. That leads me to think that there was an esoteric Egyptian religion that may have been passed down orally that underlies what you would learn about Egyptian religion in a history text book or even in some theological study.

Pythagoras, who brought the doctrine of reincarnation to the west, and who taught it openly—this is in the sixth century b.c.e.—definitely studied in Egypt and learned a lot of things there. For instance, the Pythagorean theory in geometry. People used to think that he invented it, but the Egyptian knew it and he was the one who brought it to the Greek world. And he also brought the doctrine of reincarnation. Strangely enough Pythagoras had a kind of mystical esoteric school, and one rather odd thing that's never really been explained I have any answer for. Pythagoras' followers didn't eat beans.

MC: I remember I fell out of my chair when I read that.

RS: The classical scholars try to explain this and have all sorts of utterly ridiculous theories, but the answer is quite simple. It is mentioned in Herodotus that the Egyptians didn't eat beans. They thought it was a disgusting food. And Pythagoras probably studied in Egypt. He did study in Egypt. He probably picked up their food taboos just in the way that if you study at a Japanese monastery or Hindu ashram for any number of years you might well come back as a vegetarian. But that indicates that a lot of this knowledge that Pythagoras brought in, at a very early stage in western civilization, came from Egypt.

In short, these esoteric ideas that we see in the Hermetic texts have to do with ancient Egypt is a very fraught question and I'm not sure the answers have really been pieced together, or that anyone has tried to piece them together in a really exhaustive scholarly way.

MC: Moving back just a little bit in time, what exactly are the origins of romantic love and the Troubadours, as far as you can see?

RS: One theory that was advanced by a French scholar named Denis de Rougemont, in a very famous book called *Love in the Western World,* was that romantic love as we know it was invented by the Troubadours, who elevated love and put love on a pedestal in a way it had never been before. Put in quite such simple terms it's ridiculous because if you go back and read the poetry of the Greeks and the Romans they mean something very like romantic love, long before the Troubadours of the 12th century. So the idea that they invented romantic love, although you hear this idea repeated over and over again, because de Rougemont came up with it, on the face of it is nonsense.

I think what it is fair to say is that the Troubadours and the courtly love at that period in the early medieval era elevated love itself to a central point in human life. And love in its romantic form, love in its coarser form, certainly Christianity before that had found love to be very, very central. But there's certainly talk of love in Christianity before that it was never really brought to the center even though it's implicit in the gospels, it's only really at this time that love became kind of deified. You can say, "Love is all you need, all you need is love." Every banal pop song you've ever heard has these phrases of love that are so familiar they're almost meaningless to us. But the fact that this is done, the fact that this is in the background of our culture, the fact that we have absorbed it, like it or not, is due to this impulse of the Troubadours and the courts of love in the medieval time.

MC: So basically the Troubadours didn't invent it but more than likely revived the old classical notions of eros and higher love together.

RS: They kind of put love on a pedestal in a way that it had probably never been put before, and there were lots of different aspects to it. One was the sublimation of sexuality. Everybody knows that a desire that is satisfied cools off a little bit. But if you have some woman that you're adoring from a distance, and you never get to see her or touch her, this kind of emotional frenzy keeps at a very high pace and it provides an emotional excitement of its own, its own weird ecstasy.

MC: Like Dante had for Beatrice.

RS: That's exactly it. Dante was 12 years old or something and he sees this nine-year-old girl at a party and falls in love with her and sees her in person maybe a half dozen times, and she dies very young. So there's no idea that he's going to marry her, settle down and have babies. He married somebody else that he never writes about. I don't know what Dante's wife felt about all this writing about Beatrice, but probably nobody asked her. There's this very conscious division of love into this very highly idealised love that's never realized, and the ordinary sort in which you get married and have babies and run a household. And these are two different types of love.

De Rougemont thought it you have this ideal of courtly love, this ideal lady of your dreams that you never see, it's going to set you up for being disappointed with ordinary relationships. He thinks that a lot of the tragedies of love, the tragedies of love that we see in everyday life, are a result of this kind of break made by the Troubadours. It's an interesting issue and definitely worth exploring. Our attitudes towards love are extremely strange in a lot of ways and some of it is probably due to these impulses from medieval times. There's always Christianity itself which has always tended, from its very earliest stages, to demonize physical love and idealise non-physical love.

MC: And you criticize the Gnostics for doing the same thing.

RS: Well, this is a strange thing. The Gnostics believe that the world was if not fundamentally evil, at least fundamentally problematic. The world is that much of a mess you can take two fundamental approaches to it. One is you can cut yourself off from it, in a sort of way that would stop it. There's a fictional sect in one of Jorge Luis Borges' stories, who forbade both mirrors and sexual intercourse to its followers because they both multiplied illusions. So one is to cut yourself off completely from it, and some of the Gnostics did this, as they were quite ascetic. The Cathars of the medieval times were part of the Gnostic legacy, were if anything as much or more ascetic as the Catholics of the time. And the other is to take an antinomian libertine approach, that is to say, well, if this world is a mess anyway, if it's all the creation of a secondary deity named the demiurge, what does it matter what you do down here, so you might as well do what you feel like doing.

MC: Like the Carpocratians.

RS: Yeah, the Carpocratians were accused by their enemies of having licentious orgies where semen and menstrual blood were consumed as sacraments. It's very hard to say. You have to be very suspicious about information that's coming from their enemies. If it's overstated, if you're just finding rumors, it's very hard to stay. We don't have any evidence from the Carpocratians themselves. Certainly if you're criticising and denouncing these religions you're not going to present them in their best light. On the other hand, people have used semen and menstrual blood as magical substances. They contain a certain kind of vital charge that many other types of substance don't have, so could the Carpocratians have done this? Yes, they could well have. We just don't know.

MC: Richard, moving further into the murky waters of secret societies, you point out that the Rosicrucians consider themselves Gnostic Christians. What exactly was Gnostic about them, or were they just taking the name and running with it?

RS: I don't know that in any of the early Rosicrucian texts that they make any reference to Gnosticism. I think in my book I said that there was some criticism of the Rosicrucian movement in the 17th century that said that "This is nothing but the heresy of the Gnostics updated." What they did have I think was ... if you want to say that there's a central theme, a central thread in the whole Gnostic legacy, it's the desire to know something for yourself rather than just taking it for granted because the church told you so, or because it says here in the Bible. The desire to investigate the experiential truths of religion. I think the Rosicrucians certainly had that in them, and in that sense they are heirs to the Gnostics as well. Just to provide a little background, the Rosicrucian movement in its earliest form was rather mysterious.

There were a couple of very short tracts written around 1610, called the Fama Fraternitatis, the rumor of the brotherhood, and the confessio fraternitatis, the confession of the brotherhood. And it told a story about this semi-mythical figure—we don't know if he really existed, most likely he's a fictionalized or somewhat allegorised version of a real person we don't know much about—named Christian Rosenkreuz. And this Christian Rosenkreuz went to the East, which meant in those days Palestine and North Africa, to learn the mysteries of knowledge. He came back to Germany and he taught them. One of the things he talked about was reading the book of nature. That is to say, to look at nature and explore it for yourself. Rather than just relying on what Aristotle and Galen, the Roman physician whose books on medicine were still the textbooks of the time. In those days to study science was to read the Physics of Aristotle and the works of Galen. Nobody did any experimentation.

The Rosicrucians were part of this movement that said, hey, let's look at what's really going on, really look at the secrets of nature rather than just tossing what Aristotle and Galen said. So there too, there's part of wanting to know something for yourself directly and experientially rather than just because somebody said so a long time ago.

MC: Another one of your god of the gaps, which I was pretty flabbergasted at, was that you mention that both Descartes and Sir Francis Bacon were influenced by the Rosicrucians.

RS: They were definitely part of that movement, and Descartes to this day is regarded as a kind of hyper-rationalist. People talk of the scientific worldview as the Cartesian worldview. And there's certainly that element in Descartes' thought. But there's the idea that he was very interested in these ideas. He went from France to Bohemia, today's Czech Republic, to find Rosicrucian brothers. It's overlooked. The typical conventional scholar finds all this stuff I just talked about very embarrassing. This is all occult nonsense. This is all fringe stuff. The real tradition of the west is this hyper-rationalism that started with Socrates, if you like, and continued, although there were centuries and centuries of darkness and superstition, and occult nonsense. Reason, in the way that some materialistic philosopher of today would think of reason, is the only true western tradition.

Well, obviously this is rubbish. More and more, even scholars themselves are having to admit this, because the esoteric currents were so
powerful, particularly in the 17th century when modern science as we
know it was being born. The Rosicrucian movement produced, among
other things, one of its children was the Royal Society in England, in
London, which was the first scientific society that was founded in the
western world. It still exists. Today it's a hyper-conventional scientific
society but in those days it was very much aligned with the esoteric
movement. Ironically, science is a child of these occult movements of
the 16th and 17th centuries but it doesn't want anything to do with it. It's
like some kid who goes off to college and is ashamed when his parents
come to visit. That's the way it is, but it's pretty strange.

MC: Is there a connection between the Rosicrucians and the Freemasons?

RS: This is debated. I'll give you the most widely-accepted scholarly
view, which is that the Rosicrucian movement in the early 17th century produced the tract that I mentioned earlier wasn't so much a specific secret society as a series of currents. People who were interested in
Hermeticism, in the Kabbalah, in various forms of occult philosophy,
including alchemy. These movements started to become connected with
these lodges which originally started in Scotland and they were originally stonemasons' lodges that had some version of esoteric wisdom.
And these two combined and produced what is known as Freemasonry.
Which by the time you see it really starting to surface in the 1640s
and 1650s is no longer really a stonemasons guild at that point, it's a
society. There are certain mystical ideas that are buried in its rites and
rituals, and another thing that was produced was a strong emphasis on
religious toleration.

One of the earliest meetings of the Freemasons' lodges, according to
the diary of an Englishman named Elias Ashmole, one of the founders
of the Royal Society, I think it was in 1646, and it turns out, he was an
Anglican, he was a high Anglican on the side of the king, there were
these puritans there, there was a Catholic, and this was at the height
of the English civil War, that is to say when the Anglicans on the side
of the king and the puritans were killing each other, they were having these large pitched battles. And the idea that these people could
get together and meet in peace and toleration and security, was itself a
revolutionary development.

From the Masonic impulses that we think of as religious toleration, what we think of as representative government, eventually arose. So there were these currents that kind of flowed. Just one other sideline about the Masons is that in medieval times there were these guilds which were something like a combination of professional organisations, beneficial societies, trade unions, they had a lot of different functions, insurance companies, they put out benefits for their members, if somebody died. And they did have certain esoteric teachings within them. And the stonemason guild were one of these. They provide a framework for the Freemaosns to build on. The stonemasons guild weren't the only trade that had this kind of knowledge. Many of the others did, and in France some of these guilds were known as the *companionage*. There's no real translation but they are like guilds with esoteric knowledge. Some of them are even quite strange. Like in Italy one of these esoteric lodges was for a trade known as charcoalburners because people turned dung into charcoal. These were called the *carbionari* and they surfaced in Italy in another form in the 19th century in a political movement that was aimed at unifying Italy and incidentally breaking the back of the Church as a political power because in those days the Church still owned a good chunk of Italy.

MC: You mention there was one person who was responsible for it, who was able to unite Italy, I forget the name.

RS: Garribaldi?

MC: That's it.

RS: Yeah, and he was connected with that movement and he was also head of the Masonic lodge in Italy. The Catholics have always hated the Freemasons and they had reasons for doing so, because the Masons were a force that really broke the political power of the Church in the 19th century. The church didn't like it. Today you'll see Pope Benedict XVI saying that the Church doesn't try to steer or dictate political life, he said that in a recent encyclical, but that wasn't the way they thought in those days, and they only think it now because the power was taken away from them.

MC: But still, you can't be Catholic and a Freemason according to the Catholic Church, to this day.

RS: No, no. and the Freemasons aren't thrilled about it either because they think, well, you belong to this religion and they don't want you here.

Now that is fairly recent, not recent but it started in the 18ᵗʰ century, I think the first papal bull against masonry was issued in 1738. Before that, when I said that Elias Ashmole had a Catholic in his lodge, that's because in 1646 it was okay, the Catholic church had no problem with it, it was only 100 years later. Now, I'll tell you—I didn't put this in the book because I didn't have any documentation on it, but I will throw it out as a piece of hearsay: the opposition of the Catholic Church to Freemasons has always been a bit nebulous.

It's sometimes said in Masonic circles that the reason the Pope came down so hard on it was that the Pope himself wanted to become a Mason and they were perfectly happy to have him, but in the lodge, they said, you're equal, you're not the Pope here, you're just another man like everybody else. The Pope just wouldn't go for that and he got very mad and condemned the Freemasons. Now, I don't know if that's true. I haven't seen any documentation on it. It has a bizarre ring of truth to it, to me, and it explains a little bit more about the hostility of the Church to Masonry. Because masonry is saying, no, we don't recognize the church, we don't recognize your ecclesiastical privilege, you're a man here like everybody else. If you're used to having your rings kissed, you're probably not going to like that.

MC: Very true. And moving up a little bit further, this is a view that Stephan Hoeller agrees with, but why was the discovery of the *Pistis Sophia* in the 19ᵗʰ century so vital for the esoteric movement of that time and afterwards?

RS: Because it suggested that these esoteric ideas really went back to the earliest years of Christianity. It helped confirm what people had long suspected and believed without a lot of hard evidence, that there was a kind of secret document of Christianity that isn't lost or covered over. Now, what's interesting about *Pistis Sophia* and many of the other Gnostic texts is that they have one curious feature in common. They all present Jesus as giving his teachings after his resurrection. The *Pistis Sophia* says that Jesus was around for 11 years after his death and taught the disciples. Again, whether this is so in a literal sense or not, it does point to something that is profound, that all the exoteric teachings in the gospels that Jesus delivered when he was, shall we say, alive in the flesh, are kind of the outermost court. And that after he was resurrected, and was born again in some real sense and not just if you have some real awakening, shall we say the true self, these ideas come into play. And they look very different in certain respects from the exoteric teachings that Christianity publicly promulgated.

MC: And this was certainly true for the Theosophical society through G.R.S. Mead and, I think even Mme Blavatsky was very fond of the Gnostics.

RS: Yeah, well Madame Blavatsky was operating in the late 19th century when she said this was the true Christianity that embodied the religion of the Gnostics. And this seemed a very shocking thing to say at the time, because the Gnostics were always these arch-heretics that Christianity in its orthodox form had always defined itself against. And to say that this was the real thing was mindblowing. It turns on its head everything about church history at that time. But that's of course because the winner gets to write the history. The orthodox Catholic Church won the political struggle. The Gnostics were suppressed and died out in late antiquity and their story was never really heard except for accidentally. The *Pistis Sophia* was found at some London junk shop—nobody knows where it really came from. The Nag Hammadi scriptures which have attracted so much attention over the last generation were dug up by an Egyptian peasant who was looking for fertiliser. The survival of these things is either accidental or providential, depending on how you want to look at it.

MC: I like to think of them as providential. Another thing, speaking of the Nag Hammadi, you mention that Elaine Pagels' *The Gnostic Gospels* was just as important as the Nag Hammadi in bringing Gnosticism to light. Could you explain that?

RS: Her *The Gnostic Gospels*, published in 1979, was the first clear presentation of Gnosticism to a literate reading public. The previous works, the standard works on the subject were pretty dense, and she presented these ideas in a very clear light. She also suggested, in a very creative and persuasive way, how the triumph of Christianity, particularly of Christian doctrine, was as much political as anything.

For example, let's go back to the central thread. Gnosis is about finding out for yourself, it's a knowing in some kind of deep sense. And if you know in a deep sense, what do you need the priests for? You certainly don't need them in the way you used to, which is not very helpful from the priests' point of view. They're trying to earn a living. So what Pagels pointed out is that as the church started to create its own very effective and very flexible organisation, which would eventually take over the Roman Empire, it had to do so from a different basis. And what it used was apostolic authority, and the apostolic authority was from people, from individuals who had supposedly seen Jesus after he was resurrected, and then said that if you hadn't been one of those people, or one of their followers, you really have no authority. Even if you knew something on your own. And that crucial shift, from the see and know something for oneself, to seeing and knowing something on received authority was what separated the Christian church as we see and know it today from the Gnostic movement.

For the most part people are lazy. I've got my bills to pay, I'd just as soon take it in a packaged form from somebody else. The Church is going to be more appealing on a widespread popular basis than the insights of the Gnostics which are difficult and allusive not necessarily because they put them in an obscure way, although they often did, but to see these things happening in themselves is pretty subtle. That requires a lot of introspection, a lot of inner work and inner sifting that most people just don't want to bother with, today just as much as in 100 C.E.

MC: Yes, and I guess lastly, which kind of connects to this, using your crystal ball, what is the State of the Union of Gnosticism or of Gnosis today? Where do you see it going?

RS: Well, I don't see the Gnostic religion being revived in any obvious conventional sense. There are Gnostic churches and that kind of thing. They have every right to be there. I don't think it will take that form.

What I mean by that is if you take the classic Gnostic system with its demiurge as a secondary deity and with archons as these barriers between the individual spirit and the higher realm, taken literally these are very cumbersome, but I think what they're pointing to is that these archons, the demiurge, are part of the deep-rooted structure of our minds that we have to overcome. The demiurge could be roughly equated with the ego. The archons are, shall we say, different levels or categories of experience. What do I mean by this? Well, in the Hermetic texts at one point it describes the ascent of the soul. You have the soul through different spheres, and these are the spheres of the seven planets, and each stage has a vice associated with that planet. Venus, for example, would be lust, Mars would be anger, and if you take those vices, shall we say, you know, lust, anger, lying associated with Mercury, pride associated with the sun, and so on and so on. The basic theme of condition is awareness of our experience and we see our spiritual progress as letting these things go.

The ideas of the Gnostic and the Hermetics are much clearer and more practical that the archons are not these kind of nasty archangels up in the ionosphere but are very much deeply embedded in our own minds. It's the way we see the world. A lot of our basic perception of the world is friend or foe, something you desire you go towards, something you desire you go away from, on a very deep and spiritual second by second basis. And these are the archons, and these are what the true message of the Gnostic legacy is all about.

Some might say that the Gnostics just projected an elaborate system they themselves did not understand, almost in the way that one might have a dream. Jung I think would have argued that. I'm not so sure. I suspect that they did really understand something like what I've just been talking about. They put it in these very obscure texts because it was in effect secret knowledge and hard to handle. And so the Gnostic student would read the texts and someone who actually knew what they were talking about would explain them to him or let him experience them for himself. The knowledge is not even all in these texts. The texts are only a point of departure. You can see something very similar in the way a typical Tibetan master today might teach a text with a basic skeletal framework that he expounds and the pupil absorbs and digests it from his exposition of the texts. That's how I suspect that the Gnostics worked with the *Pistis Sophia* and the Nag Hammadi scriptures and so on.

MC: Right, they were dealing with the issues of consciousness, reality, individuation basically.

RS: Exactly.

MC: More than these supernatural events.

WILLIS BARNSTONE

Willis Barnstone is a poet, memoirist, translator, Hispanist, and comparatist. He has translated the ancient Greek poets and is also a New Testament and Gnostic scholar. He is the editor of *The Gnostic Bible*.

Willis Barnstone is widely recognized as a chief translator of Gnostic texts and, as with Jorge Luis Borges (whom he knew and translated), is actually very friendly to the Gnostic ethos. Yet like the Gnostics that Willis is so fond of, he is a bit of a rogue. As we discussed in our interview, when it comes to translating ancient texts, it's far better to be poetic rather than accurate ("Literary, not literal," as he told me). His reasoning is actually logical: religious writings were meant to be read out loud, presented in plays, and pregnant with pathos. To truly understand the intent of holy texts, a scholar has to ensure they are as close as possible to an artistic expression, or else the meaning will never shine through. Both the ancient priest and the modern scholar have a duty not to bore their audiences.

Beyond that, Willis shared other techniques and challenges of translating ancient texts, as well as insights on the classic Gnostics themselves and other Gnostic-minded figures. He contended that the Gnostic literature, from the Sethians to the Cathars, is some of the most beautiful and evocative writing in all of history. During the interview, he was lyrical, he was mercurial, and he surely will always remain an ardent ally to the memory of the classic Gnostics.

MC: You've had a very illustrious and global career as a poet, literary critic, translator of a vast and varied array of genres from ancient to modern times; you've been a distinguished professor and so much more it would take hours to cover with any justice. The question the listener might have is how exactly did you run and become interested in the perennial heretics, the Gnostics?

WB: I'm not exactly sure. I'm a young squirt, still. I'm 83, which I know sounds a little obscene, but I have my marbles and I have my legs. I've had time to play with it. Let me first say that I'm a literary person and a spiritual person. I do not make any pitch for any religion. I feel closer to the Gnostics, certainly, than any conventional religious sect. I ran into them, perhaps, when I was doing a study and translation of the poems of Saint John of the Cross—*San Juan de la Cruz*—which came out with New Directions books many, many years ago, almost 30 years ago, more actually, and is still in print.

Saint John shares a lot with the Gnostics in the sense that his union with God was an internal one of union with light. In the same manner, I was educated in a Quaker boarding school and worked with the Quakers twice in Mexico, in Aztec villages with the American Friends service committee. And if there's any religion which is like Gnosticism, it surely is Quakerism, which believes in the light and the inner light, and through the inner light one has knowledge and deliverance.

Now that I've just gotten over tuberculosis, I especially am fond of Gnosticism. Because in the three levels of being which Gnostics speak of—in body, soul, and breath (*pneuma*)—for someone who has just recovered from tuberculosis, breath is very distinctly my favorite way. I don't know if that's helpful. Now, more specifically, I began to work with the Gnostics when I did the book *The Other Bible*, which I began around 1979. It came out in 1984; Harper did it in San Francisco (now I think it's called HarperOne). About sixty percent of the book is Gnosticism, and it refers to those texts which could have gotten into the Old and the New Testament, or more properly the Hebrew Bible and the Greek Scriptures. It seems 35 years or so that I have been dealing very strongly with Gnosticism.

Also, I've always been close to the books, and eventually to the person, of Harold Bloom, whose marvelous afterword to Marvin Meyers' *A Gospel of Thomas* may be the most precise, concise and well written summary of the essence of Gnosticism. And also with some knowledge of Kabbalism. I'm very interested in Gershom Scholem, who wrote the most interesting books on mysticism and Gnosticism. And he finds, even back in 1926 when he did his dissertation on the *Book of Light* in Hebrew, he equated Gnosticism and Kabbalism. So the reason it is somewhat easy to find a parallel between diverse sects which call themselves different names, is because though they translate in words the meaning of a somewhat extraordinary ecstatic experience with somewhat sectarian vocabulary, what is valid is not necessarily the vocabulary, but the existence of the experience itself.

So whether you're secular, as I am, or religious, or of the East or West, the experience endures and therefore, I wrote a book in the 1980s called *The Poetics of Ecstasy*, which deals with the experience of being elsewhere. In the case of Gnosticism it is being with the breath or the light inside us, which, once found, can give us salvation or deliverance on earth, and we need not worry about death before or afterwards. Now, I must say, with Elaine Pagels and others, I was totally taken by Gnosticism because of the prominence of women, the prominence of Eve, who created Adam.

There's a wonderful story of Eve creating Adam. Eve, Aeon Sophia, etc. They have their own cosmogony in Gnosticism. So Eve instead of being the villain, becomes the person who gives us Gnosis.

And one last thing before I finish with this diatribe. (Let's hope I use it in the ancient Greek sense more than in the modern sense.) I'm tremendously taken by the notion of women as our liberators in a Promethean sense, who have suffered the ignominious epithet of villain, of soulless, but who in Gnosticism prevail in so very many ways. I think Paul, that is to say, the historical Paul, not the mythical Paul of Acts, was tremendously influenced by Gnosticism, and obviously Augustine was equally. So, Augustine was a Gnostic missionary, but Paul was one who learned from the Gnostics, whom he was against.

In the letters of Paul you find these constant messages of "Beware the false prophets! Those who come with Gnosis!" it says in Greek. Because the Gnostics from Syria and Alexandria were the educated people. From them, and them alone, the early Christian churchmen learned about exegesis, learned about literary criticism. So, here we are, I've spoken too much. If you ask me another question like that I'm afraid we'll be here till next week.

MC; No, no. That was wonderful. So you never had a problem with the traditional Gnostic acosmic and dualistic view; you still saw beauty in their work?

WB: I've not had problems with any religion. That doesn't mean I believe it, but I understand it. I'm very fond of the essential Gnostic intention. Not all of them. I certainly don't believe the earth is evil, and that living on earth is a mistake and all that kind of thing, but I find that rather secondary to Gnostic belief.

MC: Willis, could you tell us a little about the difficulties you might have encountered or how it's different translating Coptic versus other languages? And perhaps give us an overview of the different dialects of ancient Coptic? Most listeners probably don't know there are many different dialects of Coptic in the Nag Hammadi library.

WB: Well, let me tell you something: I can't read Coptic. That's why I worked with Marvin Meyer, who is one of the world's leading Coptic scholars. In the bilingual script of the original *Gospel of Thomas*, I could pick up about every third or fourth word, because the alphabet that the Copts used is a variation of Greek. They kind of fattened up the Greek alphabet a bit. But you can, without too much problem, read the words. And I say every third or fourth word because every third or fourth word comes from the Greek. The other languages are completely different. One is the spoken language of Egypt; I believe it's a Semitic language, and I can handle Hebrew, but I certainly can't handle Coptic.

Now, you asked me about the translation. I could speak to you, I'm afraid, from here to Kingdom Come, because I did a book called *The Poetics of Translation: History, Theory, Practice*, which Yale published back in 1993. By the way, a hundred pages of that book, the paradigm of the book, is translation of Biblical scriptures and translation of Gnostic scriptures.

Let me perhaps go to first base before we strike out, and tell you: the problems of translation of any text remain the same. All original texts, since they've survived until now, must have some song. Especially if they're religious, because prose was invented long after poetry and all scriptures are meant to be chanted, either by oneself or in places of worship. And so, you have to be a poet. It has to sing in the translation. Most translators are dreadful because they're not poets in the act of translation.

Now, as far as catching the exact meaning of what the Coptic says, it's a little ridiculous, since the Coptic itself is a translation from Greek scriptures which have disappeared, not completely but largely, including the *Gospel of Thomas*. We have fragments in Greek, but those fragments in Greek are so different from those in Coptic, when you translate you say whatever you want to say. There's one passage in the 53 scriptures of the Nag Hammadi text found which is supposed to be Plato. But if you look at the Coptic translation of it you will hardly recognize Plato. So when one tries to spend hours, "What did they really mean in the Coptic?" It's so arbitrary because what did they really mean in the original Greek? So we're talking about a shadow of a shadow, which really pleases scholars, but they're barking up a very stupid tree.

It's nice to know as much as you can, especially in the *Gospel of Judas* because it's so very vital, but much of what you have to do is, as I say: it's like going to the libraries of Copenhagen and studying the literature of the time of Hamlet to find out what Hamlet's motives were. Shakespeare certainly didn't have the foggiest idea of the times in Denmark. [Laughs] There was something rotten about it.

MC: That's enough to make a story, in itself.

WB: Well, when I was at Yale, I had this wonderful professor, Rene Wellek, who was a Czech, who never lost his beautiful Czech accent though he did claim that he had lost most of his Czech. Wellek was very, very skeptical about over-erudition, of becoming too competent in a small area. He was a dean, you might say, of comparative literature, and it gave us a great deal of insignificant and misleading information, that's the great problem of scholarship. As far as translation goes, yes, you want to have a beautiful text, and the best way you can be faithful to the original is to give general understanding, be loyal to it and not create it yourself except in beauty and song. Can you imagine Elizabethan songs into Portuguese if they do not sing? Forget it.

MC: No, no, no.

WB: Why translate the wonderful Cathars, the Troubadours, some of them were women Gnostics, if we're just going to do a "literal translation." Literal is a very misleading word; as Borges says: "Literary, not literal." Literal is unfaithful. Literary can come close, but every translation is at best an approximation.

MC: I agree with you. For example, I read Spanish. When I read Cervantes, it's not the same as when I read it in English at all. So much is lost.

WB: And when you read Cervantes in the morning, it's not the same Cervantes that you read in the afternoon. Because you also are one of the instruments, and when you read it at your age, it's very different from the one you read in Spanish ten years ago, because you contribute to the meaning of the original. So there are all kinds of subjective and objective facts that go into any publication, into the translation of any text. I love the notion of translation, but if you want to read a beautiful translation it must be beautiful. Some of the translation of the Gnostics are beautiful and others are not. No names mentioned. [Laughs]

MC: Is there any Gnostic literature that, Willis, really speaks to you as a poet and an artist? That you found just sublime?

WB: Oh, well, you know, if you just look at essential Gnostic scriptures, you'll find that more than half of it is poetry. *The Gospel of Philip* and the *Manichean Song Book* it's endless, the quantity and quality of Gnostic poetry. They spoke to us through verse. They're among the great poets, and think of the enormous amount of poetry that does exist in Provence, and of course the hundred times as much that has been lost.

MC: I don't think this was an accident, that some of the Gnostics were poets, because we know Mani was a painter and the Manichaeans painted. Valentinus pretty much wrote poetry himself. It seems they were both artists and theologians at the same time.

WB: Did you say Plotinus?

MC: No, Valentinus. I'm sorry.

WB: Oh, Valentinus. Right. Because Plotinus was wonderful, and he wrote *Against the Gnostics*; but he is about as Gnostic as you can get.

MC: He's turning in his grave, Willis. [Laughs]

WB: No, no, no. I mean, it's just like Christians railing against the Jews. They were the Jews. All the early saints were Jews. Well, what the hell were they, Chinese? The things I did in translating *The Restored New Testament* that Norton published about a year ago, was restore the original Latin, Greek, Aramaic and Hebrew names. I was able to put down the philology of each word, of person and place. And so, we finally understand what it's all about—names divide. You become a new country and you change the name to disguise the original people there. That's what happened with the testament. They're all Jewish scriptures that had been copied and changed as we went along.

Every translation or copying in the past changes the work. One of the problems of the preservation of ancient scriptures is that we have copies of copies of copies of copies; and each translator twisted it his or her way.

MC: Is there an example you can give us of something that you ran into where you said, "I'm stuck, I don't agree with others, and I'm just going to intuitively come up with something."

WB: It happens every day. My examples would be mainly from Classical Greek. I did a bilingual edition, back in 1965; it keeps coming out in new editions, of Sappho. Sappho is tremendously fragmented. It is understandable, but you have to have a sense, not only of the language, but of the ways of communicating to put disparate pieces together into works of collage beauty. That's exactly what happens with someone like Sappho. Yes, one is always making intuitive guesses, but hopefully intelligent guesses, and not just willful ones. I say not just willful ones because I believe in a partnership with the past, but let the original prevail. The original, to repeat myself, must prevail in song. If you translate Homer and don't make it sing, it's not Homer.

MC: Now what specifically did you like so much about the Cathars, and what language did they work with?

WB: That's very complicated, but quickly: the Cathars were Manichaeans and they were a good part of the population in Constantinople and Bosnia and places like that, where they were very many. They spoke Slavic languages. They were a pain in the ass to the Orthodox Greeks, who were doing a little bit of slaughtering here and there against this particular heresy. They sent their missionaries to the West, and the language they used was Latin. So when they brought Manicheanism they used Latin.

But in France the surviving scriptures that we have are in the language of the servant French, which is Provençal, which is one of the many dialects. Provençal was spoken by millions of people and it's still spoken. Catalan, the language of Catalonia, is pure Provençal. It's not hard to understand. Certainly, there was very little literature by comparison with the south. The Renaissance began not in northern France. It all happened in Provence, and then Sicily.

After the Inquisition and the Albigensian Crusade kind of destroyed much of what was in Provençal, they moved to the next good place, which was Sicily. The language is very beautiful, very musical. If you know French it takes a few weeks to get used to Provençal.

MC: In *The Gnostic Bible* what were your criteria for what would go in and what would go out?

WB: We have, let's say, the equivalent of a good 350 page book of scriptures, and that's including the songs by unknown people. The two books (and I can't say which I like more, they're both fantastic) are the *Gospel of the Secret Supper* and the *Book of Two Principles*, and I included one wild one called *A Nun's Sermon*. Those were all written in Provençal. I wanted to tell you something interesting.

MC: Sure.

WB: I mentioned Gershom Scholem, but today when you go to Catalonia—I travelled with my wife all over the castles and fortresses where the people were slaughtered, one after another, the last holdout against the coalition of northern French, English, and Spanish warriors who burned them alive, and now wherever you go in southwest France, that is, the Catalonian region, instead of saying *Le pays Catalone* they call it *Le pays Cathar*, the Cathar country or the Gnostic country. It's very beautiful to see that. They don't know a damn thing about Gnosticism but they are so proud of their Gnostic past. Over every restaurant is *le pays Cathar*, and there are so many books on Gnosticism in French and largely on France's own fabulous example of Gnosticism, in the most beautiful form, which is that of the Cathars—which means "pure" by the way, like *catharsis* in Greek

MC: Who would you say influenced the Cathars? It seems there was a big soup around that time—you had the Cathars, the Troubadours, the more liberated noble women, and Kabbalists. Can we ever find out who influenced who, or was it simply everybody influenced everybody?

MC: Who would you say influenced the Cathars? It seems there was a big soup around that time—you had the Cathars, the Troubadours, the more liberated noble women, and Kabbalists. Can we ever find out who influenced who, or was it simply everybody influenced everybody?

WB: Well, look, ideas prevail in all religions. I mean, Christianity began a little later than Gnosticism. Gnosticism obviously precedes Christianity, with Hermes Trismegistus in Egypt and so on—but the same ideas prevail. Plato, who probably as most of the ancient Greek philosophers got their ideas from India, because Indian religions precede Western religions, believed in Eternity. The Jews of the Hebrew Bible had no notion of Eternity, which is very pleasant to me. They believed that the messiah was an earthly leader. But after Plato, by that time, the Jews were looking for a God who might be a little closer, who would show up. So the Gnostics had him be inside an individual, like Spinoza, who has tremendous understanding of the Gnostics. But they were all Platonized. Plato said the soul persists. He didn't say the body persists. The Christians say the soul does, and you can take your diamond ring with you if you want, it depends on the sect.

Now it's very interesting that the Jews believed in the Inner Light. The notion of light is essential to the Jews. "Let there be light." The first poem that exists in the Western world is the Biblical creation of the world through language, with the words "Let there be light" in Hebrew; and that's a beautiful poem. That is a great Gnostic beginning of the world, "Let there be light."

MC: So you have no doubt that Gnosticism was a pre-Christian system, through the Hermetics or maybe the Sethians?

WB: Marvin Meyer's really knowledgeable about the Sethians, and so is Jorge Luis Borges. Dating is always problematic, but the Gnostics probably go back a century or a century and a half before the first century. So we're talking about the first century B.C.E., and of course everything begins with Adam and Eve, you might say. There are notions of finding one's own God, which is the essence of Gnosticism, where you find it in the Gnostics, is in oneself. We are universally lights. I don't like Jung, but Jung, who kidnapped or pirated some basic Gnostic texts, smuggled some Nag Hammadi scriptures out of Egypt into Switzerland—as you know, was profoundly interested in the Gnostics and the notion of a world consciousness is totally Gnostic.

There are books now about the prevalence of Gnosticism in literature. There's one I don't own but which I saw came out quite recently in England, which speaks quite thoroughly about it. I, in my afterward for both *The Gnostic Bible* and *The Essential Gnostic Scriptures*, have a long historical meditation on all aspects of Gnosticism including its beginning; so I'd have to bone up on what I said to answer your question better, but it's all there

MC: If you would indulge me, Willis, you brg up Jorge Luis Borges; he's certainly one of my favorite writers. I always consider him very influenced by the Gnostics, wasn't he?

WB: Oh, he knew everything about them. He has this marvelous essay on Basilides. He also has an essay on Judas: "The Three Ways of Judas."

MC: I love that story.

WB: In other words, it was supposed to be a huge discovery when they found, around the time of Nag Hammadi, the *Gospel of Judas*; separately, they found it. You know, all the Humphrey Bogart intrigue about the survival. However, Borges knew the story long before they had written about it, because he knew Irenaeus and he knew Augustine. They all knew about the *Gospel of Judas*. The Church Fathers who railed against Gnosticism, including Augustine who was a Gnostic missionary for several years in Hippo, where he was born, in north Africa and also when he came to Europe. They all wrote very correctly about the Gnostics, whom they despized. So when the Nag Hammadi texts came out, this wonderful abundance of scriptures, it only confirmed what the anti-Gnostics, including Plotinus, had already told us.

Therefore people like Milton and Goethe and Spinoza and Melville—they knew nothing about the Nag Hammadi scriptures but they certainly used the word "Gnosticism" and they were profoundly influenced by it. Swedenborg would be nothing without the Gnostics.

MC: Or William Blake.

WB: William Blake. Exactly. Or Allen Ginsberg. But anyway.

MC: So Borges was definitely influenced by the Gnostics.

WB: I used to have eminent conversations with Borges in Buenos Ares about the Gnostics. I did do two books on Borges. He loved them. In fact, I do not have the book right here, but at the beginning of *The Other Bible* he said, "If Alexandria (meaning the Gnostics) had prevailed, instead of Rome, these texts, which we now consider dangerous heresies would be perfectly and conventionally normal."

In other words, what is proper and good are the winners. The Gnostics lost, therefore they are a heresy. Heresy just means "the loser."

MC: While we're having this great conversation about literature, what other literary giants do you see were influenced by the Gnostic ethos?

WB: Well I think I mentioned some of them. Those who were more profoundly influenced were Goethe and Milton and Blake and Melville and Emerson. Emerson was particularly interested in the Gnostics because of the Hermetic philosophers in Egypt. As a matter of fact, about 20 to 25 years ago when I was in southern Egypt, in a little place in the Valley of the Kings, there was a guest house that went back for a century. The man took out his guest book and rather consciously naive asked, "Have you ever heard of these people? Well how do you pronounce that name?" And I said, "Ralph Waldo Emerson." His signature was there. [Laughs]

MC: That's a great story.

WB: Called the Brahman of Boston, right. They all were interested in India and Egypt. H. D. the great poet, Hilda Doolittle, was imbued with Gnosticism and Hermes Trismegistus. Her trilogy, which my daughter edited for New Directions, it's all full of the light of Gnosticism.

MC: And we can't forget W. B. Yeats.

WB: Yeats. I love him. He was a jerk. [Laughs] Intellectually, I should not say that. I went to his country and as a poet his melodious verse is incomparable and he went off the beautiful, unreadable deep end in his visions and dreams, but Gnosticism was one of the ingredients. Don't get me started on Yeats. I'll tell you anecdotes again until dawn

MC: You can tell us one anecdote, if you want.

WB: Well, one anecdote which is really amusing: In the north, where the grave of Yeats is, you go there and you see the wonderful inscription "Pass by, so and so"a—but that's not the gravestone. What happened is Yeats died, I believe in Monaco, between France and Italy, and after a year of negotiation among the heirs, they finally got an order to send the bones of Yeats back to Ireland.

Well, they were very embarrassed because they had simply thrown the bones of Yeats into an ossuary, meaning a place where you put bones. So finally, they agreed, and gathered some bones from the thousands that were there, put them in a bag, and sent them back to Ireland. So what you're looking at or being reverent about is a nice selective Monaco reproduction of William Butler Yeats. But who cares?

MC: Willis, can you tell us a little bit about your new book with Marvin Meyer, *The Essential Gnostic Scriptures*?

WB: Well, it's about 270 pages, as opposed to a 1000 pages, and we have really not revised the text, although Marvin has revised his introduction, I believe. I left out my introduction on the problems of translating ancient scriptures into modernity, but that you can find in the older book. And then my afterword, which is a historical meditation on Gnosticism from the beginning to the present is there. About 80% or

85% of it remains.

I would like, if my life had time for it, to do a book-length media-
tion on Gnosticism, but I don't have time for it; I have too many other
things lined up. Out of great insecurity, I keep working.

MC: We're all very glad. Does it include *Thunder, the Perfect Mind*.
What do you think of that text?

WB: Oh, it's the most poetic work. It's equivalent to the Book of Revelations—*Apokalypsos*, in Greek—it is extraordinarily wonderful. My
best answer to your question is "read it." It's marvelous. It's one of the
great poems of all languages, one of the greatest—modern, ancient—
combines everything. Read it over and over again and you've taken two
graduate courses in literature. I haven't praised that one much, have I?

MC: I think you give it due honor. And you also recently, or not too far
back, did a new translation of the New Testament?

WB: Yes, that's *The Restored New Testament*. Half of it came out with
Penguin Books in 2003 as *The New Covenant*. The word "New Testament" is a mistake. It was a mistake by Jerome; he translated the Greek
word *kainē diatheke* as "testament." It's not a testament or testimony in
any way. It's an agreement; it's a pact. So it should have been "The New
Covenant." In Hebrew the word for "pact" is *brith* or *brit*—in Ashke-
nazi Hebrew—which means "cutting." The image of cutting became
the abstract word for an agreement or a pact.

The word "Christian" didn't exist in the Gospels, "Christian" meaning "the anointed" in Greek, an attribute of the Messiah. Paul did not
use the word "New Testament" but he did speak of the scriptures of as
the "new circumcision," going back to Deuteronomy saying we must
have a circumcision of the heart, not of the flesh, meaning a symbolic
circumcision.

It's rather funny, the proper name for the New Testament, *kainē pe-
ritome* in Greek. The New Circumcision.

MC: And what does this book have?

WB: What it has is the complete New Testament, plus the *Gospels of
Thomas, Mary Magdalene,* and *Judas*. We translated it into verse. We
restored all of the original Hebrew and Aramaic names. After all there
were no "James's" back in those days; it was Yakov, just as with the Ger-
mans now. And when the name is a Greek name like Andrew, we call
him Andreas. We're capable of saying "Andreas." If it's Simon, we say

"Shimon", we're also capable of saying that. Why make them all sound Scandinavian, or like people from Kalamazoo or London?

MC: That's true, that's true. And lastly, Willis, do you, in your circles, know any new translations that are coming up the pipeline that we might be excited about. It's been a while since the *Gospel of Judas*; we need more!

WB: Well, there will be many translations of *Judas*, probably in the future, but I think the supreme and beautiful one is done by Marvin Meyer. I do not know of other translations, and I don't think there's going to be another version of most of the material in our Gnostic Gospels. It took us about 12 or 13 years to do, and that's a big hunk of time.

MC: But do you know of any other texts that are right now being translated from either Greek or Coptic? I think the Ashmolean Library in Oxford has a huge amount of blackened papyruses that that they're still wrestling over or wrangling over.

WB: Oh, yes. But they're usually different versions of extant texts, and I know this mainly from Marvin because he's a Coptic scholar. They're wrangling about interpretation. It's very good, because with our new rays, I guess it's blue and infrared, they can detect texts under texts which have been lost and which are now found. We found the longest script of Archimedes whited out in a church prayer book.

There's a suggestion, and I believe it's a correct one, that people from Stanford have said, that in the coming time we may recover 35% more of ancient scripture by looking into the sublevels of ancient scripture; and I'm sure that will require a lot of translation to bring it into English and other languages. I think that's the greatest hope for the moment, more than even digging.

We can't dig very much because the Egyptians aren't very interested in Greco-Roman Gnostic things. Unfortunately, early Christianity wiped out all the traces of Gnosticism that they could. The Great Library of Egypt was not originally burned not by the Gnostics but by the early Popes and bishops, alas. And of course we know about what happened in the rest of Europe, in Provence, and Constantinople, the Inquisition, the Albigensian Crusade, all of this to wipe out the wonderful Gnostics.

It's wonderful—horrible, I should say—a wondrous horror, how each religion is so eager to award the faithful and punish the unbelievers. Faith and loyalty are the only meritocracy that exists in authoritarian cultures. We see this all the time.

It's very promising in our time because I think we're moving so far away from the notion of one idea, one rule. We're in a very ecumenical, very eclectic age, and I see great hope for the future.

DANIEL C. MATT

Daniel Chanan Matt is a Kabbalah scholar and professor at the Graduate Theological Union in Berkeley. He is the author of *Zohar: Annotated and Explained*, *God & the Big Bang* and *The Essential Kabbalah*.

It's no secret that Jewish Mysticism, specifically certain Kabbalah schools of thought, are considered relatives of classic Gnosticism. Such concepts as an emanation theology, a cosmic cataclysm, direct divine knowledge, and archontic forces are present in many Kabbalistic systems.

It's also no secret that Daniel C. Matt is considered a leading authority on Jewish Mysticism. It made perfect sense to interview him on the Kabbalah and its relation to Gnosticism, much of focus on his book *The Zohar, Annotated and Explained*. We not only discussed the theological similarities of Kabbalah and Gnosticism, but the possible historical origins and streams of the Kabbalah. Mainstream scholarship still views the Kabbalah as a primarily medieval movement, but Daniel granted other possibilities. He also provided some keen insights on Jewish Mysticism in general, revealing it to be always a vibrant esoteric pursuit for any person of any religious background.

MC: To begin more or less broadly, Daniel, as far as your research and tradition has told you, when did the Kabbalah begin?

DM: It's really very hard to pin down. I would say that there are certainly Biblical roots to the Kabbalah and roots in the early Rabbinic Judaism. But I would say it emerges as a movement within Judaism in the 12th century, 12th century Europe, in Southern Europe, in Provence, Southern France, and then it goes over the Pyrenees, you could say, into Spain, and it's really in 13th century Spain that the movement crystallizes. And that's where the greatest text of the Kabbalah, the *Zohar*, was probably composed.

MC: But isn't the *Sefer Yetsirah* long before any of this?

DM: *Sefer Yetsirah* could be called proto-kabbalistic. Many of the images of the Kabbalah appear in *Sefer Yetsirah*. The most significant is the sephiroth, the 10 sephiroth. Now in Kabbalah, sephiroth means the 10 aspects of God's personality. God's love and God's judgement, masculine and feminine powers, but in *Sefer Yetsirah*, it doesn't really have meaning yet. In *Sefer Yetsirah* the 10 sephiroth are just the numbers one to 10, the numbers through which God creates the universe. Because, according to that text, God created the world through letters and numbers, through language and arithmetic, you could say. So that *Sefer Yetsirah* is a very important part of Kabbalah, and it does predate what I'm describing, but there's no wide agreement on when *Sefer Yetsirah* was composed. Probably around the second or third century. I say that because of the style of Hebrew. The Hebrew of *Sefer Yetsirah* seems similar to early Rabbinic Hebrew of that period, second and third century. But then there is a long underground development of the Jewish mystical tradition between *Sefer Yetsirah* and this next creative period of the 12th and 13th centuries. I would call *Sefer Yetsirah* a pre-kabbalistic text and one of the roots of Kabbalah. So it's hard to pin down exactly what you would call Kabbalah. Of course, kabbalists would say that it goes back to the time of the Rabbis or earlier, or to the patriarchs, or to Moses, even to Adam and Eve. But looking at it historically, the major texts of the Kabbalah, particularly the *Zohar*, are a product of the medieval era.

MC: Back then in Provence there was a little renaissance with the kabbalists, the Sufis and the Cathars and all that, and before that there might have been problems with medieval Christianity.

DM: Yes, partly that, partly fear of criticism from outside and from within, and the mystics' own hesitancy to talk about their direct experiences. So, for whatever reason, I think you are right. The mystical tradition was kept secret for many centuries, and kept secret, but at the same time developing as it was passed from master to disciple, and then it really flowers in medieval Europe and, you are right, Provence is really a very fertile ground. You have Christian mysticism and the influence of Islam coming from Spain, the Middle East, and a lot is going on in Provence. In the Jewish community you have philosophy and rabbinics and mysticism all developing, and then it's really in Spain that Kabbalah becomes a really creative force. But even at that time, it is still relatively small circles of kabbalists teaching and copying this material, and it really takes several hundred years before it reaches a broader segment of the Jewish population and begins to influence European mysticism, and that's later in the 15th and 16th centuries.

MC: Yes, and I guess the culmination of it would have been the Shabbati Zevi movement.

DM: Yes, that messianic movement where Shabbati came to see himself as the messiah, that's 17th century, and at that point Kabbalah becomes fascinating to very wide circles. But when that figure Shabbati Zevi converted to Islam, he was rejected by most Jews and at that point didn't really arouse a lot of opposition to Kabbalah. The next stage is really Hasidism. Hasidism in the 18th century, you might call that a popularization of the Kabbalah, and at that point it spread to very wide circles in the Jewish world. That really is an arc, you know, you can trace that arc from the early teachings in very small rabbinic circles and *Sefer Yetsirah*, then more of the creative development in Spain and the 13th century, and Shabbati and Hasidism. You might say that in the age of the rational enlightenment, in the 18th and 19th century, there was reaction against Kabbalah and reaction against many mystical teachings. Many Jews were embarrassed by it and they wanted to just jettison the whole mystical and supernatural element. They wanted to redefine Judaism in purely rational terms. So it was really in the 20th century that Kabbalah was rediscovered, thanks in great part to the work of Gerschem Scholem, the great scholar of Jewish mysticism who lived in Jerusalem. Then you have this more recent phenomenon of mass media and Hollywood and the phenomenon of the last 10 years or so, where there is another explosion of interest. So it's interesting how that's moved throughout the middle ages and into modern times, and at this point or even discussing it on web broadcasts.

MC: Yes, we are. Could you tell us the why, when and where the *Zohar* was written?

DM: This is interesting. We mentioned Spain, but of course, traditional kabbalists believe that the *Zohar* goes back at least the second century, to the famous Rabbi named Simon the son of Yohar, Shimon bar Yohai, who was a student of Rabbi Akira. Shimon bar Yohai lived in the second century in the land of Israel. We know his teachings from the Talmud, he was a very fiery figure and had some creative and radical things to say. For example, according to the Talmud Rabbi Shimon said, "God depends on the human being." God says, according to Rabbi Shimon, "If you are my witnesses, I am God; if you are not my witnesses, as if it were possible, I am not God."

MC: Wow, so this isn't Lurianic Kabbalah, this is right in the *Zohar*.

DM: No, this is right in the Talmud. This is the real Rabbi Shimon that actually lived in the second century.

MC: The Talmud says that, that's amazing!

DM: It's actually in the Talmud. The roots of Kabbalah are there in the Talmud. But they are buried in dozens or hundreds of pages of legal material, and you really have to ferret them out. But the Talmud has some very radical things to say about the nature of God. And what I'm saying is that the real historical Rabbi Shimon had some very radical things to say about divinity. But as to whether he wrote the *Zohar* or not, that's another question. Kabbalists believe that he wrote the *Zohar*, or that it was written in his circle, in the second century. But most scholars today, most academic scholars, would say that the *Zohar* was really written 1100 years later in 13th centuries Spain. And the person who composed it or edited it—I would say the composer of the *Zohar*—was a kabbalist named Moses de Leon. Moses de Leon was living in Spain, he was born in northwestern Spain in the city of Leon. He may have composed it along with the other people, he may have inherited certain writings, but I think he's the major composer of the *Zohar*. So you have a book being written in the 13th century, but attributed to this Rabbi Shimon who lived over a millennium earlier. And the question is, why did Moses de Leon attribute it to this ancient figure, Rabbi Shimon? That's a complicated question. He may have believed that he was really in touch with Rabbi Shimon, that he was somehow channeling the teachings of this ancient master. Or there may be a much more down to earth explanation, that he wanted the book to be accepted, maybe he wanted the book to sell, and he's attributing it to this ancient figure. And actually, I think that both of those may be at play. It sounds like an impossible combination of motives, but I think that he may have been motivated spiritually and materially, financially, and felt that he was in touch with this ancient figure, but then he composed it and embellished it and actually tried to circulate it as ancient wisdom. Unfortunately for the history of the Kabbalah, that fantastic claim was accepted and people came to see the *Zohar* as an ancient text going back to Rabbinic times. It was seen as one of the holiest books within Judaism, perhaps only second to the Bible and the Talmud.

MC: Yes, and isn't the *Zohar* written in a sort of stilted Aramaic with Spanish expressions and so forth. Gerschem Scholem says that there's about three strata of writers he can find in there?

DM: There really are different stages of composition. It's almost a library. There are really 18 or 20 stages of composition. I would say that Moses de Leon wrote much of it, but certainly not all of it. Some things are written after him by someone trying to imitate his style, and, you're right, the Aramaic is very strange because Moses de Leon knew Aramaic not as a spoken language—probably at that point no one in the world was speaking Aramaic. He knew Aramaic from having studied the Talmud in Aramaic and Biblical translations in Aramaic, but he's trying to write this book in Aramaic without really being fluent in that language, in terms of knowing how to write it or speak it. He only knew how to read it. So his Aramaic is really unique. It is very bizarre, there are a lot of invented words and neologisms. And in translating the *Zohar* that's a real challenge. You come across a word that's really invented by him. Sometimes Moses de Leon will take a rare term in the Talmud and switch around a couple of letters, and you really have to ponder it for quite a long time to be able to estimate what is meant.

MC: So, the purpose of the *Zohar*, I'm seeing, is that it seems to be a Kabbalistic midrash on the Hebrew Bible, or was it more to clarify and bring out the hidden message in the Talmud. Which one is it?

DM: It's both and other things as well, I would say. It certainly presents itself as a commentary on the Torah. It's not written, chapter one "God", chapter two "Torah", chapter three "Finding God in the world". It's not written in any systematic way except as a running commentary on the first five books of the Bible. So the *Zohar* begins commenting on Genesis and then moves through Exodus, Leviticus, Deuteronomy and commenting on every verse, but on every significant story and many minor stories, and it tries to find a mystical, spiritual meaning in even the smallest details of the Biblical text. It's a very radical approach to the Torah. For example, the *Zohar* says the very opening words of the Bible, "In the beginning God created," we shouldn't read it that way. Rather, it's "In the beginning it created God." God actually turns into the object of the sentence, rather than as the subject. Now, what does that mean? It sounds ridiculous or heretical, "it created God." What the *Zohar* is really saying is that there is an infinite God. There is a God beyond God. This is very similar to teachings in Gnosticism. There is a God beyond what we know of this God, and that ultimate God is called infinity, or in Hebrew *Ain Soph*, literally "there is no end." This infinite divinity emanated or generated what we think of as God. So in that sense, it, the infinite, created God.

MC: And they didn't change the words, they just found different definitions or different alternatives for the words. So there was no corruption of the Torah?

DM: Right. It's accepting the Torah as it's written, but reinterpreting it. That's a technique that is used throughout all religions. In order to keep the tradition alive, it has to be interpreted and reinterpreted and applied. The technique of the Rabbis is called midrash, which is imaginative interpretation of the Bible. And the *Zohar* is just taken that a little further, or a lot further.

MC: Yeah, because really what attracts most Gnostics to the Torah, because if you read it literally... You mention one Rabbi, and it's my favorite quote, "If you translate it literally, you're a liar, if you add to it, you're blasphemous." And that makes you really think. And I realized that the Torah, as you say, has numerous meanings, and the Torah is almost an organic entity in itself. It's up there with the creator God, it's his tool, but he's bound to it in a certain way, isn't he?

DM: Yes. We have Rabbinic teachings that God actually got locked into the Torah and created the world. The Torah is God's plan or God's blueprint for the universe. He's pictured as an architect, as an architect would consult his plans, so God consults the Torah. But in the Kabbalah this is taken further and the Torah actually becomes a divine being, it is seen as if the Torah essentially one long name of God. If you reading the Torah, you're not just reading God's commands and stories, you're actually reading into the divine nature. You're pronouncing God's name as you chant the Torah.

MC: How do the kabbalists and the *Zohar* interpret the Garden of Eden?

DM: There is a fascinating description of that. Of course, Genesis describes how God expels Adam out of the garden, Adam and Eve. So who expels whom out of the garden? It really makes you wonder, and the *Zohar* says Adam through God out of the garden. In a sense, we're still in the garden but we don't realize it because we have lost touch with the divine. That's one of my favorite teachings and the whole *Zohar*. In the *Zohar* it's just written as a couple of lines and you could easily pass over, written in a kind of code. But the *Zohar* derives that from a verse in Genesis which says, "He expelled them," and the *Zohar* reinterprets it in a creative way to say, "Adam expelled God."

MC: But he didn't really expel God, he expelled the Shekhinah of God, right?

DM: The Shekhinah of God, which is a very important concept in the Kabbalah, refers to the feminine half of God, the divine presence. So she is God, but a specific quality or aspect of God, God's presence in the world, God's imminence, God's intimacy with humanity, all that is meant by the notion of Shekhinah. Literally, the word means dwelling or presence.

MC: So you would say that the culmination of creation, which I gather from your books and other books, would be somehow to get Tiphareth and the Shekhinah to be married again, or for mankind and the Shekhinah to be together, or would it be for God to get Shekhinah back?

DM: Well, it's hard to separate those options. The way the *Zohar* often describes it is the goal of life, the goal of religion is to unite the masculine and feminine within God, which is to bring together this couple, Tiphareth, the divine masculine, and Shekhinah, the divine feminine. Their union is the goal of existence. That happens only through human action. So, this is another way in which God needs the human being. The divine marriage cannot take place without our active contribution. What we have to do is act ethically and spiritually in the world. Through righteous action we stimulate the union of the divine couple. You might say that every good deed is an aphrodisiac for that divine union. So in that sense the goal is to unite God with God, God and the goddess, but in other parts of the *Zohar* it seems that the goal is to unite oneself with Shekhinah, or with this whole world of the 10 sephiroth, the aspects of God. The *Zohar* goes back and forth between aiming at the divine union and trying to participate in that union.

MC: And the sephiroth are not really explicit in the *Zohar*. It's pretty implicit, it doesn't come out in the form of the diagram, does it?

DM: Right, we don't find diagrams in *Zohar* itself. On almost every page there are references to the sephiroth, but you're right, they're often cryptic. The *Zohar*, for example, will often not use the name Shekhinah or Tiphareth, it will say the King, or the Queen, or the river of emanation.

MC: Or the bed, that's another one.

DM: The bed, the ocean, the garden, and the *Zohar* much prefers that kind of poetic imagery than a systematic presentation of the sephiroth. Other books of the Kabbalah do it more systematically, but I think the secret of the *Zohar*'s success is that it is more allusive and poetic, and it really forces the reader to join in the search.

MC: Yeah, I understand how it could make the reader very interested, because there's a lot of romance and a lot of talk about kings and maidens, maidens with veils, that you have to take her veil off and find the secrets. It's a journey for the reader as well.

DM: Definitely. The romantic search and the erotic element is certainly key to the *Zohar*, the eros within God and the celebration of human sexuality too, if it's pursued in holiness, that's is seen as part of the secret of existence. You have the secret interpretation of the Torah, and also the secret level of existence, and the two go hand in hand.

MC: Can we find the doctrine of reincarnation, the *gilgul*, in the *Zohar* or was this conceived beforehand?

DM: We certainly have no references to reincarnation in Rabbinic Judaism. We have to distinguish between reincarnation and resurrection. Resurrection of the dead means that when the messiah comes then the world will be renewed, but all those who have died will be bodily resurrected. That you do find in Rabbinic Judaism, although it's very hard to find it in the Bible itself, except in very very late parts of the Bible such as the book of Daniel. In the Torah you would not have any explicit teaching even about the resurrection of the dead. But resurrection is different from reincarnation. As I've said, resurrection of the dead, that the dead will someday be revived, that you find in Rabbinic Judaism. What's new in Kabbalah is, of course they accept resurrection, but introduce the notion of reincarnation, that when a person dies, even in present history, he or she may be resurrected, the soul will roll into a new body. The word *gilgul* means rolling. The soul will roll into a new body. Now, this is introduced a little bit before the *Zohar* in Kabbalah, in a book called the *Bahir*. The *Bahir* was written in Provence, or I should say was edited in Provence, towards the end of the 12th century, and that's probably the first Kabbalistic text that mentions the theory of reincarnation. It's talked about in the *Zohar*, but very secretly, very cryptically. You really have to decipher the references to reincarnation in the *Zohar*. Later in the Kabbalah it's talked about much more openly and it becomes a universal principle. But I would say that in the *Zohar* itself, it's not that everyone undergoes *gilgul*. *Gilgul* is seen as something that happens only if you fail to observe certain very important *mitzvot*, certain very important tasks, most of all if you haven't brought new life into the world. If you haven't married and had children, then you will be reincarnated. It's not clear whether it's punishment or more an opportunity, so you have a chance to fulfill this essential commandment. That's really how it's presented in the *Zohar*. Later by the time we get to Isaac Luria, the famous Kabbalistic who lived in Safed in the Galilee, in the 16th century, by then already *gilgul* becomes a universal principle, and everyone, or nearly everyone undergoes *gilgul*. But in the *Zohar* it's more selective and more secret.

MC: How is the concept of evil explained in the *Zohar* or the Kabbalah for that matter? How is evil explained besides being the punishment of God?

DM: Yeah, this is interesting. For the *Zohar*, evil is really the shadow side of God. In other words, God as we know him is good and loving and caring, but there's a dark side. The *Zohar* refers to this as *sitra achra*, the other side. In some ways it's opposed to what we think of as God, but in another sense it emerges from God. It's not clear how. According to one theory of the *Zohar*, when the divine powers are balanced, goodness goes into the world. For there is a balance between love and strict judgment. But when things are out of balance because of human evil, human evil will bring about an imbalance in the cosmic forces, and then harsh judgment overwhelms God's compassion or love or mercy, and evil results from that imbalance. So you have different theories, there's not one unified theory about it. What's most striking is that evil is seen as somehow emerging from the divine and ultimately as serving a purpose either of testing or punishment or temptation, and part of the divine economy and that sense.

MC: Another question, I know we got past the *Ain Soph*, but what would be the ultimate concept of godhead is that the *Ayin*, nothingness, and is that found in the Torah?

DM: *Ain Soph*, the infinite, you could say is really the ultimate level of divinity. It's very hard to distinguish between *Ain Soph* and what the Kabbalah calls *Ayin*, which is literally nothingness. Technically *Ayin* is the first sephirah, and *Ain Soph* is beyond all those sephiroth. But that first sephirah is really inseparable from Ain Soph itself. You might say that infinity manifests as a *Ayin*, this paradoxical nothingness. Now in Kabbalah as in Sufism and Buddhism, nothingness is not a negative term, it's just really means nothingness. That which is beyond material existence. So nothingness is seen as undifferentiated divine reality. It's not yet any one thing. It hasn't yet turned into the world. It's pure potential. In that sense it's no-thing-ness. So infinity and nothingness are seen as almost identical. Both of those, you could say, and the top of the ladder have to find existence. From them all the specific qualities of God emerge.

MC: So you would say that the reason we have existence at all is simply God manifesting himself. Is that why God created the world, as the kabbalists look at it?

DM: Yes, there are discussions occasionally about why did this all come about? Why, as a modern philosopher would put it, is there something rather than nothing? Nothing with a small "n", nothing as a blank. One answer is that God was lonely. God wanted someone with whom he or she or it could interact. So God created that which seems to be separate from God, but this is all part of the divine dance of eventual reunion. God yearns for the divine spark within our soul to reacquaint itself with the divine source, and that will bring about fulfillment of union and mystical oneness.

MC: Is the divine feminine in Judaism something that has evolved since the Kabbalah? Or has it always been present but only surfaced periodically and then gone back down?

DM: This is profound, because certainly if you look at the Bible it's very hard to say anything about the traditional picture of God. God seems purely masculine. It's very rare to find any feminine images. There are a few here or there, in Jeremiah or in some of the later poetic books, but in general God is the King to judge the warrior. The radical innovation in Kabbalah is that God is half-male and half-female. So one wonders where did this come from? Did this just emerge out of nothing? And it seems that there are roots of the divine feminine in earlier traditions. Certainly if you look at ancient Canaan itself, there were definitely goddesses, there was a widespread worship of the goddess under different names Ashirah, Maat, Astarte. So there were goddesses worshiped in the ancient world and the Mediterranean east, and of course the prophets are always railing against this worship, seeing it as a betrayal of God to go after the goddess. But we know now from archaeological finds that there were Israelites who tried to combine the worship of of the Israelite God, *Yod He Vav He*; they tried to combine that with the feminine. So, for example, they've dug up pieces of pottery and which you will see written this is to *Yod He Vav He*, to the Israelite God, and his Ashirah, and his goddess. And this isn't something you find in the Bible. It's criticized, this kind of worship, of syncretism, but we know that there were Israelites who were attracted to it, and apparently it was suppressed, it was defeated, it mostly disappeared, but it must have continued to exist underground as well, as you say. It surfaces and resurfaces and what you find in Kabbalah is really a reemergence of this ancient goddess material. One scholar, Gerschem Scholem, has called this the revenge of myth. This mythic image of the feminine had been eliminated almost entirely, but it came back with a vengeance in Kabbalah. Another way to say this is that the Kabbalah now turns the goddess into something kosher. The goddess really becomes kosher in Kabbalah, and you have a feminine and masculine divinity.

MC: Aren't there are some hints in the Song of Songs and other places when they're talking about wisdom, and wisdom was there from the beginning. In Gnosticism that's considered obviously to be Sophia. How does Judaism, or the Kabbalah see it?

DM: Kabbalah would accept that. In the book of Proverbs and other wisdom literature you do have a feminine entity it seems, that apparently is God's helper and assistant. You don't find in the Bible a description of God being married to wisdom. God is creating the world through wisdom, so wisdom is a divine quality, a divine helper, a divine helpmate, so there is some feminine imagery there. But in Kabbalah it's made much more explicit, and they take all those verses, many of those verses, and apply them to the Shekhinah. So there are hints of raw material that are developed further by the Kabbalah.

MC: Yes, because another character that I've always found very interesting is the figure of the judge Deborah. For some reason I've always seen her more as a goddess than as a human being. Maybe a lot of the judges, I don't know.

DM: Well, they're historical figures, but they also become turned into divine or heavenly versions in the Kabbalah, many of them.

MC: Yeah, like in the Psalms, "Ye are gods of the Most High." Backing up just a little bit, you mentioned, and other people mention, that's there is that word in Genesis called *et*. What exactly does it mean and how to the kabbalists define it?

DM: It's a Hebrew word pronounced *et*, it consists of two Hebrew letters, Aleph and Tav. And that is interesting because of course Aleph is the first letter of the Hebrew alphabet and Tav is the last letter. So it's a little word that contains the first letter and the last letter. As to what it means, it's very hard to pin down. In many uses, in many senses, it has no independent meaning. It's just a marker, it has to appear in a sentence in between the verb and the direct object.

MC: This was from the earliest scriptures, from the Masoretic text and so forth? It just appears there?

DM: It appears there, for syntax. For example, in Hebrew you can't say, I threw the stone. You have to say I threw *et* the stone. It precedes the direct object; it has no independent meaning. But in the *Zohar* it becomes a symbol of Shekhinah. Why? Because she is the last of the 10 sephiroth and she includes all of the others. She includes everything from the first to the last. In some ways it is similar to what Jesus says according to the new testament, "I am the alpha and the omega, I am the first and the last." Shekhinah includes in herself the entire flow of divine being. And the *Zohar* uses that very often when it wants to interpret or reinterpret a verse. But I should say that you also find that in Rabbinic Judaism. There are interpretations of the word already in Rabbinic Judaism.

MC: And, lastly, do you agree with Rabbi Ezekiel, who is in your introduction, the man you met, that in recognizing the divine feminine in all the faces is the only way to have a feeling of mankind?

DM: I should say that the book you're referring to, *Zohar Annotated and Explained*, I wrote that book, meaning I translated passages from the *Zohar* and interpreted them. There's a preface written by Andrew Harvey, and it's there that you find the story about Rabbi Ezekiel, but he talks about the need to rediscover the divine feminine. I would say that it's very important to move beyond the notion of God just as a masculine power or male power or authority figure, and to celebrate the divine feminine, the intimacy of God and the presence of God in nature and the world. I think that's a very important balance.

MC: You won't find anybody who agrees with that more than I do. Could you just tell the listeners what you are working on right now?

DM: I could tell you a couple of things that other than that are available first of all. The book I can talk about most immediately is the *Zohar Annotated and Explained*. It's published by Skylights Paths, or Jewish Lights, that's a small paperback. There are a couple of other paperbacks, one is called *The Essential Kabbalah*, which is published by HarperCollins of San Francisco. And that's a selection of texts and Kabbalah translated with some written notes. There's some other material too, there's *Sefer Yetsirah*, the *Bahir*, Isaac Luria, a little bit of Hasidism. But mostly traditional Kabbalistic texts organized by subject, the sephiroth, divine nothingness, Torah, how to find God in the material world, meditation, sections such as those. Then another book that I've done is called *God and the Big Bang*, which is on parallels between Kabbalah and contemporary cosmology. That was published by Jewish Lights. And my current project, which will take me many years, is a full annotated translation of the *Zohar*. The book we talked about, *Zohar Annotated and Explained*, that's a tiny percentage of the work, but I think it's a good place to start. What I'm working on now is called the *Zohar Pritzker Edition*. The Pritzkers are a family in Chicago who are enabling me to do this work. The full edition is published by Stanford University press. So far three volumes have appeared, and these three volumes cover the entire book of Genesis. I'm now working on the book of Exodus, and I imagine the entire thing will run to something like 11 volumes.

GNOSTIC SCHOOLS OF THOUGHT

DAVID BRAKKE

David Brakke is Joe R. Engle Chair in the History of Christianity and Professor of History, Ohio State University, as well as author of The Gnostics: Myth, Ritual, and Diversity in Early Christianity.

In an odd (and Gnostic twist), one of the most heated debates concerning Gnosticism is whether the Gnostics even existed (while the Gnostics argued in their texts if reality even existed). Scholars like Karen King, Michael Williams and Elaine Pagels advocate using the term "alternative Christian" or just "Christian" when discussing the forces behind the Nag Hammadi library and in church father polemics. On the other hand, academics like Birger Pearson, Dylan Burns, and April DeConick feel Gnosticism is a sensible term defining a specific school of thought in early Christendom, and beyond.

David Brakke falls in the middle of this debate, much like Bentley Layton and a few other academics. His book, *The Gnostics*, draws from and compares the many arguments and ideas on the history of the Gnostics, concluding with some utilitarian ideas such as the notion that the Sethians were the authentic Gnostics, while others like the Valentinians were simply Christian. Beyond that, Brakke's book and our interview explain the latest scholarship on the Gnostics, other academic debates, and his own insights on the complex and vibrant early Christian communities.

In the end, what is most startling is not whether Gnosticism was ever a movement but that early Christianity was nothing like the monolithic movement most have been lead to believe.

MC: You write in your book, The Gnostics, that there are two models in understanding the development of Christianity. One is the Irenaeus model: Christianity grew uniformly but then splinters of heresy broke from it; the other is the horse-race model: where all these groups—Gnostics, Montanists, Marcionites, Encratites, proto-Orthodox and so forth—just shot out of the gate in the second century, fully mature, all racing to the finish line of respectability in Roman culture.

DB: [Laughs]

MC: It's a great one, just the mental image. But you also offer a third and more sensible alternative. Could you tell us about it?

DB: Sure. First of all, we want to understand the horse-race model, as I called it. It is actually a very good model on the one hand. We want to give it props for doing what it does, because it really highlights the fact that Christianity was diverse from the beginning. Different groups had different traditions, interacted with each other. We shouldn't see it as there was simply one dominant Church from which other Christians, just like the Montanists or the Gnostics or the Valentinians, broke away from. We want to say the horse-race model is a good one.

The problems with the horse-race model that it creates stable groups that are just uniform within themselves and separate from one another. This leaves one side known as proto-orthodoxy—that there is one form of Christianity that included such people as Irenaeus, the Bishop of León, Origen, the great Christian thinker in the third century, or Cyprian of Carthage. They all belonged to one brand of Christianity, proto-orthodoxy, and it triumphed in the end.

I think what scholars are moving toward now is not really so much a third model in the sense that we have a new overall way of seeing everything; but I think scholars are now thinking more in terms of how different groups formed their identities in interaction with each other, and that these identities were and are always in flux. Christianity—or we should say perhaps Christianities—are always being invented and reinvented in interaction with one another. There really isn't a kind of single entity that we could call "proto-orthodoxy," not perhaps until the late third century and the beginning of the fourth century. Whether in the horse-race model or in the Irenaeus model, there isn't that one Christianity we can put our finger on.

MC: As you mention in our book, there perhaps never will be because even up to today, Christianity is always evolving, interacting and mutating.

DB: That's exactly right. Some historians of Christianity, I think, would say that there might have been periods, like the Middle Ages or Byzantium in the east, when there was a kind of hegemonic single Christianity from which groups could break away from. But scholars would notice that even with those two examples there were always various practices that people were doing; and there was very seldom a tight control of what Christianity was, even in those situations. But certainly today the varieties of Christianity and the ways they define themselves is astounding, even within large organizations like Roman Catholicism. It's just an ongoing process of people making and remaking Christianity and what it is.

MC: You give some great illustrations in *The Gnostics*, like how all these Christian thinkers and their schools and their churches overlapped. For example, I was floored when you said that Irenaeus—who I often call "old battleaxe" because he's always complaining about something—believed in seven heavens and seven guardians of heaven.

DB: Very true. We like to think "Oh, Irenaeus is just so different from the Gnostics," and of course Irenaeus would like you to think that. But when you look at what he is doing, you see that he is in the same worldview as the Gnostics, which is that God really can't be seen. There isn't just a single God and us. There's God in multiplicity and there are divine beings above us. So yes, he had this notion that there are seven heavens, and there's a different spirit or angel ruling each of these, and they have names like Prudence and so on. We read that, and it's simpler than what the Gnostics had, but it's not so different from our perspective and the way we conceive things. The Gnostics and Irenaeus are not as distant from one another as the church fathers would like you to think that they are.

MC: Another example—and of course this breaks Michael Williams' concept of simply calling Gnosticism "Biblical demiurgists"—but the truth is there were a lot of Biblical demiurgists back then, weren't there?

DB: Almost everybody who was Jewish or Christian and thought about things at all philosophically was a Biblical demiurgist. That is, practically no one who was Jewish or Christian thought that simply God by himself or itself created the world. All of them thought that there was some lower divinity that actually did the hard work of creating. You already see this in the New Testament where "In the beginning was the Word and the Word was with God, and the Word was God, and all things came into being through the Word."

MC: In Galatians Paul says angels handed Moses the Torah.

DB: That's exactly right. So, if "Biblical demiurgical" means you believe in a demiurge that is a lower creator God than the highest God, and you use Biblical traditions to talk about that God, then Philo of Alexandria was one, the Gospel of John was one, the Book of Hebrews was one, Justin Martyr was one, practically everybody was one, and the Gnostics certainly were as well—among them the Valentinians, and so on. So everybody was doing it.

MC: So they basically made Jesus the demiurge and there was no concept of the trinity. He was the creating force.

DB: Right. Certainly in certain thinkers you have what we might call the "raw materials" that would later become Trinitarian thought. Justin Martyr, who was in mid second century, talks about the fact that there's also this spirit—you know, the Holy Spirit—but he's much more interested in the relationship between Father and Son. So he's much more into a binitarian God with this spirit thing over here that he doesn't quite know what to do with.

So the materials are there, but it's certainly not the trinity that we think of, or that later became normative in the fourth century. They all think of what we would now call the second person of the trinity—what we would now call the Son of God or the Word of God—as less fully divine than the Father which, by later standards of Trinitarian orthodoxy, that's not the right way to think. But everybody thought that way at that time.

MC: Another important issue, David, that you bring up in *The Gnostics* is the concept of heresy, which originally might not have meant what we have been accustomed to believing. What did heresy mean in the early stages of Christendom?

DB: At first, in just general usage—before there were even Christians— the Greek word hairesis from which we get "heresy," was simply a neutral word that meant "a school of thought." So, for example, the field of medicine could have multiple hairesis, in Greek or "heresies" we'd say. That is, different traditions of thinking about medicine that might go back to an original person like Hippocrates. You would have the

Hippocratic hairesis. And you do have early Jews and Christians who do use the word hairesis in Greek in a kind of neutral way. The Jewish historian, Josephus, in the first century, identifies different groups of Jews—the Sadducees, the Pharisees, and so on—as hairesis. He doesn't mean to say they're heresies, he just means they're different schools of thought within Judaism. And he says "I belong to the hairesis of the Pharisees." He would certainly not want to say "I'm a heretic."

The word slightly changes as Christians become more and more suspicious of divisions among themselves. What happens is that they start accusing of each other of not being really the truth but being merely a school of thought. They start to use "school of thought" or hairesis as an insult that means "You're just an opinion or a way of thinking; you're not 'The Truth,' which is what we Christians have," or at least, "We group of Christians that I belong to."

Originally it was a neutral word and it became negative, no thanks to the work of certain Christian authors. The notion of heresy isn't just there to use; it's one that's actually invented through this process of identity formation that I was talking about earlier.

MC: So basically terms like "heretics" and "proto-orthodoxy" are just as problematic as "Gnosticism"?

DB: Certainly. And at least "heretic" and "heresy," to their credit, are words that ancient people actually used. Justin Martyr and Origen, for examples, were happy saying "Those people over there are heretics and belong to a heresy." But proto-orthodox is a completely modern invention. It's a word that we have come up with to talk about people who we see now as orthodox in retrospect.

It was a good thing to come up with this word, because we don't want to just say "Justin Martyr was orthodox" because he simply wasn't, and he wasn't there yet when orthodoxy had really been invented. So "proto-orthodox" is a good word, but it's also something that I think can obscure difference among people who we now see as proto-orthodox.

MC: And now to the main event, David. There's always the two paradigms or sides in the whole Gnosticism debate. On one side you have the Williams-King paradigm that thinks the term is problematic and should be discarded for something just like "Christian" or "Biblical demiurgic," and of course on the other side you have Birger Pearson who believes there were Gnostics—nobody's ever going to convince him otherwise.

DB: [Laughs]

MC: You also have Marvin Meyer on that side as well. But you propose a sort of middle way. Don't you propose there were not only Gnostics but actually two types of Gnostics?

DB: Yes. What I argue is that King and Williams are right: the scholarly concept of Gnosticism is not productive. It's too big and includes too many different groups of people that are simply not the same. We group them together in this thing called "Gnosticism" and it's not right to do so because it distorts the groups who are put into that category. There wasn't actually one giant religion in antiquity called "Gnosticism." I agree with their basic point. In many ways, I belong to that camp—the King and Williams camp—than to the camp of Birger Pearson and Marvin Meyer (who are great scholars as well), who want to argue that there really was an ancient phenomenon called "Gnosticism."

What I want to say is a variation on both those ideas: there was in fact a group of Christians, a school of thought—to use the term "heresy" in a neutral way—which was known as the Gnostic school of thought, in which people thought of themselves as Gnostics; but it's a limited group and not inclusive of a whole bunch of other groups. I would separate that group, for example, from the Valentinians, who I would see as a different movement from these Gnostics. I want to continue to use the word "Gnostic" but I want to use it in a very limited sense.

MC: But you also use the word "Gnostic" as the others who thought of themselves as perfected Christians, like Clement of Alexandria?

DB: That's right, a good point. We have to keep in mind that "Gnostic" in antiquity had two connotations. One was as a proper name of a school of thought—"We belong to the Gnostic school of thought"— just as today Christians might say "I'm a Lutheran" or "I'm a Presbyterian." But then it was also a more general term to denote a person who had reached some form of spiritual perfection, and it did not then constitute some kind of particular doctrinal affiliation or something. Clement of Alexandria, who's proto-Orthodox, called the ideal Christian a Gnostic. There seem to have been other groups who did so as well, and this use continued. A famous example is Evagrius Ponticus, who was a fourth century monk, and probably one of the most brilliant theorists of the monastic life in antiquity. He called the most advanced monk, the spiritually adept monk, also a Gnostic.

There are kind of two sense to the word "Gnostic" in antiquity, and we need to be attentive to those different uses and keep them both separately and together at the same time.

MC: And the way you found out who the Gnostics were was very interesting. A lot of people miss it but by reading Irenaeus, who keeps saying, "Well, the Valentinians did this," and "The Marcionites did this," and then, "The Gnostics did this." Most people assume that Irenaeus was just lumping them all together, but he was really talking about one specific group when referring to "the Gnostics."

DB: That's right. At this point I think I'll pause and say that I am not the only one to say this; so I'm not inventing this. So, you know, you shouldn't credit me totally with discovering it. It's a hypothesis that's been out there among scholars, but people haven't really thought about it seriously enough. The idea is that if you read Ireneaus, he seems to be making a claim that there is this group called the Gnostics or the Gnostic school of thought, that is separate from other groups and that influenced Valentinus. Valentinus was not a member, but he was influenced by them.

If you pay attention to what he says about that group—and people have always noticed this—he attributes to them a myth that is narrated in the *Apocryphon of John* from the Nag Hammadi library, or *Secret Book of John*. That's the myth that we as scholars have traditionally called the Sethian myth, and have called the people who adhered to that Sethians or Sethian Gnostics. I guess my proposal really is that the Sethians were the Gnostic school of thought. We should call them the original Gnostics, and not call anyone else Gnostics, in the sense of the school of thought.

So that's what I'm using Irenaeus for, and that's probably one of the more controversial parts of this, because I'm actually suggesting that Irenaeus isn't always lying. [Laughs]

MC: That's always hard.

DB: Irenaeus wrote his big work in the year 180 c.e., and it's clearly polemical, called Detection and Overthrow of Gnosis, Falsely So Called. With a title like he's not being neutral in what he's doing. But he's certainly not writing so that historians from the twenty-first century can have an accurate view of the religious life of his time. That certainly is not his goal.

I do think that in his effort to smear his opponents—and his main opponents are really the Valentinians, the people who are threatening his congregation. He does at times offer us accurate descriptions or does say things that actually were happening in his time. I think this was one of them, because we can check it out, and it does check out when you look into it.

MC: But what if somebody says, for example, Marcellina, who was a Carpocratian, she self-designated herself as a Gnostic. Do you think she was speaking in the context of a perfected Christian?

DB: Yes, that's what I think. So Irenaeus does say, "Well Marcellina, she said she called herself a Gnostic," but it's interesting that he identifies her primarily as a member of the Carpocratian movement. I think what he's saying therefore is that she used that term as Clement did. Remember, Clement of Alexandria, who was called a proto-Orthodox, used the term "Gnostic" as a term of spiritual perfection. I think this is most likely what she is doing as well.

At this point is where my argument is most vulnerable, I would say, because I am trying to distinguish between the use of "Gnostic" as this term of spiritual perfection, rather than as a designation of one's philosophical school allegiance, which is what I think the Gnostic school of thought was doing. That's the kind of argument that I can have with people; and I'm perfectly happy to understand that people would see it differently, but that's how I would see Marcellina.

I would also see that as the case of this group that Hippolytus and other heresiologists talk about called the Naasenes. They too seem to have made the claim, "We're so spiritually perfect that we are Gnostics."

MC: What exactly is the problem with the term "Sethian"?

DB: First of all, we mostly made it up. It's not a term that Irenaeus uses; it's not a term that Porphyry uses. Porphyry is a Neoplatonist philosopher who also talked about the Gnostics, saying there was a school of thought called the Gnostics. The Neoplatonists don't use the term "Sethian." The term really first occurs with Epiphanius, a late fourth century heresiologist, rather removed. It's not a bad term in the sense that these people did identify themselves as the seed of Seth, the descendants of Adam and Eve's third son, Seth. But it seems as though their preferred term for themselves was Gnostics, so we might as well use that.

If we go around talking about Sethian Gnostics I think that kind of opens the door to other varieties of Gnostic. My argument is that we should just call these people the Gnostics. Once you start saying

"These are the Sethian Gnostics" well then over here are the Valentinian Gnostics, and over here are the Marcionite Gnostics, that's precisely the route I don't want to go down, and that's the route that Karen King and Michael Williams have said is so unproductive, and I agree with them. So that's why I am kind of hesitant to continue to use that adjective, but I understand its use and certainly don't jump up at meetings and say "Stop using that!" or anything like that.

MC: I don't know if it was synchronicity, but even before your book, I was reading Philo and he also uses the term "the descendants of Seth" and "the descendants of Cain." This might have already been in the air for Christians.

DB: The Hebrew Bible, in Genesis and so on, just lends itself to this because it's so interested in genealogies. It's always stopping and saying "So and so begat so and so . . ." If you are someone like Philo or Origen or Irenaeus or any of these people, you have to make sense of that; and one way of doing that is talking about these different lineages representing different types of people or different communities. This kind of reaches its climax with St. Augustine of Hippo, in his City of God, where he talks about two different cities on earth: the city of God and the city of humanity. He too will trace this through lineages in the Hebrew Bible.

But he's not meaning this to be literal, like being a part of the city of God is transmitted genetically. He's interpreting these stories to say something symbolic. I think that's what Philo's doing. Descendants of Seth are virtuous; descendants of Cain are not virtuous—it must be saying something to us about different kinds of people. So it's no surprise that the Gnostics used this as well and identified themselves as descendants of Seth.

MC: David, could you give us some of the characteristics of the Gnostics, or the artists formerly known as the Sethians, and what set them apart?

DB: I'm going to have to come up with some unpronounceable symbol for them, right?

MC: Yeah, some Greek letter.

DB: Well, I think the main thing that is most distinctive about their teaching, obviously, is their myth, and that they see the ultimate God, the highest God, as essentially unknowable, remote and indescribable.

This is a very typical way that people indebted to Platonist philosophy thought in this period. God must devolve, in order to communicate with and to engage with lower levels of reality. God must expand as well. Because God is mostly a thinker—God thinks, the nature of God is kind of intellectual. When God thinks, it becomes multiple.

One of the distinctive features is to tell a myth that really unfolds and celebrates the multiplicity of God, whose multiplicity reflects the multiplicity of our own minds and their complexity. There's a lot of interest in the different aspects or modes of thought of the mind of God that are called aeons, residing within the Eternal Realm. It's kind of hard to say. They're both actors but not really actors.

And of course one of the most distinctive teachings, then, is that one of these aeons, Wisdom, kind of went wrong somehow. The result is this lower form of divinity or divine life that they call Yaldabaoth, who is identified with the God of Genesis. And it is actually this Yaldabaoth who created this world in which we live as a rather imperfect copy of the Eternal Realm. In so doing, he dispersed into humanity some original life or power from that upper realm, that his mother, Wisdom, inhabits.

The story of humanity and of God is of God's attempt to return this dispersed spiritual power to the Eternal Realm. The coming of Jesus is a way of making this news available to people and bringing them back to the knowledge of who they truly are, which is forms of this dispersed power.

What distinguishes them very much from other Christians is this view of the God of the Bible, of Genesis, the Lord God in Genesis as essentially being this Yaldabaoth, who's not some wonderful divine character but who's actually hostile to humans. The Gnostics also had a distinctive form of baptism, as well as practices that lead them to have some form of mystical contemplation of God and the aeons. We can look at that in greater detail if you like.

MC: Right, like for example the Five Seals. I think most believe it's just a ritual baptism.

DB: They definitely had some form of baptism that was central to their ritual life because they talk about it constantly. In one text, Revelation of Adam, the author criticizes other groups for defiling baptism and having bad water and so forth. A distinctive part of their baptism, apparently, was something called the Five Seals. One of the most fun things about studying these people is trying to figure out what these Five Seals were. I mean, no one knows the correct answer, really, until some other text shows up in an Egyptian cave somewhere.

But they could be five steps of the baptismal ritual. Like taking off your clothes, putting on some new robe; they could be five different kinds of anointing. Anointing with oil is always an important part of baptismal rituals. So people wonder about what this is, but one of the distinctive features of the texts that belong to this school is this mention of the Five Seals. You don't find the Five Seals of baptism in a Valentinian text. That wasn't not part of their ritual life.

One of the things that makes them distinct is not just a myth or a bunch of thoughts, it's an actual ritual, which is why I think they were an actual group of people, as opposed to folks just writing myths on their own and ripping off other people's myths without any kind of real religious life to them.

MC: We talked before the interview about how much I really enjoyed April DeConick's The Thirteenth Apostle, the second edition. She focuses on the astrology, the astro-theology, the magical rituals of the artists formerly known as the Sethians. But you actually compliment her book very well, because you focus on how philosophy and tuning the mind must have been very important to these people.

DB: Yes. There's always been this group of texts, within the Gnostic set of literature that we've called "the Platonizing treatises," which sounds very scary. They are kind of difficult, but they focus very much on what we would call mysticiSM: some form of direct knowledge of God or contact with God. So, I think one thing that's been lacking in the study of Gnosticism is that there has been such a focus on the myth and how strange it is, that we've devoted not enough attention to thinking, "What would be the payoff for people doing this?"

I do think that this kind of interest in some sort of mystical contemplative experience of God that's very philosophically based—definitely comes out of a Platonist tradition—must have been important to at least some people in the group. I'm excited when I go to meetings now because a lot of younger scholars are picking up on this aspect and writing about this in their dissertations, like about how the Gnostics' interest in knowing God is actually influential on other individuals such as Plotinus. There's a guy named Mazur doing a PhD in Chicago; there's a young man named Dylan Burns. It really excites me to see that kind of work happen, because I think mysticism is an important part of what the Gnostics were about.

MC: Exactly. After all, as you point out, if they believed that God was this gigantic mind of a computer up there, they figured out, "Well, to become God, don't we have to get the circuitry of our mind correct before we can know God?" That's what Gnosis is.

DB: I think God for them is, in a way, our minds but much larger; that's our way of seeing their imaginative process. Far better from their point of view is to imagine that our minds participate in God, and so the structure and nature of our intellect mirrors that of God. One reason that the myth of the Gnostics must be so complex must be that the mind is complex. So, when they talk about mysticism, they have two ways of thinking about it, which must be complimentary for them. One of them is a turning inward and examining one's own thoughts and thought structure as abstractly as possible. Not just thinking about what you're thinking about, but how you're thinking.

They believed that once you do that, you gain greater insight into God, because our minds are modeled after that mind, and eventually you can have some sort of acquaintance with God, which is what Gnosis means, a direct knowledge. Not just knowing that, for example a city exists, but knowing a city once you've been there and experienced it. That's what Gnosis is supposed to be. But our minds are in tune with God, and that's why God is complex is that our minds are complex.

MC: And would you say that the Gnostics saw themselves as the highest branch of Christianity? April DeConick agrees with me that they really thought they were Christian Bodhisattvas; they were full of compassion, but they still saw themselves as above everybody, head and shoulders.

DB: I'm not sure about that. Let's put it this way: I'm sure they thought they were the most accurate form of Christianity. They were the true Christianity. They were bringing the message that Jesus meant to bring. I'm hesitating about the adjective "above" because that might suggest that other Christians were forms of them, or were on their way to be them. I think the Valentinians thought of themselves that way. The Valentinians thought of themselves as a more advanced form of Christianity, and other Christians are kind of "junior Valentinians."

The Gnostics really saw themselves as being the right Christians and other Christians being wrong, in the same way Irenaeus thought other people were simply wrong. If the newly discovered *Gospel of Judas* comes from these Gnostics, or Sethians as others would call them, it's very critical of other Christians. It's not like "We're just better than you. You're not even right about who God is." I think they were Christians and they thought their form of Christianity was the true one, the most accurate one.

One of the points of my book is to say, we like to sometimes think "Oh, the Gnostics, they're like cool people who are inclusive," but in reality they were just as adamant about the truth of their beliefs and the wrongness of other people's beliefs as anyone else was in antiquity.

MC: But they weren't like these rebellious individuals a lot people like to paint them to be? The "protest exegetes" Kurt Rudolph talks about.

DB: Right. I think this is a very important point that Michael Williams made in his book, Rethinking Gnosticism. That's one of the great things about Michael Williams' book. It's hard to believe it's been like fifteen years now.

MC: I know!

DB: But one of the great things about is that he pointed out that the Gnostics were much more engaged with the wider philosophical thought of the day than for example Irenaeus. We think of them as rebels and protesters. They really are part of the fringe to the extent intellectuals are a fringe—but they're not really rebelling against something. They are actually participating in a wider conversation about God and how we know God. They're not radical, wild protesters—they are participants in that conversation.

The fact that a major philosopher like Plotinus, in the third century, felt that he had to write tractates against the Gnostics and explain how he really is different from these people shows that they really weren't so different from people like him.

Protesting the most about being different than others is a usual sign that you're like them!

MC: The lady doth protest too much, right?

DB: Exactly. If you have to spend page after page saying, "We are not like them and they're not us," that usually is a sure sign that there's something close between these two groups.

MC: And if Plotinus is giving somebody attention when we know what

Plotinus thought of himself, that's huge. That's like a celebrity talking about you.

DB: Exactly. He was not one to spend a lot of time worrying about people he thought were not worth thinking about.

MC: What about their origins? Birger Pearson states that there were once Jews who later became Christianized. I think John Turner or April DeConick has this model—where they might have been Jews and then they became Christian and later they were thrown out of the churches. Where do you stand? A lot of their scriptures have Jesus as a kind of Johnny-Come-Lately, or there's no Jesus at all. So how do you explain these scriptures like the Apocalypse of Adam, Marsanes, and so many others?

DB: The prevailing hypothesis among scholars right now is that Gnostics emerged as a kind of disaffected Greek-speaking Jews. Somehow you've got to have a Jewish element because these are people so obsessed with Genesis. It's hard to imagine that some non-Jewish Pagan person decided to pick up Genesis and decided to create a whole mythology just around that book.

The Jewish hypothesis is that Jews started making this myth before they had even heard about Jesus, and that Jesus is indeed added later in a kind of secondary way. I think there's a lot of virtue to that because it explains why they were so interested in what we now call the Old Testament; it avoids the Irenaeus model of seeing them as bad Christians who've gone off the path. Unfortunately, in this model, they become kind of bad Jews who've gone off the path. But that's what all Christians were, we should say, at the beginning, right?

MC: They were heretical Jews.

DB: Right. I tend to belong to the school of thought that they were Christian from the get go. We've got to be clear about what does it means to say a person is Christian. What I mean to say by that is that from the beginning these were people who knew about Jesus and felt that something had changed with Jesus; they needed to respond to that in some way. That doesn't necessarily mean then that they would, for example, make their religion completely about Jesus. Certainly Christians did and do—that's what we'd think Christianity would look like, completely Jesus-focused.

One reason I believe this—and I'll come back to the issue of the lack of Jesus in certain Gnostic texts—is the decision to make the God of Genesis this malevolent, ignorant deity, Yaldabaoth. It's very hard for me to understand any ancient Jew doing this without some message saying something has radically changed and is completely different: that we've had a revelation of a new and higher God, which is what they're interpreting Jesus is.

Jews throughout history have suffered various ills, but never say, "Therefore our God is evil." They always say things like "We have sinned, God's ways are inscrutable," these kinds of things. So I think that what's needed here is not just Jews who feel disaffected and are heavily influenced by Platonism. Something new needs to have happened that says, "Here's a new revelation of a God even higher than the God we thought we knew." That's what they see happening in Jesus.

You're exactly right that some of the texts that come from this group— Jesus is not a hugely prominent character. The *Apocalypse of Adam* is a good example because it doesn't mention Jesus at all, at least overtly. I still think, though, that this human being the Rulers were chastising his flesh could be a reference to Jesus. It is true that, in a document like the *Apocryphon of John*, Christ is a very important figure. Jesus seems to come at the end of these things, and sometimes seems tacked on. But I think that from the get go they thought something new had happened with this Jesus person. Some new revelation had occurred. Maybe for them it wasn't really all about Jesus, it was all about God. Jesus isn't as prominent in this literature as we might think.

Certainly, the external evidence that we have seems to say they were Christians because of the people who talk about them, like Irenaeus. Of course, Irenaeus doesn't say they were real Christians—they were false, horrible Christians.

Almost certainly they were from a Jewish background, but that something had happened that to their minds revealed a higher deity. And that something was Jesus for them. So I don't think they were something that happened before there was Jesus and they later learned about him and said, "Oh, let's add him to our story." I think they were thinking about these issues post-Jesus from the start. I want to say that I and others who think this way—and I think Karen King is one of them—we are not adhering to some sort of Irenaeus model where there was original Christianity and the Gnostics kind of went astray from that.

But when the Jesus event happened, things went off in all sorts of different directions. All sorts of movements and trajectories formed around what Jesus meant. There wasn't just one Christian thing from which the Gnostics derived, but they were one of these many ways of thinking that developed in the light of what happened, in the light of the Jesus event. They may not look as Christian to us as other groups did, but Christ and Jesus were part of it from the start.

If it's the same *Gospel of Judas* Irenaeus was talking about, and I think it is, then the *Gospel of Judas* is thoroughly Christian, along with the *Apocryphon of John*, one of the earliest Gnostic texts. That's one of the most important pieces of information in this question: were the Gnostics Christian from the beginning or not?

MC: Another point, David, where you seem to go against the grain is the concept of dualism. You seem to think that the artists formerly known as Sethians were not as dualistic as other scholars say.

DB: I think dualism is not a helpful word when you apply it to this group, because there are different kinds of dualism, but strictly speaking is the view that there are two eternal principles—good and evil, light and darkness—and one does not derive from the other.

The Manicheans, who come later in the third century with Mani, seem to have been actual dualists—believing in two principles from the beginning. The Gnostics are not this because they seem to believe that the Great Invisible Spirit, who is the ultimate God, the Father of the Entirety, is the source of all that is. Even the world in which we live, as flawed as it is in their view, ultimately has its source in the Father. So they are really monists.

You can use dualism in a softer sense: people who distinguish very sharply between the spiritual or intellectual realm of existence and the material type of existence. In that case the spiritual type of reality is what is truly real, and this material world isn't quite as real or maybe isn't even ultimately real. That's just basic Platonism. In that sense you can call them dualists because they do make that distinction pretty sharply.

To say "Oh, they're dualists, as opposed to other Christians who are not dualists," I don't think is very helpful, because other Christians can in fact be very intense on distinguishing between spirit and flesh. I don't want to call them dualists in that kind of strict sense of having two ultimate principles because they really don't think that way.

MC: What do you think happened to the Gnostic school of thought?

People want to have this romantic notion that Constantine went from house to house with a sword. But that's not what happened.

DB: No, I don't think so. Part of the problem is that in the end we don't really know, let's put it that way. My own view is that they were probably were never a big group to start with. I think that by the fourth century there were really not many Gnostics left. This for a couple reasons:

One, in reaction to them and in dialogue with them, other groups had formed. Among them were the Valentinians, which were a much more successful movement. I could see the Valentinans as being a good alternative for Gnostics.

When Porphyry talks about Gnostics interacting with Plotinus in the middle of the third century, they seem to be much more engaged in discussion with other Platonists than with other Christians—which may be a sign that they feel less at home—although they probably never felt at home in the wider Christian network. You just don't hear that much about them in the fourth century. In the fourth century you have people like Epiphanius with these wild stories accusing them of ritual cannibalism. That seems more like, "Oh, in the old days there were these evil people that did all these terrible things, and they're still around. Watch your children, lock your doors!"

MC: [Laughs]

DB: I think what happened to them is that they just kind of petered out. Other groups like the Valentinians picked up some of those other people who had mystical interests. As you pointed out, the later Gnostic literature doesn't feel, from our perspective, particularly Christian. Jesus isn't a big deal anymore.

As time went on, and the lines between who was a Jew and who was a Christian became more a matter of clarity, the Gnostics found themselves in an increasingly difficult position as well. I think their unique mode of Christianity became increasingly less possible. Not because some government saying, "Don't do this!" but because the ritual and communal life and thought-world of Christians and Jews just evolved in a way that gave them less space to have a productive existence.

The Valentinians lasted longer, and then perhaps you can give Constantine and the bishops and emperors who followed him some credit for getting rid of groups like the Valentinians.

MC: It would be reasonable to say that the Sethians, or original Gnostics, might have been absorbed into Neoplatonism. Furthermore, as Jason BeDuhn explains, and we always forget about the Manicheans who were just as successful at converting people, they might have converted the Gnostics in Alexandria and other parts of the empire.

DB: I totally agree with that. I was holding up the Valentinians as just one option for them, but I they might have just as well gone off into other Neoplatonic groups. The Manicheans would have been another great place for Gnostics to end up because—despite the fact that I don't want to call them Gnostics—I do want to agree with people that point out the resonances between Manichean teaching and the mythology of the Gnostics. And yes, Manicheans were extremely successful.

Often people who study Christianity, third century and later, totally underestimate the importance of Manichaeism as a movement and its attractiveness to a lot of people

MC: I will, but you won't convince Birger Pearson, I know that.

DB: I don't think so, and that's okay. What a great contribution he has made to scholarship. All of us are in his debt. I do disagree about the way he sees Gnosticism, as a larger phenomenon, but few people are as knowledgeable about all of the different movements in antiquity that contributed to what I'm calling the Gnostics, especially Hellenistic Judaism. Great scholar; great guy.

MC: What's the legacy that the Gnostic school of thought left on Christianity?

DB: One of the things I want to say in this book is that we often hear that the Church rejected Gnosticism. One of the things I want to say is that there was no big Gnosticism. There was this Gnostic school of thought, and there wasn't of course a single Church, and "reject" is too simple for what was going on. I think the Gnostics contributed to how Christianity developed in several ways.

Of course, one of them was negative. Not negative because I think it was bad, but a lot of how Christians felt was a response to them. To say, "We don't agree with that so we have to come up with an answer for what they're saying." One way they left a legacy was simply by having ideas that other Christians were like, "No, no, no, we don't like that! So we have to come up with our own thought about the questions they're raising." I think they left other things.

One of them—Karen King pointed this out and she's exactly right— is that the *Apocryphon of John* is really the earliest datable book we that provides a Christian comprehensive account of human salvation from God to the future consummation of all things. The Gnostics set a precedent of saying one of the tasks of a Christian intellectual or thinker is to come up with such a comprehensive vision. They left this audacious act: come up with a comprehensive vision of God and the world. That is as a legacy.

Another legacy is their interest in the demonic rulers that oppose human beings and prevent us from being virtuous. They're very interested in the various demonic cohorts that are around Yaldabaoth and obstruct our quest to be good, virtuous people. That's picked up by not only by people like Origen but later by desert monks. Christians develop a great interest in that.

And their mysticism. As I said earlier this is one of the things that really interests me about the work of some younger scholars. They're showing how texts like Zostrianos and the Foreigner—the Gnostic texts that talk about mystical acquaintance with God—actually influenced other people like Plotinus and so on, and through him people like Pseudo-Dionysius. That's also part of their legacy, part of the things that Christianity as we know it has actually taken from the Gnostics.

The Gnostics weren't just rejected—they interacted with them and some of their ways of doing things were actually assimilated into other forms of Christianity.

ISMO DUNDERBERG

Ismo Dunderberg is Professor of New Testament Biblical Studies at The University of Helsinki, as well author of *Beyond Gnosticism: Myth, Life Style, and Society in the School of Valentinus*.

In *Voices of Gnosticism*, we were honored to provide the interview with Einar Thomassen, an original translator of the Nag Hammadi library and a noted authority on the Valentinians. In this book, we present another leading expert on the elegant school of Valentinus, Ismo Dunderberg. A second perspective is very sensible, in my view, for the Valentinians were perhaps the most complex Gnostic school of thought (and many scholars don't even regard them as being Gnostic at all, merely a more sophisticated form of early Christianity). Their cosmologies, notions on the nature of the soul, interpretations of the death of Christ, and other theologies are varying and layered—with disagreement among the many successors of Valentinus in the second and third centuries.

Much is written on the byzantine mythology of the Sethians, but the Valentinians matched their span and depth—albeit with a kinder attitude towards creation and its ruling angels, as well as the human condition and sexuality. This all points to the speculative and creative aspect of all Gnostic schools of thought. Regardless, Dunderberg managed to capture the Valentinian ethos with precision and even empathy.

In the spirit of the Valentinians, our interview revealed that Thomassen and Dunderberg disagree in certain respects on the Valentinians. What they agreed on was that lofty ideas twere never truly a divergence from early Christianity and moreover became a foundation of Christianity, even to this day; and that the legends concerning Valentinus only reveal a larger than life figure that was honored in the Christian community—until later church fathers like Irenaeus of Lyons felt threatened by this broader, philosophical, and even inclusive movement.

MC: Could you tell us from your research who was Valentinus and how did he come to establish his schools?

ID: Valentinus was an early Christian teacher often designated as a Gnostic. I approach him as an early Christian teacher who received his education probably in Egypt and from Egypt he came to Rome around 130 C.E., and then he became obviously quite successful as an early Christian teacher, so a later rumor even added that it was a very close call for him to be elected the Bishop of Rome. It may be that the rumor isn't historically accurate but it shows his relevance and importance in Roman congregations. We don't know for sure if Valentinus ever left Rome after he went there. It seems that he established a group of people, probably quite educated people, and we know quite a number of Valentinians who were associated with Valentinus and were usually described as his followers or members of the school of thought established by him.

MC: Would it be safe to say that stories that he almost became Bishop of Rome and came in second place? Or that it's Eusebius quoting somebody that he came up with the concept of the trinity? These things you have to take with a grain of salt, don't you?

ID: Yes, the thing with the bishop is that the story continues, and you find the story in Tertullian. The story goes that Valentinus, because he wasn't elected, became bitter, and only for that reason became a heretic. So it was a polemical story, and we have a competing version of why Valentinus became a heretic, and the competing version is that he shipwrecked in Cyprus and therefore he went mad. I wouldn't say that either of these stories is true. Probably they are both based upon later malevolent rumors. All these kinds of stories, regardless of who told those stories about whom, should be taken with a grain of salt.

MC: As you mentioned before, it seems like the problem, especially with all the research that has been done with the Nag Hammadi library and so forth, is the concept of Gnosticism. Do you see Gnosticism as a problematic term, and can it even be applied to the Valentinians?

ID: The problems are well known in research. The term Gnosticism itself was coined only in the seventeenth century. It doesn't appear in the early church, although there are some early Christian groups designating themselves as Gnostics. For example, we don't find that word as a self-designation in Valentinian sources. I often think of the problem that has been pointed out by Karen King and Michael Williams, especially Karen King, that as soon as we begin to talk about Gnosticism people think that we are talking about something different than Christianity. I found it more fruitful to try to locate Valentinus in the Christianity of the second century and I think that there are many things that support that location rather than portraying him as an exotic Gnostic teacher. But of course there are different views about that and we probably can't get rid of the term Gnosticism. But I think when we use that term we should be very careful of what we achieve by using that term.

MC: But isn't the term second-century Christian also problematic? It seems it was very fluid and very speculative in the second century. There were so many sects with different ideas.

ID: That's exactly why Valentinus fits well in the second century, because it's kind of a laboratory when people were experimenting with different ideas of how to integrate Christianity when faced with classical Greek and Roman education and Greek and Roman philosophy. I think what makes the whole thing in the second century so interesting is that everything seems to be in motion still. There are no councils yet which decided how Christianity should be understood. People were approaching that issue from different perspectives.

MC: Could you tell us how Valentinus' theology and philosophy were unique or different than the Christianity around him at the time.

ID: It's actually quite a complicated question. We know that many followers of Valentinus differed from other Christians by assuming that the world was not created by the supreme God but by an inferior ignorant creator God. That is actually quite unique. There is only a certain amount of historic Christian groups maintaining that and that certainly stirred controversies among Christians and also stirred controversies between these Christians and platonic philosophers. So that actually seems to be the greatest difference. We can't tell, because we only have a dozen fragments coming from Valentinus' own writings, so we can't be quite sure what his stance was in this discussion was, but it seems that he also taught that the world was created by inferior and probably malevolent creator angels, so he accepted that idea. But it doesn't seem to be very dominant in his thinking. There are several fragments that do not differ in any significant manner from the standard early Christian teaching in the second century. You wouldn't recognize the difference.

MC: Some have posited that Valentinus may have come with early mystical Christian ideas and it was his followers like Ptolemy and Marcus who began to create these grandiose cosmologies and neoplatonic ideas. Do you see any veracity to this idea?

ID: As far as the evidence goes, it's true that the best evidence we have for these grand mythical accounts comes not from Valentinus, and not even from his first generation students like Ptolemy, but Ptolemy's followers. But, as I said, I don't exclude the possibility that Valentinus already had some background in that kind of thinking, that he may have accepted cosmological myths as we find also in non-Valentinian Gnostic writings, or in the so-called Sethian writings, but I still think that what dominates the picture in the fragments we have from Valentinus is, for example, that he interpreted the same Christian scriptures as other Christians would have done as well. He quotes Paul and he quotes the Gospel of Matthew, for example, so in those senses he seems to have been a very standard early Christian from the second century. And he's also interested in moral aspects.

I'm not really sure whether Valentinus was very heavily mystical. Of course, it's a tricky term and has problems of its own, but when I'm reading the fragments of Valentinus, I rather see his concern about, for example, how one soul could be purified from demons, so it's one important aspect of his teaching. There is one poem where one could think that he is having mystical apprehension of the world and there is one story where he met Logos—that is Christ—in the form of a child, so that could be something like mystical experience, but it's awfully difficult to know because we don't really know the context of that text at all, it's only a few lines of text and we don't know what he meant by that story.

MC: What about the idea of the Valentinians, that each person was given a sort of angelic counterpart once they became part of the body of Christ. Is that from Valentinus? Where did it come from, do you think?

ID: I don't think we find the angelic counterpart in the fragments of Valentinus. Of course, it doesn't necessarily mean that Valentinus didn't have that idea, but we don't have any evidence for that. We have that idea, for example, in the teachings to survive from Theodotus. My understanding is that you can follow that line to Jewish traditions, but that also might be one quite important idea of Valentinians, that they have angelic counterparts, and it was also very important in the anti-

Valentinian polemics because Tertullian expressed horror at the pros-
pect of being married to an angelic counterpart after death, because he
thought that angels are male and he made fun of that idea, insinuating
that I don't want to be an angel's sex toy after my death. This is pretty
much what Tertullian says. It's quite gross, I would say.

MC: But it meant that you were simply joined to your angelic counterpart, the daemon or the eidolon, or later on Mani meeting his divine
twin, and so forth.

ID: Yes, I think basically the idea is the same. I'm not sure that Mani
or the Thomasine Christian would speak about angels in that connection, but basically the idea is very similar—that you have part of your
soul stored somewhere else, and you have become separated from that
original connection, and you are returning to the original state and it's
expressed in different ways. For example, in Thomasine literature the
same idea is expressed in terms of twinship in many cases, that it's not
only of angels but also of the idea that one's heavenly twin or heavenly
spouse, all these possibilities.

MC: And another question that is often brought up is the notion of
dualism. Do you consider the Valentinians dualist? Or some sort of
qualified monists?

ID: It's a very difficult question because when it comes to the theological system it seems to be dualistic in the sense that there is a strict
separation of this world and the other world, the supreme God's world.
But on the other hand it seems when we compare Valentinian teaching to other, for example, Sethian texts, it seems that the Valentinians
held a much more positive view about the physical world. They didn't
think that the lower inferior creator God would be very hostile towards
mankind. They rather thought that this demiurge might be ignorant
but he's not malevolent and they thought that especially the Valentinian Christians themselves were especially loved by the demiurge, so it
doesn't sound in the practical level very dualistic and it also seems their
views about this physical world weren't particularly negative I think, at
least for most Valentinians.

MC: I guess the question is, although for example you read the *Tri-
partite Tractate*, or let's say the *Gospel of Truth*, everything happens by
the will of the Father. But ultimately matter and spirit are completely
different, or come from different sources, or that's how the Valentin-

ians played it. They weren't going to blame matter on the Father, even though he allowed it.

ID: Definitely the idea for Valentinians is that matter won't be saved. It was also commonplace in antiquity, though of course it may sound somewhat blasphemous for present-day Christians, that the flesh won't be saved. But most people in antiquity would have agreed that the flesh wouldn't be saved, because everybody saw what happens to flesh after death. We can speak about monism and dualism in Valentinianism on very different levels. Unlike in other so-called Gnostic systems, in Valentinianism there are no two different original principles. There is no original evil principle, so it's monistic in that sense, that everything, including this physical world, emerges and goes back originally to the supreme God. There is only one original principle and there are not two opposing principles as in some other views. Later, for example, it is my understanding that in later Manichaean texts you may find this kind of original opposition between good and evil. But in Valentinianism it is rather that the whole thing stems from a single source.

But, on the other hand, there is great variation in the physical world, in how hostile they would find it. Valentinus himself believed that people can be possessed by demons. So you may call it a dualistic understanding as well. Some Valentinians like Heracleon thought that even the soul, which most people think in antiquity that the soul survives, so Heracleon thought that the soul itself wouldn't survive after death. I'm not sure whether that should be called dualism but it certainly shows a certain attitude towards the visible world. It's not overtly negative, I would say, after all.

MC: It seems that the Valentinians came up with a sort of compromise that was basically the psyche, right, and the tripartition of man? The psyche was sort of a compromise and I believe some—I don't know whether it was Valentinus or another Valentinian—believe that the psychic human could gain salvation but he would gain a lower form of salvation.

ID: That's one Valentinian theory. On the other hand, it was perhaps a more common notion in antiquity that the soul or psyche is the place where the decision between good and evil is taken, where the human being takes the decision whether he wants to follow good things or whether he is inclined to evil things. We also have that other notion, also attested in Valentinian writings, where it would then mean in that concept it's rather the soul should become something else in order to be saved. Or it unavoidably becomes either spirit or matter if the soul inclines to matter or material things then it becomes matter and it will be destroyed as matter will be destroyed. So that's another theory which we also have in Valentinian writings which actually seems to make more sense even in our present world than perhaps this very strict distinction between psychic inferior Christians who don't have the knowledge and spiritual Christians who already have knowledge.

MC: So basically you have a choice to make, whether you want to go back to matter or whether you want to go to the spiritual. They weren't universalists, let's put it that way.

ID: I should emphasize that I think we have in the Valentinian sources evidence for both understandings. Usually Valentinians are described as having the idea of three fixed categories for human beings, but that's only one theory and the other seems to be more flexible in the sense that it gives room for transformation, for example.

MC: You say that everything comes from the monad, or Bythos however they would call the ultimate source. But matter ultimately is destroyed. Why is matter destroyed? Is it a deficiency?

ID: It seems that matter is, in Valentinian mythologies, a by-product of the cosmological myth. In ancient philosophy, in most philosophies matter was as original as God. The Greek and Greco-Roman philosophers usually didn't find the idea attractive that the creator God would have created something out of nothing. So they thought that God needs matter to create something. As soon as God begins to create matter it no longer is matter, it becomes something else.

But Valentinians thought that matter has an origin and they also thought that matter has an end, so in that sense they were adapting Jewish-Christian eschatology. They thought that matter emerged at the same time as the demiurge, and the demiurge, the lower God, worked at matter. At the end of times matter disappears and that also means that material human beings disappear or are destroyed as well. It probably was the idea if they promoted that idea among philosophically inclined people those people found something familiar about matter and they found something quite new in the idea that matter plus people inclined to matter would be destroyed at the end of times.

MC: How did they view Jesus Christ? Obviously I'm sure they had different views of him. But in essence he was an aeon who came to restore Sophia who committed transgression that gave us matter with the demiurge and to save the spirituals, those with the seed, from matter.

ID: It seems that they usually spoke about "Christ" or they used some other forms for that aeon or eternal being who came to visit the fallen Sophia who was left outside the divine realm. It sounds awfully mythical but when we begin to look closer at the myth it describes what the Christ has to offer Wisdom is what Jesus has to offer the believer. So it's kind of the Jesus-believer relationship transferred into a mythical account.

I think they are describing that by means of cosmic myth as well. And one thing that Christ was for Valentinians, perhaps more importantly, was a teacher and they emphasize his role as a teacher rather than as a ransom for our sins. But also one important aspect which I find interesting in the ancient context was they also portrayed Christ as the healer of emotions, because in antiquity there was a whole lot of discussion how one can get rid of noxious, wrong kind of emotions. There were different theories of how people can achieve peace of mind, and I think that Valentinians offer one theory. They wanted to portray Jesus as meeting that kind of expectation that he was the doctor of emotions, as the ancient philosophers themselves were often portrayed as doctors healing emotions.

MC: He was a sort of heavenly psychologist, a heavenly Freud.

ID: A heavenly Freud, or heavenly Heidegger, yeah. Perhaps even more a philosopher, no? In most cases I'm not sure what he would qualify as the heavenly Freud because I don't remember if we really have any accounts where Christ is portrayed as listening to your problems, it's more like he takes them away.

MC: We're going back to the church fathers who split the Valentinians between western and eastern. They saw the nature of Christ himself very differently. One side saw him as coming in the flesh, while the other side, didn't they see him as just taking a psychic form, perhaps?

ID: Yeah, there's a discussion about that, whether all Valentinians seem to have agreed that Christ had a different kind of body, but they couldn't agree whether the body was psychic or spiritual. They didn't think that Christ could have had a material body because matter was reprehensible, not a good principle, so it's impossible to think that Christ could have had that kind of matter. But we should also remember that in Valentinian dichotomies, matter is not flesh, so it doesn't necessarily mean that people disagreed with the idea of Christ's becoming flesh, but it's certain that they won't associate Christ with matter.

MC: Matter's not flesh? What do you mean by that?

ID: Yes, matter is not flesh. For example, we can see that these three essences: spirit, soul/psyche and matter, they are all present in all human beings except for Christ. Only after then the human being has all these essences already, only then the human being is provided with leathern garments, and that comes from the Genesis creation story, where God sews leathern garments for Adam and Eve after the fall. It was quite commonly thought that this describes how the human being was provided with a body, with a visible body. And Valentinians had that notion as well, and probably accepted that notion as well. So matter is rather a wrong kind of principle working inside the human being and this body of flesh is only a cover for the human being. The Sethians really describe the body as a prison of the soul, or as the prison of the spirit, but Valentinians rather seem to have thought that the body is something we must have. They didn't really think that body itself is matter. Matter is a rather more profound principle.

MC: Another interesting question, and I don't know if there is an answer. We do know that the groups we can put at least somewhere in the category of Gnosticism, that we do actually have writings for, are the Sethians and the Valentinians. Do you see them as completely parallel movements, or could they have crossbred at certain points?

ID: They are usually grouped together because they belong together as Gnostics. I sometimes play with the idea that if Valentinians would have met Sethians, would they really have thought that "we are thinking the same things" and perhaps they would have felt more like normal early Christians because we know that's probably the biggest different, at the level of myth it seems the Sethian myth is much more radical or extreme in its condemnation of the Old Testament and its portrayal of the inferior creator God as evil, while Valentinians seem to be more moderate. They think that the demiurge is ignorant but not necessarily evil. And in terms of social organisation we know from Irenaeus that for him the big problem for that bishop of Lyons was that Valentinians attended the same meetings as other Christians. That's a particular problem for Valentinians. I would assume that Sethians were also socially more distinct from other Christians. If we would use the terms "sect" and "church" Valentinians were certainly more church-oriented people and were not so distant from the surrounding society as Sethians, who seem to have been more rigid and supporting more radical distance from society.

MC: But we don't know if their ideas were parallel? Like you said, there's no evidence of a Sethian and a Valentinian having a conversation in a pub in Rome?

ID: They certainly had common ground when it came to their myths, and certainly their myths of the fall of Sophia and that kind of thing, the myth of the demiurge and the myth of how Adam was created, they are so similar to each other that there must be some comparison. In my book I compare the Valentinians, using a family metaphor: in some terms they are like sisters in comparison to their more distant cousins. But even though they would have agreed on having similar points in their myths, I'm not quite sure whether they would have agreed with the consequences or whether they would have wanted to associate with each other.

MC: Ismo, what are some of the sacramental practices of the Valentinians that we know of?

ID: I read in Thomassen's great analysis of Valentinian writings he reconstructs a sacrament of initiation that is strikingly similar to what all other Christians would have gone through. In most cases we could also interpret the same texts as being witness to Valentinians discussing the importance of the use of Christian sacraments. But of course we have some evidence, for example, there was one Valentinian group led by Marcus, who was also called the magician in the hostile sources, by opponents, and it was told that Marcus and the followers of Marcus, practiced, for example, there were even bishops conducting a kind of deathbed ritual, to those about to decease. So the dead ones were anointed before their deaths and provided with secret keywords or codewords which they should use in the hereafter, and that certainly is a ritual practice we don't have in that form in other Christian circles. In some Valentinian groups they had their distinct ritual practices as well.

MC: Do you mean they were given these secret words, in other words, while they travelled up the heavens to get through the gates of the archons?

ID: These are the answers in that form of Valentinianism. They were in a sense hellfires because they assumed that when you go to the hereafter, then you meet angelic or some kind of rulers commanded by the demiurge himself, and you must be able to give the right answers to these gatekeepers in the hereafter in order to be released, in order to get back to the pleroma, to the realm of fullness. The picture of the demiurge in this ritual is more negative than in Valentinian sources in general. Therefore, I assume that this wasn't commonly practiced by all Valentinians but by a certain group of Valentinians.

MC: Ismo, do we have any evidence that some Valentinians might have believed in reincarnation?

ID: I'm not quite sure. In the Sethian writings we would have, as far as I can recall, but I might be wrong. I don't recall that we would have any clear evidence for reincarnation in Valentinian sources.

MC: And what about the sometimes romanticized sacrament of the bridal chamber, about which I've heard different ideas from the more common that it was simply a form of chrism or baptism to the more occultist radical one that they actually practiced sex magic? What is your view on the bridal chamber?

ID: That is something we hear only from the hostile sources, and of course we know that even very innocent rituals in the hands of their opponents can turn into very vicious things because we know that Christians altogether in antiquity were accused of, for example, cannibalism, because they have the Eucharist, so the rumors developed that Christians were eating human beings in their meetings and because Christians are meeting at night they must be orgies. I think that when the church fathers in their hostile sources describe the Valentinian sacraments I'm inclined to think that they are not much more reliable than these other people accusing all Christians of similar non-moral behaviour. We don't have any first-hand evidence for any of those immoral rituals taking place. Of course everything is possible in the region of religion. We know that these things may take place in religious groups but we don't really have any sexual evidence we have only malevolent accounts.

MC: So you think the bridal chamber was just another sacrament?

ID: I find it possible that there was some additional sacrament at least practiced in some groups, because it is sometimes mentioned in the connection of baptism and Eucharist and bridal chamber it looks like it could be a ritual at least in certain groups. Irenaeus tells us that the bridal chamber was practiced among Valentinians in different ways and somebody thought that it was simply some kind of spiritual initiation that didn't require any sacramental aspect to it in terms of material things. It's very difficult to know. We have much less evidence than we would want to have about the bridal chamber. Irenaeus certainly wants us to believe that Valentinians had this immoral ritual which they wanted to practice everywhere and in every place that they go.

MC: And the question of free will. I believe April DeConick writes in *The Thirteenth Apostle* that when you had baptism the rulers of the stars were actually replaced with the apostles. And that was the way Valentinians were able to get rid of *heimarmene* (fate). Do you agree with this, or how do you think they saw the concept of free will and fate?

ID: Yes, it's a plausible explanation. It generally comes from the text called *Excerpts of Theodotus*. In any case the text clearly states that fate is valid only before baptism. After baptism we are liberated from fate. I've been thinking about that, whether that means that after baptism you understand that fate doesn't exist or whether it literally means, as we may gather from the text itself, that fate is a real factor before baptism. But in any case it claims that after baptism people are free from fate. It's actually quite interesting as well because almost all people who were discussing fate in antiquity claimed that all other people are subject to fate but we are free from it. It's also not so unique as we would assume in the beginning.

MC: So, to say the least, if we were to travel back in time, we would not be able to tell a Valentinian from a Christian if we were walking down the street or going to church? Perhaps they had meetings on the weekend where they discussed philosophy, but outside of that they were one and the same.

ID: That was Irenaeus' big problem.

MC: He had a lot of problems.

ID: He wrote a massive five-volume work to make the difference clear. So it shows that ordinary Christians didn't know that Valentinians were other kinds of Christians. Even for these Marcosians, the followers of Marcus. it is told that some faithful women attended the meetings and only during the meeting realized that this is not a normal Christian meeting. People didn't know in advance which Christian groups were those which Irenaeus would have liked or which were the opposed one. So it certainly was a big problem and I'm not sure how many Valentinians would define themselves as Valentinians. It's quite clear that their first and foremost self-designation was that of a Christian rather than a Valentinian. Some of them certainly designated themselves as students or followers of Valentinus as well.

MC: One last question Ismo, if you don't mind. This is from a friend who has been studying Coptic and Greek. He told me that Einar Thomassen suggests that the really beautiful poem *Summer Harvest* can be read in a strictly dualistic sense, but he says that when he read your book you say that, no, it's a very monistic poem. What is your argument to counter Thomassen's view of *Summer Harvest*?

ID: I think that the poem has been interpreted in that way. Where we find it in Hippolytus there is a short commentary but I agree with Einar that the commentary is secondary. I think Einar starts from the Valentinian mythology of Christ to figure out how the poem reflects the whole thing, while I'm rather seeing that what the text affirms is a chain of being coming from bottom up, from the lowest element to the highest and from flesh to soul to air they are all held together by the spirit. So I think that even the flesh belongs to the cosmic chain held together and sustained by the divine spirit. This isn't my arguments to begin with, it's Christian Markies who pointed out it doesn't sound awfully dualistic, rather it sounds much more monistic in the sense that the whole cosmic world, including the visible world and including the body, they are all part of that great chain of being and that whole being is provided by the divine spirit. There is no rupture at any point in the poem. That would be my main argument. That's certainly one of the points where the scholars' interpretations of Valentinians differ is how much Valentinian mythology we should read into the fragments of Valentinus.

MC: If you don't mind, one last question I have: the *Tripartate Tractate* has always confounded me. I don't get a feel that it's completely Valentinain, maybe because of the switching of the mythos, and the lack of Sophia, maybe because it's more monistic than others. What is your take on the *Tripartate Tractate*?

ID: Although the figure of Sophia is lacking there, we have the very similar figure of Logos or the Word there. What I find intriguing about the text is that it's so much concerned about society and the structure of society and what it does with the cosmic myth. It explains why things are as they are now, and it explains how and why society has heresies, and why the church must suffer at the hands of those who have power. I would be inclined to think that it's a Valentinian writing, but it certainly sees or makes different points than for example the Valentinians whom Irenaeus describes. So it's quite a different take on Valentinian myth and a different application concerning what we should do with the myth and what we should explain with the myth. It's not so much focused on human beings and their different classes but it also shows interest in how society is structured and I argue that it can be read as mild criticism of the ways things are right now. That makes it much more interesting for me.

MC: So it's sort of a pastoral version of Valentinian thought?

ID: It's a pastoral version but it's also a political version of Valentinianism.

MC: Alright Ismo, well I think that's all the time we have today. I'd like to thank you very much for coming on Aeon Byte and giving us your time.

ID: Well, thank you Miguel, it was pleasant talking to you.

SEAN MARTIN

S ean Martin is the author of *The Cathars*, *The Knights Templar* and
The Gnostics, as well as an independent filmmaker.

Even before the publication of one of history's greatest bestsellers,
The Da Vinci Code, the Cathars have been a perennial favorite of oc-
cultists, Medieval romantics, and conspiracy theory buffs. They represent the engaging motif of the enlightened few crushed under the fury
of intolerant powers. Consequently, legends and lineages sprout like
weeds from the fecund soil that is the rise and fall of these alternative
Christians from Provence, France, in the middle ages.

The Cathars might not have even been Gnostic, but that's a subject
of great debate. Some scholars even contend the Cathars didn't exist,
and were merely rebellious Catholics in a time of no real centralized
authority. After all, championing Mary Magdalene and her marriage to
Jesus, reincarnation, vegetarianism, or a dualist cosmology wasn't out of
bounds in the history of Christianity.

Enter Sean Martin, an independent scholar with an incredible ability to simplify and organize esoteric subjects without losing any scholastic depth. In our interview, he did just that, granting a clear picture of
the Cathar culture and the Albigensian Crusade of the 13th century that
actually sparked the Inquisition. Additionally, Sean offered the possibility the Cathars survived in some aspect, beyond their sensationalistic
manifestations still found today in novels, occult revivals, and non-fic-
tion books of questionable scholarship like *Holy Blood, Holy Grail*.

MC: I noticed both of your books deal with the important issue of dualism. Could you tell us what dualism is, and what are its origins?

SM: Yeah, dualism is basically the belief that instead of just having one all powerful God, you've actually got two. In the sort of Judeo-Christian take on things—that's basically God and the Devil. In other words, the dualists believe that the Devil is as powerful as God. Life is a constant struggle between good and evil. It sounds like something out of a fantasy movie. That is essentially what Hollywood blockbusters do is, in its very filtered down version, it's all dualist idea that evil is as strong as good. That comes out in *Lord of the Rings* for instance.

Its origins are quite obscure. As far as we know, the earliest—I mean dualism could be older than recorded history—but the earliest recorded dualist faith is Zoroastrianism. Zoroaster or Zarathustra as he is sometimes known, is a man of uncertain dates himself. We think he may have lived around the year 1200 B.C. but that's give or take a couple of centuries. Zoroastrianism is probably the worlds oldest revealed religion. The role of evil—the evil principle in Zoroastrianism—it originally started out as the evil principle not being as strong as the good. Then it underwent changes over time. Eventually the evil principle in Zoroastrianism became as powerful as the good, especially in an offshoot called Zurvanism. From there Zoroastrianism influenced all sorts of religions. Most of the main Western ones certainly. It has influenced Judaism and Christianity quite profoundly.

It then later flourished with the Gnostics who seemed to have been active around the time of Christ up until the fourth century of the common era, and then sort of went underground, and then the trail goes very cold. Then it re-emerges in the high middle ages with the Bogomils and the Cathars, and then it kind of goes underground again. It's an interesting tradition. It's a long tradition, and it's one that does intermittently kind of just reappear into historical visibility, but its origins are fairly murky.

MC: And as far as we can tell, were the Cathars true dualists? Did they really see Satan and God as equal, coexistent, or was God going to win in the end?

SM: Well, in the Zoroastrian version of events, God will win at the end of time. There were different types of dualism, it has to be said. The Cathars, when they first emerge into the history books in the 1140s in Germany in the Rhineland, they seem to have been what's called mitigated dualists or moderate dualists. That means that if you're a moderate dualist, it's a bit like the original Zoroastrian idea that, although the power of evil and the Devil or Satan or whatever you want to call him is as strong as God, eventually God or good will triumph.

We know that in the 1160s or 1170s the Cathars became absolute dualists. They were converted by a Bogomil priest who came over from probably Constantinople; Istanbul in modern parlance. There was a big Cathar convention in the South of France—well, what is today the South of France, but then was the independent Kingdom of Languedoc. This guy came over and there was a big meeting, a big Cathar convention. He seems to have persuaded them all to become absolute dualists. The absolutes believed that God and the Devil are completely equal, and there is no guarantee that there will be a happy ending.

Mind you, it has to be said that a lot of these guys—the absolute dualists including a lot of Cathars—believed in reincarnation, and the idea that time is cyclical so, if the devil wins this time maybe God will win next time--history can repeat itself—which is quite an eastern idea. Reminds me of—in Hinduism, you have the Great Yugas, the Great Ages. We're currently in the Kali Yuga, which is the age of darkness and violence and oppression.

So that's kind of a brief summary of dualism in regards to the Cathars. I think the Gnostics of the classical era—from the time of Christ, up until about whenever they kind of fall off the map really, in about the fourth century—they were probably moderate dualists. They often talk about—all of the very colorful and detailed Gnostic creation myths—all talk about the active role of what they called Yaldabaoth, who is basically the same as the God of the Old Testament. They didn't really have—the classical Gnostics—didn't really have a Devil, or an evil principle in the shape of the Devil of medieval Gnosticism—the Gnosticism of the Cathars and the Bogomils.

The Gnostics of classical antiquity basically said the God of the Old Testament is, as it famously says, "I am a jealous God . . ." and spends much of the Old Testament giving the Israelites a really hard time. [Laughs] It's sort of their take on it—with a God like that we don't need a Devil.

MC: Right. [Laughs]

SM: The God of the Old Testament—as I said the Gnostic name is Yaldabaoth, which is translated in various ways. Sometimes it means

childish God or selfish God—They said this God claims to have created the world but he didn't get it right because evil exists, and war and
hunger and famine and so on. Their take on it was—This God thinks
he knows what he's doing, but he doesn't. There's actually a higher God
above him. I obviously now know why your website is called *The God
Above God.* [Laughs]

MC: Right. [Laughs]

SM: That kind of idea that the God who is overseeing the material
world is not the highest authority, there is somebody else higher up
the food chain as it were. I think this is sort of reflected in mainstream
Christianity to some extent where the Devil is known as the Lord of
this world. I think that is a reflection of the old Gnostic idea that the
Deity who was supposed to have created this world is actually not
the "main man" as it were, he just thinks he's in charge but he's not.
[Laughs]

MC: You mention the Cathars—their origins were in the Rhineland?
Do we really truly know where they came from?

SM: The Rhineland Cathars were the first Cathars to emerge onto the
pages of the history books. I think they got found out in about the year
1143 or 44. Apparently they blew their cover by having an argument
about some point of doctrine, and somebody tipped off the local bishop.
They all got hauled up in front of the Bishop. The Bishop of Cologne
I think. The Bishop managed to persuade them all to come back to the
Church. A couple of them didn't, and got burned at the stake. Before
they got burned, they said that their Church was a really old tradition
that dated back to the time of Jesus and the Disciples. There is actually
no way of proving that, although there is no way of disproving it either.

What we do know, or what we can kind of piece together is that
the Cathars were basically the Western version of the Bogomils. The
Bogomil faith flourished in the Balkans starting in about the year 930
or 940. In other words, the second quarter of the 10th century. It was
said to have been founded by a priest called Bogomil, whose name we
think was an alias or a pseudonym meaning beloved of God, or words
of that effect.

The Bogomils were pretty extreme guys. The only scripture they
used was *The Lord's Prayer.* They were violently opposed to the ruling
Church in the Balkans at the time. They were kind of revolutionaries.
They didn't want the priests to go about in fine clothes. The Bogomils

were firmly on the side of the peasantry who were getting a bum deal from the Church.

What we think happened is that the Bogomils came over in waves, or maybe small groups to start proselytizing Bogomilism. The interesting thing is though with the Bogomils, none of them ever got caught, at least in the West. They did in the East in the Byzantine Empire. We know of one guy, Basil the Physician, who got caught and was interrogated and questioned by the Emperor—this was around the year 1100—and quite unusually got burned at the stake. They didn't really go into burning at the stake very much over there at that time. That was very much a Western thing.

For the Bogomil missionaries who came to the West, it was one of the best undercover jobs of all time, because they kind of came in and started converting people, then disappeared almost like phantoms. One of the things that I find quite interesting about them is they managed to slip in under the radar and start this new religion off. They only came to the attention of the Church in the West as I say in about 1143 and 1144 in the Rhineland. By that time, it was quite prevalent because then these guys who called themselves Cathars started to appear all over the place. In Holland, in the low countries, they made it to England as well during the reign of Henry II.

What's confusing is they were all known under different names according to which area they were in. One name—for instance—they were known by is Texerands, which I think was particular to the Netherlands. Nobody knows what Texerand really means. They think it's something to do with weaving and weavers. Weaving was a profession that was often associated with the Cathars for some reason. Then in England they were known as the Publicans—which didn't mean they were running bars, which is what the word means now. I'm not sure what Publican meant in the 12th century. It was probably a corruption of a continental word. Then they become known as Cathars, largely in Germany and the South of France. There's differences of opinion as to what it means. Some people say it's derived from the Greek *katharoi*, which means pure ones.

Interestingly enough, at the Council of Nicea in 325—which is really where the official Western Church got its act together, and started to draw up things like the *Nicene Creed*, and try and decide what they actually believed in. One of the things on the agenda to discuss during the council was what to do with the group called the Cathars, or the

Katharoi, who were quite extreme ascetics. It would be nice to think there was a link between the 4th century Cathars, and the 12th and 13th century Cathars but it's really difficult to prove. Although the medieval Cathars would say there was a link, no historian has yet managed to uncover a link, so it's really conjectural.

The other etymology of Cathar is that it means somebody who kisses a cat's bottom, [Laughs] which is what Devil worshippers and all sorts of evil people, including heretics like the Cathars were supposed to have done. The Medieval church was really good at demonizing its enemies. Obviously they said a lot of similar things about the Jews, that they were eating Christian children. This was completely unfounded. Also, in the case of the Cathars, they weren't going around kissing cats' rear ends or anything. It's just stuff they were making up for the purposes of propaganda. But anyway, the name stuck so they were called Cathars. To this day we're still not entirely sure which one is the right derivation.

In terms of what the Church thought the deadliest of heresies, as far as medieval churchmen were concerned, these guys probably really were going around doing things to cats, and all sorts of very Satanic ways. [Laughs]

On the other hand, the Cathar priesthood—who were called the Perfect, who were both men and women—really were very pure people. They were quite noticeably Good with a capital G. So, the idea that they were the pure ones—that works as well. They were pure in that sense—they were abstaining from all of the vices that the rest of us mere mortals get up to. [Laughs]

MC: What are some of the other theological beliefs that separated the Cathars from mainstream Catholicism?

SM: Essentially—I've got a list here, it's in no particular order—some of the main defining differences between the Cathars and the Church were that the Cathars rejected pretty much the whole of the *Old Testament*. They regarded the God of the *Old Testament* as not the creator God. To them he was Yaldabaoth or the childish God who was basically synonymous with the Devil: what became the Devil because the idea of the Devil underwent a lot of philosophical changes. That's really interesting in itself. The idea of how evil became personified. As more of the *Old Testament* came to be written, people changed their ideas about what evil was.

The Cathars believed this world was created by either an evil or, at the very least an incompetent deity who is not the real God. Obviously the mainstream church would say that the creator God and the true God are one and the same, who is also the God of the *Old Testament*.

The Cathars also believed that because of that, creation itself, material things were evil. Having said that, they saw the necessity of earning a living. You might be trapped in an evil creation, but you've got to pay the rent. They were fairly practical people, and they got involved with lots of artisanal professions like weaving, which is one thing they became particularly associated with. They also worked as carpenters, for instance, or blacksmiths. They felt like they were in the world, but not of it—as the saying goes.

They also didn't venerate the cross. To them the cross was the instrument of Christ's torture and death. Obviously in the mainstream Church at the time, and also in the Orthodox Church and the later protestant churches, the cross is venerated as the emblem of Christ's suffering and sacrifice. The Cathars didn't go for that sacrificial thing at all. To them the cross was the instrument of Christ's death and suffering. His role in coming to the world was not to be a sacrificial lamb, but to actually bring knowledge. Knowledge that would save us all.

They also built no churches. They held their services in people's homes usually. They were sometimes also known to have held services in barns or fields or woods or by rivers. That is really beautiful actually. Brings the spiritual life into the everyday in a really tangible way, especially if you are holding service, or giving a sermon in somebody's place of work or where they live rather than in a church.

MC: Were they vegetarians, Sean?

SM: Yes, kind of. Basically you've got the two main ranks of Cathars, or the normal believers. Then the Perfects—who were the priesthood. Once you became a Perfect you weren't allowed to eat meat, but you could eat fish. So they were fish-eating vegetarians—or rather the Perfects were fish-eating vegetarians. The normal rank and file of Cathars—what we call the believers, or the listeners—basically could eat meat, or eat anything they wanted really. It was only that point they decided they really wanted to commit to the faith, that is when they underwent the ceremony known as consolamentum which means the consoling. Once you've been consoled you couldn't eat meat again, although you could eat fish. If you did accidentally eat meat—somebody accidentally slipped a steak in under the radar, as it were—that meant you were no longer a Perfect, and you had to be re-consoled. So you had to start from scratch. They were pretty strict and extreme.

You couldn't make a mistake once you were a Perfect. A lot of them seemed to have stuck it out actually from what we know. Even when they eventually began to clash with the mainstream Church—a lot of the preachers who were trying to spread the message—the Church realized that these guys were actually winning the hearts and minds of people because they were conspicuously holy. Once the Perfects became the Perfects, once they had been consoled, a lot of them didn't slip up. I think to our 21st century minds, it's quite impressive actually. Some of them did accidentally eat meat or have sex. Then they were stripped of their rank, and had to start again.

MC: You say they didn't use the Old Testament. For the New Testament, didn't they pretty much only use the Gospel of John?

SM: Yes, they had a particular fondness for the Gospel of John. Nobody really knows why. I think the Bogomils revered the Gospel of John as well. Sometimes at a push, they could be persuaded to read the other Gospels. When a Cathar was being consoled for instance, it was the Gospel of John that was placed on their head. They had a ritual where—part of the ritual meant you had to have the Gospel of John laid on your head while the Perfect who was consoling you recited certain verses. If they couldn't find the Gospel of John, they would actually put a New Testament on your head instead. Where this veneration for John comes from is a bit of a mystery. It's one of those things related to the esoteric side of Christianity that we don't really have any answers for. Obviously the Gospel of John is quite different to the other three canonical gospels. A lot of people have wondered why that was. I don't know, but it's interesting.

MC: What about the accusations that they performed ritualistic suicide, or helped each other suicide once somebody was enlightened enough to leave this world. Is there any basis for that?

SM: Yes, there is actually. The rite was called the endura, which I guess means the enduring or words to that effect. This seems to have been a ritual that Cathars from the 12th century had. It's usually associated with what's called the Autier Revival, which happened in the early years of the 14th century. It was named after a guy called Pierre Autier who was from the South of what we now call France. He kind of got the faith in a big time—in the 1290s. From about 1299 to about 1310 is the era of the Autier Revival. Pierre Autier, his brother, and a couple of converts—including a couple of women. Cathars had women priests. Because of the nature of the time they were in—this is a good 50-55 or so years after the fall of Montségur, which was the big Cathar citadel in the Pyrenees which fell in 1244. So after that, Catharism goes underground in the South of France. By the time Pierre Autier comes along and tries to do a one man revival—and does a pretty good job I must admit.

Those years were quite amazing—but it did mean that Catharism was totally underground by that time. What that would mean is, if somebody was consoled—underwent consolamentum—it often became, in that era, a deathbed rite. What would happen is—in order to ensure their soul was saved—they would undergo this rite called the endura, which basically meant, after you were consoled you were allowed to only consume water. If somebody in your family, who you thought was a Cathar, had been consoled, and you wanted to make sure they went to the Catholic Heaven, not the Cathar Heaven as it were [Laughs] you could try and feed them meat while they were on their deathbed, or make them drink wine. The Cathars weren't totally against wine, but certainly in this environment, when somebody was consoled on their deathbed, they really shouldn't have had wine. In other words, they were sort of hastening their own end if they were really on death's door. Just drinking water, not taking any other nourishment would bring about the final journey.

We do know of one or two cases where people took the endura, they got consoled, and then they took the endura, and they don't seem to have been particularly ill. These were people who were basically intent on dying by the sound of it. This is one of those cases where somebody is just hell bent, as it were—pardon the expression—on seeing something through. We do know that one woman—in the time of Pierre Autier and his gang, in other words the early 14th century—was consoled, and lived on nothing but water. Apparently, she took about seven weeks to die. That's a really extreme case. Not many of those cases have come down to us, but we do know about that woman. That was obviously—she wanted to die. As a whole they weren't particularly suicidal or anything.

In the context of the Autier era, the Inquisition was founded to root out the Cathars. The Cathars by that time, by say 1300-1310, were hunted people. The entire faith was going on underground, so things like the endura became a kind of practical necessity really.

MC: Is there any evidence of the legends surrounding the Cathars, like they possessed the Holy Grail and were affiliated with the Knights Templar? Any evidence of that?

SM: Yes and no. The Templars themselves were associated with the Grail. The Templars definitely had Cathars in their ranks. The Templars, the Cathars, and the Grail are three overlapping areas. What we know about the Templars for instance—I'll take it one step at a time, try and keep it simple because there are no easy explanations to all this. We know that the Templars were particularly strong in the Languedoc. One of their great Grandmasters from the 12th century, he was the Grandmaster in the 1150s I think, was a guy called Bertrand de Blanchefort, and he was from a Cathar family.

This is really early Catharism, well before any military moves had been made against them. The Templars were really strong in the Languedoc. When the crusade against the Cathars started in 1209, which is called the Albigensian Crusade, I'm sure that's something we'll come to discuss. When that started, the Templars refused to participate. As far as they were concerned, they didn't want to go to war against what they saw as fellow Christians.

If you were a Cathar being persecuted or were on the run, you could join the Templars and you'd be safe because the Templars were answerable only to the Pope. Because the Templars had this Cathar connection going back to the 1150s they seemed to have been sympathetic to the Cathars. That could have been for a couple of reasons. They had a lot of support in the Languedoc, and to turn against the Cathars during the Albigensian Crusade era, in the early decades of the 13th century, would have been politically really difficult for them. A lot of the Templars wealth in terms of land, holdings, and castles and so on was in the area, so if they started to go against their supporters, the nobility of the Languedoc, that would have been difficult for them.

The Templars were always short of manpower because of the main crusades in what we now call the Middle East, what the Templars called Outremer, the land beyond the sea. Obviously, the death toll was pretty high, we are talking about medieval warfare which is pretty bloody, a lot of carnage and gore. So the Templars were always looking for new recruits, they would even accept ex-convicts. They weren't particularly fussy, which probably added something to the Templars reputation for being necromancers, and being evil.

I think it was just a long tradition of the Templars being good friends with Cathar nobility. That's where I think the Templar-Cathar link comes from, they were basically friends. They were all together in the South of France, and had decades' worth of friendships and alliances going back to the 1150s, if not earlier than that. That kind of puts the Cathars in bed—as it were—with the Templars. They were allies, largely by dint of being together in the same area.

The Grail stuff is really interesting. All the Grail stories start to get written towards the end of the 12th century. We don't really know where they came from. It's traditionally said it's Chrétien de Troyes. He wrote the first one, that's a fact, or the earliest surviving one. Whether or not there is a Templar connection with Chrétien I don't know. Chrétien came from Troyes, hence being known as Chrétien de Troyes— Chrétien of Troyes. The Templars were actually from the Troyes area. It could be that Chrétien was talking to the Templars and, according to one version of the story, the Templars found something under the Temple Mount and knowledge of this, rumors, filtered back to Europe. This is all sort of speculative history, but there's no way of disproving it. The Templars do seem to have been excavating under the Temple Mount, but again it's a kind of really contentious issue amongst modern archeologists. Some of the Templar tunnels under the Temple Mount have been closed about 40 years. Whether anybody will get back in there is kind of dependant on the political situation in this realm and the Middle East.

Anyway, I'm sort of going off the beaten track slightly. It was known by about the early 13th century that the Cathars had treasure. Whether this was financial treasure or spiritual treasure or the Grail as well, we don't know. These stories were definitely circulating at the time. They're not the invention of later writers. There's been lots of romanticization of the Templars and the Cathars by 19th and 20th and indeed, 21st century writers. I think its a case of there's no smoke without fire. The Cathars were certainly rich in terms of having rich benefactors. Not all the nobility of the South, but certainly a lot of them were either Cathars themselves, or let Catharism to flourish in their lands. That became one of the major causes of the Albigensian Crusade. Now the interesting thing—it's one of those moments in history where you really—well I personally start to wonder—When the fortress of Montségur was being besieged in 1243 and 1244—it finally fell on the 16th of March 1244.

What happened was, there were about 200 Cathar Perfect on this incredibly, inaccessible Pyrenean castle. They had a number of mercenaries fighting for them—by this time some of the Cathars had decided nonviolence just wasn't an option. Some of them formed breakaway command or units—sort of Cathar version of the Marines or something, and would indulge in a bit of violence here and there--killing the odd person. That was the nearest they ever got to being—the Church was much more violent toward them than they ever were in the other direction against the Church. This is one of these moments where the Grail almost becomes visible in history. A fortnight before Montségur fell, I think they signed a truce on the 2nd of March give or take a day, I forget. It was around early March. The deal was that the Cathars could continue doing their things in Montségur for two weeks, and then they would surrender on the 16th. What actually happened was, the offer they were given was that if they all renounced Catharism they would be allowed to live. Obviously they would be questioned by the Inquisition, but if they didn't renounce Catharism, then they'd be burned at the stake. It was pretty clear cut what was going on. The Church was happy to accept these people back into the ranks as repentant sinners.

What actually happened, which is really interesting, is all 200 or so Perfects refused to convert back to mainstream Christianity. A number of the people, the mercenaries, actually converted to Catharism, knowing that it was certain death. They converted about a week before. That's a fascinating thing because then, literally the night before the fortress fell, the sacred Cathar treasure was smuggled out. Apparently a couple of guys scaled down the cliff face in the middle of the night, and were never seen again. Whether these mercenaries converted because they had seen the Grail or not I don't know, but it makes me wonder. Having said that, we do know for a fact that they definitely did convert to Catharism and they definitely, as a result, went to the stake with the 200 or so Perfect. So that's really intriguing. We do know that something was definitely smuggled out of Montségur never to be seen again. That's pretty much a fact. What it was, we don't know. Some people think it's the Holy Grail, other people think was just a lot of gold and silver and precious rubies and stones and so on. I don't know, and I try to keep my options open really because I think these stories are the most potent when you keep all your options open.

I say in my book *The Cathars* that maybe, in one interpretation, this Cathar treasure is actually their simplicity. They were a very simple faith. We've been talking about how they held their services in people's homes or in barns or fields or in the woods, so it was a very simple faith. I think that kind of emphasis on simplicity and goodness and, in the main, they were nonviolent. There were a couple of incidents towards the end in France where they killed Church delegates, but they never endorsed violence. Maybe that was the real Cathar treasure, something that seems to me to make sense. History is often misinterpreted, and what starts out as a metaphor then becomes a historical concrete, supposed fact. The Grail is a good example where some people think it definitely has to be just a kind of symbol of inner spiritual attainment. Some other people think it was a definite physical object, a cup or a stone. Maybe the Cathar treasure, the Cathar Grail if you like, was actually their simplicity and their devotion and their goodness.

MC: Sean, how exactly did the crusade against them begin? What was the turning point?

SM: The last straw was the murder of the papal legate to the South of France. A guy called Peter of Castelnau, or Pierre of Castelnau. He got killed in early 1208, January 1208. Nobody knows who killed him. He was apparently hacked down while waiting for a ferry to cross the river Rhône in the South of France. Pope Innocent III believed it was people sympathetic to the Count of Toulouse, Raymond VI who was a famous Cathar sympathizer. That's never been proved, Raymond VI denied all knowledge. It's possible this guy was killed by either somebody sympathetic to Raymond and the Cathars, and wanted to get this awful papal legate out of the way. I mean this guy was really unpopular, everybody hated him. So it could have been a case of some local guy thinking, well let's get rid of this guy.

It's not impossible that this guy was killed by papal agents just to kind of precipitate a war. They needed a really good excuse to start a military campaign. The jury is out I think. We'll never know for sure, but the guy definitely got killed and that's what triggered off what became known as the Albigensian Crusade.

The whole problem had been boiling up for decades. As we were saying earlier, the first Cathars came to light at about 1143 in Germany. A couple of those guys, the ones who didn't recant, got burned at the stake. Then there was a little bit of a military campaign against the Ca-thars in the South of France in the early 1180s.

Anyway, there was definitely a campaign that didn't really do much because—it was I think 1 nobleman and some knights. They went down to the South of France and didn't really manage to either kill that many people or convert many people.

Yes, just looking at the back of my book here, it was 1181. There was a short lived campaign against the Cathars in the area around Lavaur led by Henry de Marcy. Shortly after that in 1184, the Cathars and oth-er heretical groups like the Waldensians were finally, officially declared heretical. Then eventually, by the early 13th century the Church started sending representatives down to the South of France, and to other plac-es to try and win them over by debate. We know that in the South of France they had a number of public debates between the years—I think it was around 1204 to 1207. Usually the Church guys lost the debates to the Cathars, they just kind of argued them out of court.

Then what happened was this guy called Dominic Guzmán turns up and says to the Pope, look, there's no point in sending in your priests if they're in all this regal finery because the Cathar Perfect are just walk-ing around barefoot, and are men and women of the people. Why don't we try that? So this guy does that; he eventually becomes Saint Domi-nic. He goes around with his men trying to preach to the people of the Languedoc in a kind of Cathar-like way. They walked everywhere, they were barefoot. That seemed to have had some success, but the Langued-oc was still pretty much defiantly Cathar.

Then as I said, the papal legate got assassinated. I imagine a lot of people could be heaving a sigh of relief that this awful man was dead. Then the Pope decided this was the end of the line and called for cru-sade. It was the first crusade managed against fellow Christians. Be-cause the various nobility and various kings he'd asked to join were all kind of busy doing their own stuff, the campaign didn't get under way until the following year.

We do actually have precise dates for the start of the Albigensian Crusade. As I say, Peter of Castelnau, the papal legate was bumped off on the 14th of January of 1208. On the 10th of March, Innocent the Pope called for Crusade. It didn't actually get under way until the 18th of June, 1209, when the Count of Toulouse, Raymond VI was publicly flogged, and he was forced to apologize for shielding Cathars.

Then a month later on the 22nd of July, which was the feast of Saint

Mary Magdalene, the town of Béziers was sacked. This is the first atrocity of the campaign. They surrounded the town which held at least 10,000 people. The papal legate was asked by the military chiefs—who should we kill? He then comes up with the notorious command "Kill them all, God will know his own." So that's what they did, they basically killed the entire town. There's got to be at least 10,000 people in Béziers that day. Some people say as much as 20,000, but we know that probably around 10,000 people got killed in a day. Most of them weren't Cathars, but they just went in there and basically carpet bombed the whole place.

MC: Isn't that where they burned the church?

SM: Yes.

MC: They burned their church with all the people in it on Saint Mary Magdalene's feast day?

SM: That's right, yes. Because obviously the whole idea of going into a church—church was sacrosanct, and was traditionally the place where you could always find safety. You would never be harmed in a church, but not this time. This was the first time when the Church broke its own rules, and they burned the church down full of people. It kind of really went from there. I think the first two or three years of the Albigensian Crusade were the most notorious. That's when they were killing entire towns on a regular basis. Then it kind of became more of a protracted, intermittent thing with the atrocities getting smaller. It lasted 20 years all together. It was basically a Church sponsored crime against humanity, there's no two ways about it really. Even critics at the time who were normally pro-Church were kind of saying, wow, this is horrendous.

They were trying to blame the violence on mercenaries because all medieval armies had mercenaries. There was no such thing as a standing army apart from the Templars. That actually wasn't the case. The violence was actually authorized by the Church. Pretty soon into the first campaign—just after Béziers, about a month later—Simon de Montfort (5th Earl of Leicester) became the leader of the crusade. He sounds like a complete psychopath.

MC: I read his stuff. Horrible.

SM: Yeah, dreadful. He obviously saw himself as a very pious Christian. We've got to remember, these people were living in an age of extreme piety, but even so he was incredibly violent and sadistic. He eventually got killed at the Siege of Toulouse in 1218 where his head got destroyed by stone fired from a catapult. The story goes that the catapult was operated by women. I've always thought that was a bit of poetic justice.

MC: I agree.

SM: [Laughs] If any man deserved to have his head smashed in, it was him.

MC: Right. What's funny is when you read, let's say, Dan Brown and other novels, romantic novels on the whole issue, and people believe that the genocide was one swell swoop, but the Crusade was just a long campaign of small fights, peace treaties, a comedy of errors. Really a chaotic endeavor, wasn't it?

SM: Yeah, that's right. As I say, the first couple of years, well about 1209 to 1212, it was pretty full on. Then the Pope decided, he'd obviously heard stories about the brutality and the cruelty which even for medieval standards was terrible, and actually stopped the Crusade in 1213. Unfortunately, he was persuaded to relaunch it about five months later, so then it carried on. Then Simon de Montfort dies after having made a little money out of it. Shades of Iraq here, I think he made a lot of personal gain out of the war, out of the crusade.

Then that's where it starts to really fall apart because his son takes over. His son is not really a military strategist, and he's far less cruel. He starts to lose all the gains his father had made. Then some of the main Cathar nobility start dying off. Saint Dominic, well he wasn't Saint Dominic then, but he dies as well in the early 1220s. Then I think de Montfort's son cedes all of his lands to the French King. At that time, the Kingdom of France was the area around Paris. By about 1226, you've then got the French King involved in the whole thing, which then starts a new phase. By that time the Southern nobility who were fighting for the Cathars couldn't withstand yet another invasion this time from the North. The whole thing kind of peters out around 1229 with what was called The Treaty of Paris.

You're right in saying that it was pretty intermittent. You'd have several years of offensives, then it would tail off a bit, then it would start up again. One of the tailing off periods was the mid 1220s, when the Cathars felt sufficiently safe to hold another council. There was a major council in 1226, but unfortunately for them, that was the year the French King started to head south.

Yeah, it was kind of intermittent. It was generally 20 years that just decimated the Languedoc. Regardless of its intermittent nature, it was a really really terrible period.

MC: Yeah, and it wasn't just the Cathars who got it, it was Catholics and Jews too.

SM: Yeah, there were certainly instances of both Catholics and Jews being killed by the crusaders as well. They were just totally ruthless. Such was their desire to root out the Cathars that they would just kill anybody.

MC: The fall of Montségur was pretty much the end of the Cathars in Southern France or, the end of the crusade.

SM: The crusade officially ended in 1229. Then about two years later, the Inquisition is formed to root out the Cathars. Although the crusade had officially ended in 1229, there were still a lot of people who were still Cathar. That's when the Inquisition started, and they were the first secret police almost. They managed a huge campaign which lasted for decades to root out Cathars, and were encouraging people to inform on their neighbors and so on. It's kind of the forerunner of the secret police in Eastern Europe in the 20th century. It's a Western invention. [Laughs] These guys are pretty scary.

Then what happened was there were a number of fortresses that were sympathetic to the Cathars. Montségur was the last remaining major one, and that fell in 1244. Then after that, Catharism becomes much more low profile in the South of France. It wasn't actually the last Cathar castle to fall, there was a castle called Quéribus which fell in 1255. That's a bit of a mystery because we don't know much about it. It might have actually been fallen by negotiation so, all of the Cathars inside it might have actually got away. I think, having read around the subject, that seems to have been what happened. I think if there was a blood bath, we would have heard about it. I think the Quéribus Cathars managed to escape, but where they went we don't know.

So, then it becomes an underground thing in the early 14th century of the Autier revival. The last Autier Perfect is burned at the stake in 1321, but Catharism is still going on in places like Italy where the last Cathars were actually burned at the stake in 1389. The fall of Montségur in 1244 isn't really the end of it. It does carry on.

A number of the Italian Cathars cross the Adriatic into the former Yugoslavia, to places like Bosnia. The Bosnian Church is one of those big, sort of historical riddles. We don't know whether they were actually a Cathar Church, or a Bogomil Church. Obviously, Bogomils had passed through Bosnia on the way to preach in the West. Bosnia was called land of many heresies by one churchman, and he was dead right. They were pretty much a heretical country. When the Ottoman Turks invaded in the 1450s it's thought that a lot of the Bogomils, or Cathars, whatever you want to call them, converted to Islam, but we don't really know for sure. We know that the Cathars were active in Bosnia much later than anywhere else. I'd say well into the 1450s. In fact, the last reported sighting of a Bogomil was 1867 so we just don't know. They could still be active today, I kind of hope they are.

MC: [Laughs] Somehow they survived, somehow one or two.

SM: Yeah. Reminds me of a story by—I think a British researcher, I forget who it was now. They were in the South of France maybe 10 or 20 years ago—in the Languedoc. They were researching Catharism, and all the associated stories about Mary Magdalene and the Grail and so on. All around the Château type stuff. They got talking to a local woman. The Cathars came up in conversation, and the woman just says—I think she was quite an old lady, probably in her 60s or 70s or whatever, or even older—said "We are still Cathars, but we don't talk about it." And that's all she would say.

Anyway, I think the Cathars do still survive in the South of France today. More in a sense of folklore or just tradition. Something that's kind of in the air or in the blood. They're all sympathetic to the Cathars, and they always have been. In a way, the story does come from the middle ages down to us today. There still are people out there who claim to be from Cathar families in that area.

MC: Well I think that should do it for today on the Cathars Sean. I'd like to thank you very much for coming on.

SM: Thank you Miguel, it's been a pleasure talking to you and I hope we can talk again.

NATHANIEL DEUTSCH

Nathaniel Deutsch is author of *The Gnostic Imagination: Gnosticism, Mandaeism, and Merkabah Mysticism,* Professor of Literature and History at the University of California, Santa Cruz and co-director of the University's Center for Jewish Studies.

Since the dreadful wars in Iraq, the reclusive Mandaeans have made the news as a Middle Eastern minority on the verge of extinction. They might also be the last Gnostics, as some have called them, a group with an unbroken lineage to the classic Gnostics. Perhaps the unbroken lineage is what makes the Mandaeans (which means "Gnostic") so hard to understand—as their texts and rituals have remained hidden but also evolved depending on the conquering empire surrounding their culture.

Interviewing Nathaniel Deutsch took me a long way towards understanding the Mandaeans, from their possibly origins to why they viewed Jesus as a usurper and John the Baptist as a luminary. Furthermore, Nathaniel is an active advocate in their humanitarian aid. I've always said that academics truly begin to empathize with their subjects by scholarly osmosis, and with Nathaniel it's even more severe. He truly cares about this endangered culture, which seems to be a reflection of the classic Gnostics cast in the middle of a volatile and growing Christian Roman Empire.

Will the Mandaeans, along with other Gnostic-leaning ethnic groups like the Yezidi, survive or become another bygone esoteric religion? The answer, the classic Gnostics would say, depends on the Gnosis and goods works of humanity. Nathaniel possesses plenty of both.

MC: Although it seems it's a much discussed topic and I've read several theories and so many books, what would you say are the earliest origins of the Mandaeans?

ND: It's actually a very complicated question because no one knows exactly where they come from. The Mandaeans have their own origin story, which is that they date their origin to Adam, the first man, who is both a prototype and, in a genealogical sense, the first Mandaean. There are other stories within Mandaean literature that link their origin to the land of Israel, to the area around Jerusalem, and link it in that case to tensions that arose with the Jewish community there, and a kind of splintering off that occurred and the Mandaeans moved east to Mesopotamia. Another possibility is that they grew out of the indigenous Mesopotamian community. So there's a kind of Mandaean mythological explanation tracing back to Adam. There's this idea that they come from the land of Israel, or Palestine. There's the idea that they are descendants of indigenous Mesopotamian people. There are a few other theories. The earliest texts that or extant date back to around 200 C.E. One of the ways that you date Mandaean texts is they have what are called colophons. They have scribal notes in the books and scrolls that they composed. So as a scribe recomposes or copies a scroll in his possession he will write down information, and based on those genealogies you can date, it's one way of dating the scrolls. And I think the oldest one is 200 and something, if I'm not mistaken. So we know at the very least that they go back that far. There's been a debate for pretty much as long as there's been Mandaean studies in the West as to whether the Mandaeans are pre-Christian or post-Christian, and what their relationship is to Christianity and Christian texts, like the Gospel of John, for example. It's unclear. I don't think anyone knows exactly when and where the Mandaeans first emerged as a distinctive community. There were a lot of baptizing groups in the first few centuries of the common era. Most of them are extinct. A couple of them—Christians, Mandaeans—are still around.

MC: And it seems a lot of people have said maybe they were a part of the John the Baptist sect. In the Acts of the Apostles Paul meets a group of them, and I think the Pseudo-Clementines talks about Simon Magus and others being the splinter group that didn't go with Jesus. What do you think of this, is this just speculation?

ND: It's speculation. It's worthwhile thinking about those kinds of things. In my own work I've tended to focus more on the possible connections between Mandaeism and Judaism than the Christian angle, though there are other scholars who focus on that aspect of it. It's clear that there were a lot of different groups. Ultimately, Manichaeism is going to be another one. Some of them are in Palestine, some of them are in Mesopotamia, they are in Syria, Egypt. It's a very fertile time for these groups. They were sharing a lot of traditions: the Hebrew Bible, both what are going to be canonical and extracanonical Christian writings, Plato, and other Greek writings, Neoplatonic writings. They are also drawing on the common pool of magical traditions, on ritual traditions. So to identify particular communities, particularly at their originary moments, is not always so easy. It's easier when you have a founding figure, for example in the case of Manichaeism. But other than that it becomes more complicated. So I think it's worthwhile to explore all those things, particularly when you have textual connections. For example, people have explored the connections between some of the Mandaean texts and early Manichaean texts. Most recent scholarship would say that Mandaeism was one of the cultural influences in the milieu that Mani grew up in and developed his own theology in.

MC: Why would you say the Mandaeans are considered to be Gnostic?

ND: Part of that designation has to do with their name and there's a debate as to the etymology of their name. One of the etymologies relates it to a Semitic root for knowledge. So their name would mean "knowers" in the same that Gnostic in Greek means "the one who knows". That's one reason that people identify them as Gnostics. But there's another explanation for that, another common one, which has to do with the Mandi, which is a fenced off area in a river or other body of flowing water that is used for ritual purposes, or the Manda hut, which is the hut which is used again for ritual purposes. So they would be the people of the Manda, the people who use this hut or this fenced-off area. So that would not support, at least in the etymology of the name, a connection to Gnosticism. More than that, though, there are texts—and these are one of the reasons why it's so significant and so fascinating—is that although it's been a small community for its entire history, relative to others such as Islam or Christianity, it has a very rich body of literature that has been produced over the centuries. It's not as if there was one period 800 years ago when people produced texts and that was it, but they've been continuing to produce them In those texts we find a number of significant parallels to Gnosticism, to what's called western Gnosticism or western Gnosis.

MC: Aren't the Mandaeans perhaps more dualistic than the classic Gnostics, that makes them closer to Manichaeans in that sense?

ND: There is a tendency among scholars of Gnosticism or dualistic religions like Manichaeism, Gnosticism, Catharism, Bogomolism, the various traditions that have been described as dualistic, to distinguish between radical dualism and more moderate dualism. The Manichaeans are the poster children for the radical dualism, in so far as they posit a very originary or even existential distinction and break and opposition between good and bad, light and darkness, and that there's this kind of ongoing conflict between those two from the very beginning. Whereas the more moderate dualism that often people would attribute to western Gnosticism, would be the idea that you start out with a good principle, usually described as the Father, the One—there are various names for it. In Mandaeism it's Life. And then through usually a series of emanations you move away from that, until finally there is some kind of rupture, in the western Gnostic tradition it's often associated with Sophia. Then her "abortion," Yaldabaoth, who's the demiurge, and then you have the creation of the Bad. But first you start with the Good, and then you move away from it, which was probably influenced more by a kind of neoplatonic notion of the Good being degraded the further you move away from the source.

Mandaeism is interesting, because Mandaeism has an enormous number of texts that reflect different periods in Mandaic history. Some of the texts are more Manichaean in terms of the way they describe the opposition between the world of light and the world of darkness, and some of them are more moderately dualistic in that they describe a more emanatory or, in the case of Mandaeism, they often talk about different aspects of Life created through a Call, for example, or emanation, or even some kind of creative process. So, depending on the text, and this is something you cannot give a definitive answer to when it comes to Mandaean theology—I hesitate even to use the word theology because to me theology implies a marriage between Greek philosophy and the Hebrew Bible, which is definitely not philosophical. So what happens when you merge Greek philosophy—and typically Platonic philosophy of some sort—with biblical stories—to me Christianity really invented theology because that was the combination—so you have an attempt to apply certain philosophical principles to texts like the biblical stories of creation, which already poses a problem from a philosophical point of view, that really don't lend themselves that easily to philosophy in terms of things like logic, no contradictions, all those sorts of things. So you end up with these efforts to systematize thought about things like Jesus' christological nature. If you look at the New Testament there are a lot of stories that in some sense the versions contradict one another but at least give different versions. And then you see the early church fathers who are in many cases influenced by philosophy, trying to derive a certain almost philosophical portrait of Jesus' "being". Is he God, is he man, is he always man or always God? Is he both, is he sometimes one, all of that.

In Mandaeism, although there are sometimes places where you could detect the influence of philosophy, perhaps through the influence of some western Gnostic traditions that may have entered Mandaeism, in general it tends to be more mythological and earthy than the western Gnostic texts, some of which are extremely theosophical, as I'm sure you know. The Mandaean texts tend to be less so, although again you can sometimes see some influence of philosophy. In my opinion, when you have the influence of philosophy the more likely it is you will have a move towards a more definitive account. In the case of Mandaeism you don't have that effort to systematize, to choose one version over the other. That's more akin to Jewish midrash, where you have multiple versions of different events that are allowed to co-exist, even though you could point out to someone, "Well, wait a second, this story contradicts that story." That hasn't seemed to be a problem for Jews or Mandaeans. Sometimes people try to choose, but within the literary traditions you can have all these multiple versions. So in the case of Mandaeism, to get back to the original questions, you have some texts that evince a more radically dualistic view, some that evince another one that's more moderate, different stories about where the word came from, that in some cases are much more radically dualistic than others. It's very hard to pin it down in that respect.

Manichaeism, for example, tends to be much more uniform. Although it's quite complex too, one of the reasons Manichaeism could be a worldwide religion is because it could be so easily translated into different idioms. A lot of the basic ideas would remain the same, you could just plug in different figures that were local, whether it's Buddha or Jesus, or whatever, and use a lot of the same concepts and mythology and translate it into Uighur and into whatever other languages, Latin, whatever, and the basic ideas would remain the same, so Manichaeans in different places could understand one another and share a common body of traditions. What's extraordinary about Mandaeism is that here you have this very small community living, really, in one place, they're producing this enormous variety of views that, if you were to take it all together, would show the whole spectrum of dualistic traditions, all produced by this one community over time.

MC: But don't the Mandaeans, unlike classic Gnostics, or I guess like any of the "people of the book," don't they turn things upside down by making Jesus the villain of the cosmic play?

ND: That's actually an excellent point, because when you describe the Mandaeans as Gnostics, the issue of Jesus should then be addressed, because a lot of the "western Gnostics" see Christ—as a divine being rather than as a human being—he is one of the more popular saviour figures. In some of the "Christian Gnostic" texts he is a saviour figure, sent in order to provide people with knowledge of the true self so they can escape this world. Now of course there are differences between the way Gnostics would see Christ, in terms of did he really have a physical body, but nevertheless a lt of it is quite Christocentric. Even the Gnostic texts that don't focus on Christ as the saviour, as far as I know, there aren't any in the western Gnostic tradition that attack him as a false prophet. That isn't the case in Mandaeism.

In Mandaeism there is a polemic against Jesus as just that, a false prophet, a false messiah, a deceptive messiah, a deceptive prophet. So this shows a number of things, one that they are very well aware of Christianity, and there is actually an extended polemic against Christianity, against Judaism, against Islam. So they are aware of all these traditions and they're interacting with them to some extent, and for example in the Christian case there are some polemics against what appear to be maybe the Syrian monastic tradition. In cases like that you might be able to in fact situate where attacks might have come from, what period they might have come from. I'm not sure if it helps really to tell whether Mandaeism preceded Christianity or not, which was certainly one of the more important questions for the early scholars of Mandaeism, but it does point to a complex relationship between Mandaeism and Christianity.

MC: Also with Judaism, don't they also see Moses as someone who was given the law by the demiurge? They're not too keen on Moses either.

ND: No, they're not. My view is that Mandaeism probably emerged out of a Jewish context at some point, and that over the centuries in Mesopotamia they had very close relations which were probably much more amicable than the texts would suggest. Not only Mandaean texts, but if you look at pretty much every religious tradition in the Middle East, if you look hard enough you will find negative things said about other people. But on the ground, particularly if you look at the so-called magical tradition, one example of which would be magic bowls, which we have a fair number of examples of, that survive, that archaeologists have discovered, where it becomes clear from the language that's used, from the different divine beings, angelic beings that are evoked, the names of the scribes, the names of the customers which are sometimes inscribed on them, that there was a lot of cross-cultural contact going on between these different peoples. Even if officially in their elite texts they were antagonistic, they were neighbors, in the case of the Jews, the script is different but the spoken dialect of Aramaic was very similar. Mandaean and the dialect of the Babylonian Talmud, for example, are quite similar.

In some cases, they were living in towns or areas that were over-lapping one another, so it may be one of those cases of the anxiety of influence, where they generally get along with their neighbors, but when they fight it can take on a different connotation when you fight a neighbor versus a complete stranger. One of the things I've studied is the possible relationship between Mandaeism and Jewish mysticism, and the fact that some of the Kabbalistic traditions that emerge, or at least are written down in Spain and in Provence in southern France in the medieval period, may in fact be rooted in earlier Babylonian Jewish traditions that have a lot of parallels to some of the things you find in Mandaean texts.

So while on the one hand you see a big effort on the Mandaean part to distinguish themselves from Jews, and to criticize Jews in a variety of ways, claiming that they don't follow purity laws properly and describing them with a word that means something like "abortion" and all sorts of negative things, on the other hand they have stories that suggest that way back in time they lives together with Jews and maybe split off, or maybe some of them were Jews—it's a little hazy. And then, as I mentioned before, historically, there was probably a lot of contact between Mandaeans and Jews.

My guess is that a lot of that did not reflect the hostility you see in the texts themselves. So that's another thing that's important to keep in mind, you have the texts and you have the way that people live on the ground. One of the things that is significant about Mandaeism in terms of the broader context of Gnosticism is that you actually know very little about the way the Gnostic communities that produced the texts, say the Nag Hammadi texts, how they lived. People have tried to extrapolate, like Elaine Pagels for example, in *The Gnostic Gospels* made certain sociological arguments about what kind of people, what kind of communities these were, on attitudes towards women, things like that, attitudes towards authority and how they differed in turn from orthodox Christians. And to some extent you can do that, but in no other case do you have a community like the Mandaeans which has existed from late antiquity, and that are still around, and you can still ask these questions about how they live now, for example.

Let me give you another example in terms of Christians: there have been different periods in Mandaean history where people have either thought that they were Christians, or where the Mandaeans may have allowed them to think that they were some sort of Christians, just to make it easier on them. It's not only because of John the Baptist, whom the Mandaeans revere as a teacher, also because there are a number of rituals like baptism, for example, like a staff that Mandaean priests have that resembles a Christian staff. So there are other parallels that make that kind of association possible, even though it should be said that Mandaeans are not Christians. Even in the New York Times, a month ago, an article mentioned the Mandaeans and it referred to them as a form of Christianity. That's just not accurate.

MC: Nathaniel, what are some of the more notable rituals that the Mandaeans have. You mentioned baptism. Don't the Mandaeans baptize each other every day?

ND: In Arabic they're actually known as the Baptizers. Their baptism is typically on Sunday. A priest, called the *Tarmida*, typically performs the baptism in flowing water—living water, it's called. In Mandaic they called it a *yardna*, it's basically the Mandaic form of "Jordan", as in the Jordan river. There's a celestial Jordan river, and then flowing waters on earth are earthly incarnations of that heavenly Jordan. So you have to do it in tis living water and the priest does it. People can do ablutions themselves, there are different rituals that they perform with water themselves. Mandaeism is very concerned with purity, in terms of eating, in terms of menstrual purity. In this way there are a number of parallels with Judaism and Shia Islam in particular. And so baptism is an important ritual.

There are rituals for them to make someone a priest. There are different feasts, sacrifices. Wedding rituals are important. The funeral ritual is very important. I was speaking to a Mandaean on the phone last week, and he was saying that one of the most difficult challenges for Mandaeans in the diaspora, outside of southern Iraq and Iran, is where you bury people. He was describing a community where they purchased a plot of land to make a Mandaean cemetery, and they were forced to do that because someone died suddenly. They had been talking about doing it, but when this person died they realized they had to do it right away, and they got a permit, and someone donated land, and they were able to do that. But the funeral is particularly important because (and here a kind of Gnostic element comes in again) your soul is seen as leaving this world and returning to, to use the western Gnostic term, your pleromatic home, and you have to make it through different obstacles, and rituals will help you to do that, and your soul will be weighed by this figure called Abatur, you'll cross over water and you'll make it into the world of light. So you want to make sure that everything is done in a ritually correct way. When a child is born there's a baptism. People have weekly baptisms, there are various festivals, when you make a priest, funerals, weddings, these are all events that are marked with various rituals. And access to flowing water is very, very important to Mandaeans.

The priests, to use the English term, are very important to Mandaenism as a lived tradition. One of the things that has happened as a result of the war is that the priests, many of them or maybe most of them, have gone into exile as well. In Syria, this friend of mine was telling me, the priests have the most difficult time because the other Mandaeans can often blend in with the other Iraqi refugees in terms of the way they dress, but the priests are very distinctive in their clothing—white clothes, turban, a few other things that would identify them, and long beards—so he was saying when they go to the market, for example, to go shopping, people know, "What are you?" They may not know they're Mandaean, but they know they are something else. Traditionally the other professions in Iraq were goldsmiths, metal workers. Some of them continue to do that, as jewellers of some sort, but more recently a lot of the younger people have become professionals, they've gone into professions. In that sense they often tend to be quite well assimilated in many ways. But the priests are very distinctive in their appearance and so that has caused some problems.

MC: Nathaniel, before we move on to their modern plight, do the Mandaeans actually believe in Gnosis?

ND: Yeah. One of the things that makes it, if not a branch of Gnosticism then certainly related to it are the stories about Adam—and here you see some real parallels with both western Gnosticism and Jewish rabbinic midrash traditions about Adam being this big kind of blob like a golem that needs to have spirit to become animated. So they take some spirit, *ruha*, and they animate Adam and then Adam is enlightened by a figure that is sent from the Pleroma. So Adam and the creation of Adam and, if you want to use that term, the "enlightenment" of Adam, is a prototype for what Mandaeans are supposed to experience as well. As in the western Gnostic case Adam has this spirit and this knowledge, and yet is stuck in this world, which is dominated by these, malevolent at worst and ignorant and foolish at best, creatures. Powers is a better term. So that's what makes Adam the first Mandaean and he serves as a prototype for other Mandaeans. Now there is a split between the laity, if you want to use that term, not as extreme as in the Manichaean case, but there's more fluidity between the categories, between the lay Mandaeans or the Mandaeans who don't know as much about their tradition and Mandaeans who are much more in the know. So even within the Mandaean community you'd have people who were identified as much more knowledgeable. The priests are expected to be that way, but there are non-priests that possess more knowledge of Mandaeism too.

So there is some division within the community, although all Mandaeans—here's where the rituals come in too. It's not just a matter of possessing knowledge. Sometimes when you read the western Gnostic texts you might get that impression that it was, and maybe for some of those communities it was more focused on that, we just don't know the role of ritual. For example, when it talks about the bridal chamber in a Gnostic text, was that a ritual, or was there a ritual that accompanied that? And was that the source of some of the heresiological critique where they accuse some Gnostics of eating semen instead of the Eucharist or whatever it is. Was there in fact a ritual that they are transforming in the heresiological writings on one hand, and then describing in more spiritualized terms in the Nag Hammadi texts but at the core there is in fact a ritual that some Gnostic community or group was engaging in that then is reflected in these different literary ways. In the Mandaean case the rituals are the more consistent and systematized and the texts are the more complicated, varied, even at times contradictory in terms of different versions that don't necessarily jibe with one another.

MC: It seems that the Mandaeans, like the Jews in the diaspora, were able to survive all these centuries through the Christian and the Muslim empires. What happened that their situation became so dire, what was the turning point in recent times?

ND: If you look at each of the minority communities in the Middle East, there have been different periods when things have been better or worse. So you can look at Mandaeaism just like you can look at Jews in Iran: in Iran in the nineteenth century there was persecution against Jews. But alternately there have been periods when it's been better. In the case of Mandaeans it's the same way, that some periods were worse. Some periods depended on whether a local religious leader identified them as being the protected people according to the Qur'an. There has been a debate in Islamic jurisprudence over whether the Mandaeans should be identified with a group called the Sabeans which, along with Christians and Jews, were one of the three peoples identified as protected people of the book in the Qur'an. The Mandaeans would like to have that identification because they would then be tolerated as an acceptable religious minority. Some Muslim jurists have in fact accepted that and others haven't. So some of the toleration or lack of toleration has depended on that. Under Sadaam Hussein the Mandaeans were a religious minority like Yazidis or Chaldeans or Syrians (there's an enormous variety of religious minorities there) who were more or less tolerated but were still in different ways discriminated against, but in general were tolerated. All those people I mentioned had been there for many, many centuries and were really woven into the local fabric.

Under Sadaam that continued. So for example in a town in southern Iraq you might have a street called the Subi street, where all the Mandaeans had their metalsmith workshops and they knew their Shiite neighbors and people might have stereotypes of one another, and maybe there might sometimes be some tension, but people would generally speaking get along. What happened with the invasion was that fabric, those local connections between peoples, the neighborhoods, all of those had been, in many places anyway, just torn apart. Neighborhoods that were integrated at one time are now segregated. People who leave can't come back. Either they don't want to come back or their homes have been taken over, or don't exist anymore. For a group like the Mandaeans it's particularly difficult because in many ways they are the most vulnerable of the vulnerable. They don't have a safe haven as some of the groups in the north in particular have. Their religious rituals are performed by priests who are very distinctive looking and they are done out in the open in flowing water. That has been the source of harassment and in some cases violence when they've tried to perform some of their rituals.

It's one thing if you've lived with your neighbors and you've known them and their grandfather knew your grandfather, etc., there's a certain tolerance that's built on that. But when you're a refugee and you're in a new place and no one knows you from Adam, and you're different and you're from the south and now you're in the north, you're in Baghdad, you become even more vulnerable, particularly at the time when a lot of people there are engaging in different forms of ethnic cleansing based on people's backgrounds, religious and otherwise. Because the Mandaeans have historically been involved in metalwork, which actually may have something to do with religion in the sense that in the Middle East a lot of minority groups, for instance Jews in Ethiopia or north Africa, end up getting involved in metalwork because that profession is seen as polluting. So often the dominant group doesn't want to engage in it. So you end up with a minority group engaging in it. But because they're involved in that profession they're seen as having a lot of money.

Therefore, they've also been targeted by people because they think they can get their gold. They don't have a larger community elsewhere to count on. It's not like there's a million Mandaeans in England or America that can help this wave of refugees. They're all they have. There are probably fewer than 100,000 of them in the entire world. It's amazing that they've survived for this long, and that's one of the most tragic things that, here they survived various invasions and reversals and now for this to be the thing that puts them into in certain ways a greater crisis than they've probably experienced. So they're really trying to figure out ways of ensuring this isn't the beginning of the end, but rather the beginning of another chapter in their history.

MC: Is anything being done actively by any of the governments, like the United States or England to help them out?

ND: The short answer is no. Unfortunately, the United States has taken in very very few refugees. I think last year it was 7000. Maybe that was even what they pledged and they ended up taking in fewer than that. But that's a drop in the bucket compared to the number of refugees, five million externally and internally displaced Iraqi refugees. There was some recent American legislation that opened the possibility for a group like the Mandaeans to be let into this country, to given what's called Priority 2 status, which is a privileged refugee status, where the process is expedited. Only a few have been granted that thus far, but if they were granted it large numbers of Mandaeans from Iraq could come into this country. I think that in Iran—it's a smaller Mandaean community in Iran—that they actually already have priority 2 refugee status because of the American government's relationship, or lack of relationship, with Iran. The American government has taken a stance on religious minorities, on providing expedited refugee status for religious minorities from Iran, but not from Iraq. But ironically in recent years more Mandaean refugees from Iran have come into this country than from Iraq. So the United States has not done very much thus far although there was this legislative opening that was worked on a few months ago and hopefully something can be built on. Sweden, of all the western countries, has probably taken in more Iraqi refugees than any other country, although now I think they might be trying to restrict the number. Australia has a fairly large Mandaean community, like a few thousand people.

    Dr Wee Sambriji has been trying to establish a group which will focus on specifically helping Mandaean refugees. He and I spoke about trying to bring in a critical mass of Mandaean refugees into the United States and settling them somewhere. That's actually one of the things that's good about the United States, is that historically it has been a place where religious minorities and communities which were persecuted elsewhere have been able to find a home here and to thrive here. It is possible for Mandaeans to come to America, or to Canada or Australia, and create enough of a community that they can perpetuate themselves. Part of the issue is that you cannot convert to Mandaeism. In order to be a Mandaean both of your parents have to be Mandaean. So there really is a need to have enough Mandaeans in a particular area so that people can find marriage partners, so that the religious life and the cultural life can be replicated and passed down. If there are just small pockets all around the world it's going to be very very difficult to do that.

MC: And what can we do as private citizens to help the Mandaeans, what are some of our options?

ND: I know Mandaean Crisis International has a petition that has been circulating. Any time there's a crisis like this, like in Darfur or Bosnia or here, the more voices that are heard, or the more contact you make with your congress people, is always helpful. You have to encourage congresspeople to include the Mandaeans in any legislation, to specify that there are particular reasons why the Mandaeans should be singled out as requiring expedited refugee status. There are a lot of Iraqis that should be getting refugee status and they're suffering tremendously, but there's probably no other group that as a community could become extinct as an indirect result of the war in Iraq. Those are a couple of things. I wish I could go beyond letters to the editor, writing to your congresspeople. Mandaean Crisis International. Going online, looking for Mandaean activists, Mandaean groups, that have a number of websites, sending an email asking Mandaean activists what you can do. That's really what I've done. I don't presume to speak for the Mandaean community at all. I really want to try to help the Mandaeans who have taken a lead, to try to help them do what they think is right.

I know a number of Quaker individuals and a number of Quaker groups have expressed an interest in helping to relocate Mandaeans. There are models for this: refugees from Somalia, refugees from Sudan. Whether they are religious minorities or just people who have suffered during war, America has a long history of bringing in people from south-east Asia and settling people, so if you belong to a not-for-profit or a human rights organisation, or a church or another religious organisation that has had a history of doing that, bringing up the plight of the Mandaeans and seeing whether your group would be interested in trying to help them and reaching out to them, then contacting one of the Mandaean organisations that's listed on the web would be very helpful.

You're also welcome to contact me. It's really a question of helping Mandaeans to figure out what is right for them. Mandaeans have lived in what is now Iraq and Iran for 2000 years, if not more. It would be great if they could recreate their community there. The Mandaeans I've spoken to just don't think that that's a realistic option for the foreseeable future and feel like a better option is to try to create vibrant communities in what's now the Mandaean diaspora.

MC: That's all the time we have today. I'd like to thank you for coming on the show and hopefully we can reach as many people as possible.

ND: Well, I want to thank you. As amazing as the Nag Hammadi texts are, and Manichaean texts, it's also wonderful that you've devoted a show to flesh and blood people who have been carrying on these traditions for thousands of years and are really in dire need of knowledge, of people knowing about them. Talking about Gnosis, if knowledge is the beginning of the journey, for people to know about the Mandaeans, because a lot of people just don't know, and they would be willing to help if they did know, I really want to thank you.

GNOSTIC SAGES,
ANCIENT AND MODERN

Robert M. Price

Robert M. Price is the author of *Deconstructing Jesus*, *The Incredible Shrinking Son of Man*, and *The Amazing Colossal Apostle*.

Part of the ethos of Aeon Byte Gnostic Radio was to be a rogue media, a sound but edgy alternative to mainstream broadcasting. My first guest back in 2006 was Robert Price, whom one might also call rogue—being an academic who embraces the Mythicist position of Jesus being a fictional character, one of many dying/rising godmen of mystery religions. Thus, our joining of forces, if you would, for the show's maiden broadcast made sense.

And so did a later interview on another rogue figure, Paul of Tarsus, who spearheaded a radical form of Judaism centered on the character of Jesus Christ. Yes, Paul was rogue, as Robert explained in our interview, based on his book, *The Amazing Colossal Apostle*. Paul was so radical and mercurial that the early Gnostics likely embraced him before Orthodoxy adopted him as a main founder of Christianity before they embraced orthodoxy or before orthodoxy appeared. Many claimed Simon Magus was a cipher of Paul, and a uniform religion was the last thing on his mystic mind. Never to be outdone as a rogue, Bob is extremely radical on Paul—suggesting that Paul might have never been Paul at all, but a patchwork character whose main creator could be none other than the arch-heretic Marcion of Synope, writing the initial Pauline epistles early in the second century.

It's doubtful our interview will settle the identity and thrust of Paul after centuries of debate and scholarship on him. But for those seeking an alternative to the mainstream press release of Paul, this is the space you will be welcomed.

MC: This is the Aeon Byte interview, and with us, we definitely have the pleasure of being joined again by Robert Price to discuss his book, *The Amazing Colossal Apostle: the Search for the Historical Paul.* How are you doing today, Bob?

RP: Well, doing great. I hope you're the same.

MC: Ah, everything's wonderful on this side of the Kenoma!

RP: [laughs]

MC: So, tell us, you begin your book by telling us that Paul has become—in a way—the new Jesus, the main mouthpiece for various factions in the religious agendas. Could you expand a bit on that, Bob?

RP: It seems to me that orthodox Protestants—whether evangelicals, Lutherans, whatever—though they are unaware of the parallel, have done the same thing with Jesus and Paul as the Gnostic, esoteric Ismailis and Druzism in the Middle East has done for many centuries. The idea that when the manifestation of God would appear, then He would preach to the public, and be followed then by someone who would explain the esoteric sense for the elite—they called the first one the Proclaimer, and the second one, the following, the Foundation—much like the idea of the Paraclete in the Gospel of John. Jesus is going to go, so he can prepare the way for the Paraclete to give deeper teaching.

Well, that's in effect—I mean, they'd repudiate that—but that's what's going on. In Protestantism, with Paul, Jesus is the Savior. He did the work of salvation, and he taught some good stuff. But if you really want to know the truth of Christianity, it's Paul of the Pauline epistles. He was the one that came to clarify, really. Very difficult to find any kind of justification by faith teaching in Jesus, but there is apparently in Paul. And so, he's really the one that C.J. Carnell once said, "the epistles interpret the Gospels." In other words, they pull rank over, and then the Gospels are read through the lens of the theology of the epistles.

Just like Harnack and the liberal Protestants used to say, Paul was the second founder of Christianity. That's almost the same language. And by that, they meant that Jesus came and preached a simple, ethical gospel. And Paul came, and corrupted the whole thing with a religion of metaphysical formulae and dogma that Jesus would never have recognized. So, they didn't like Paul, whereas the conservative Protestants do. But in both cases, they kind of portray him as the second founder of Christianity.

Well, that means that you've got to make him the authority for things Jesus never speaks about. And this is true not only of conservative Protestants, but of today's more liberal ones. Because the pendulum has swung, and I guess because it's widely recognized among liberal Protestants that the historical Jesus is quite problematical. They figured, "Well, we've at least got seven epistles by Paul, and we can make use of him." And so Paul gets treated as a ventriloquist's dummy, just as Jesus does.

Now, it's not an either/or thing. Often, people (like the Jesus and Paul seminars of the Westar Institute) are busy making Jesus and Paul the mouthpieces for progressive agendas of various kinds, which I find extremely unconvincing. But the same problem exists with both—we really don't know if we have any reliable source material about what either man taught, or even whether they really existed. So, if you realize there's a problem with Jesus, I'm afraid there's no refuge to the comforting embrace of Paul—same problem.

MC: And don't you see that sometimes—like you said, with more liberal movements—for example, in more of the New Age neo-Gnostic movements, people like Timothy Freke, or Tom Harper just going, "Well, Paul was a full-blown Gnostic." That's pretty inaccurate, right?

RP: Well, they're on to something there, because as I argue, there's a whole lot of Gnosticism near the bottom of the Pauline tradition, Gnosticism and Marcionism. But there's also other layers, but some of the subsequent layers, I think *are* out-and-out Gnostic. Like certain chapters of First Corinthians, which, like all of them, I think is pretty much patchwork quilt. But the letter to the Colossians certainly appears to me simply to be Gnostic. Parts of Philippians, too, which a lot of people admit is a patchwork.

So, they are sort of right, there is a lot of out-and-out Gnosticism, and the ancient Gnostics saw it there. The first Gnostics we actually know existed—and not just inferring from the Pauline epistles themselves—the first ones we know of from any external sources were the Marcionites and Gnostics. They were the first to make any references to the Pauline letters, to write any commentaries on them; same with the Gospel of John. And so, yeah, I think they are right, to some degree, but especially in the case of Freke and Gandy. Freke and Gandy are sort of right, but from book to book, they tend to dilute the meaning of Gnosticism to the point where it's just like *Oprah*-ism. And *that*, I cannot really find in the epistles or the Gospels.

And then Harper, he wants to say, "Yeah, the Bible teaches this, and I'm behind it." But what he comes up with just seems to me to be very vague and insipid, without any distinctively Gnostic content. He seems to like them, because they were allegorizers and esotericists. I don't know that he really comes up with anything when he's panning for gold there, either.

It's just like Schweitzer said about the historical Jesus, once you find out who this guy was, or who wrote the stuff, it's an embarrassment to modern intellectuals. Nobody really believes this mythology; we like to see in it some kind of self discovery and independent thinking, and that did exist in there. But it does in the New Age movement, too, which comes up with all kinds of silliness.

Harper and Freke and Gandy are trying to use the Bible as a Scripture in some ways, still. And I just think, does it really teach the message you want to teach? So, there's a lot of funny business going on, even there. You want the authority of the Bible for what you're saying, but you don't really like what it says. So, you make it say something else.

MC: Why do you think the Valentinians were so enamored by the Pauline corpus? What exactly about it spoke to them?

RP: Well, I believe that a lot of it was written by people like them, possibly with earlier versions of what they thought. This is tough to say, but in my view, the historical Paul was the guy also known as Simon Magus, Simon the magician, or Simon the wise man. There may even be a scrap of Romans written by him. But he was already a pretty beefy Gnostic, with the idea of fallen souls from a fallen godhead, and the need for a Gnostic redeemer to gather them by converting the elite, and revealing the true identity.

It wasn't Valentinianism, but nobody ever said Paul was a Valentinian. It's just that the Valentinians said that they were taught by Theodus, the disciple of Paul. Which I think is a way of saying they bear the same relation to Paul as Platonism does to Socrates. It's not just quoting him, but starting there, and developing the ideas. And they believed in the essentials of it.

And when we run across things like the three classes of humans—the *sarkics*, the *psuchikoi*, and the *pneumatikoi*—in First Corinthians, that is the classification of the Valentinians. Did they get it from Paul or Simon, or is this part of a Valentinian fragment of that letter? It's really hard to tell. But they certainly saw themselves in the mirror in much of the Pauline epistles. Whether it was put there by the founder, or just an earlier generation of Valentinian writers, we don't know.

MC: The crux of your book that really explains a lot—and this is an idea by Walter Schmithals—says that the concept of the apostle didn't begin with Judaism or Christianity, but with Gnosticism. What exactly did he mean by that, Bob?

RP: From a look at all these esoteric sources in ancient Middle Eastern religions, especially Syrian, Schmithals said that given the way apostleship is depicted in the Pauline letters, he sees the emerging Christian idea of the apostolate as partly reflecting the Pauline epistles, and partly developed more, as in the twelve apostles idea of Luke's Acts. But he does say the basic idea goes back to Syrian Gnosticism, which he thinks is pre-Christian—no reference to Jesus yet.

And the idea was, again, there was a pre-human fall in the godhead, and that one sought salvation by recognizing the sparks of fallen, forgetful, amnesiac divinity within oneself and others. The *apostoloi*, the sent ones, were individuals who had somehow seen this in themselves, probably because they had a larger concentration of it in them. And the elite among humanity had a divine spark within them; not everybody did. But the ones that did might have more or less of it, and the ones with more came to an awakening, a self-recognition, like the guy does in the *Hymn of the Pearl*—a Gnostic text contained in the *Acts of Thomas*. And these guys became the apostles because they had some vision, or somehow knew that their appointed task was to go out, and like Diogenes, seek those who also had a spark of divinity, but didn't know it.

This is exactly like Morpheus in *The Matrix*, which is pretty much explicitly based on Gnosticism. Well, Morpheus would be the Gnostic apostle, the Gnostic revealer, and the idea was, that the more of these people that were recruited and awakened, the more the divine sparks would be re-collected. Which is also very much like later Kabbalistic Judaism. But also, much like the Sankya yoga doctrine, and Vedantic Hinduism, and so on.

Well, the more of them that could be awakened, that meant that upon death, they would not be reincarnated into this salt mine of incarnate, fallen existence. They would know how to elude the Archons, the planetary guardians, the fallen angels, who were like guards on the Berlin wall, trying to keep the merchandise in the store. They don't want people to catch on to the truth, because that will be the end of their customer base. But the Gnostic revealer awakening the pneumatics, the spiritual ones, shows them how to cut to the chase, and get back to the divine Pleroma, from whence they once came.

In the *Gospel of Thomas*, the disciples ask Jesus, "Tell us what our end will be?" And he says, "Have you discovered the beginning, that you ask about the end? Rather, go back to the beginning, and then you'll know the end." You have to know where you came from, what you really are, and then you'll know your destiny, and be able to attain it. So, the more of the *pneumatikoi* who are awakened, upon death they will return to the Pleroma. And eventually, this world will collapse on itself, because it was only the divine sparks that kept the whole mess going.

There was a plan B for the conventionally religious; they didn't just say, "the hell with you." They weren't necessarily elitists. The Gnostic revealers were again, like Diogenes, and they were the original *apostoloi*. This got Christianized, and the figure of Jesus was made into the chief Gnostic revealer, as it were. And the death of the channeler, of the Gnostic revealer, Jesus—his death provided salvation for the guys in "business class". They could get to heaven by faith.

But the original idea of these wandering preachers seeking out the elect must come from the Syrian Gnostics; you don't find it in Judaism. And it's almost made more clear by the fact that some seek Jewish origin for *everything*, because they want everything to go from the Old Testament, via Judaism, into Christianity. They don't want anything like Zoroastrianism or mystery religions involved. Jews, more or less in New Testament times, had the idea of a *shaliach*, a sent one, a delegate for the Sanhedrin, delivering the decrees of the religious authorities to Diaspora Jews. And it wasn't their views that they were promoting; they were authoritative conveyors of whatever the rabbis had said. They say, "That's no doubt where they got the idea of Jesus and the apostles."

But Schmithals says, "No, it's got to come from Gnosticism," even though he thought Paul *did* write all of those letters, except for the Pastorals, and that he wrote them in the middle of the first century. So, he's very radical in some ways, and very traditional in others.

MC: So, basically, what we have is Paul, Apollo, Cephas—these gurus walking around with their inner Christ, competing for a piece of the pie?

RP: Well, they might have worked together, but probably they were competitors. And I think that's what we have preserved in a little snapshot in First Corinthians, to which you refer. One grouping says, "I belong to Paul." Another, "I belong to Cephas," another, "I belong to Apollo." What is this? Is Christ divided? Did *Paul* die for your sins? Were you baptized in the name of Paul? I think that it really cannot mean anything, once you through Christ into the mix. This is the stage of things Schmithals was talking about, that these people were apostles of a Gnostic man of light who had never come to Earth.

They became, by default, the saviors of these "fan clubs", and Christ was one. Apollo was another; Cephas—perhaps to be identified with Peter—was another. Eventually, the Christ faction won out and subsumed the others, just as Christianity had assimilated many members of the John the Baptist sect. I think there was competition. You certainly read about apostolic bickering and competition in the Pauline epistles—it doesn't matter who wrote them, or when.

MC: In our past interview on Paul and Marcion, we certainly covered the "Simon Magus is Paul in drag theory," as one scholar called it. But in *The Amazing Colossal Apostle,* you bring even more evidence. One of the truly astounding pieces of evidence is found in the Jewish writing, the *Toledot Yeshu.* Doesn't it come right out and say that Paul's original name was Simon, and that he *was* a magician?

RP: Yeah, that is shocking. They're obviously using older ideas, and this is admittedly, a speculative way of putting together the pieces of the puzzle so you can prove this, but that is shocking to me. And the similarity of some of the material in the *Toledot Yeshu:* especially the aerial battle between Jesus the false prophet, and Judas Iscariot the good guy, the secret agent of the Sanhedrin—this appears again with Simon Magus versus Peter. The pattern just keeps repeating, and I think the *Toledot Yeshu* almost is a smoking gun, except that we can't really date those traditions.

MC: Like you said, the magical battle is with Simon and Peter. And for the Protestants, here's another little tidbit that you point out: Irenaeus says point-blank that Simon Magus preached salvation comes from faith and not works. I mean, what else do you want, Martin Luther?

RP: Yeah, and Irenaeus thought this guy's a heretic? That's not too surprising, because it's far from clear, as Roman Catholics have known, that the Pauline epistles teach the Lutheran doctrine. Even a lot of critical Protestant scholars are willing to say he wasn't talking about what Martin Luther talked about; he's just saying that the law is not binding on Gentile converts. He's not talking about whether you have to keep your nose clean—he says you do. You've got to show up before the judgment seat of Christ, to answer for what you did in the flesh. So, Roman Catholics have never thought he's teaching what Lutherans think.

Irenaeus gives this as a doctrine of heretic Simon Magus. And Simon is depicted in the Pseudo-Clementine novels as preaching freedom from the law. He seems very clearly to be a stand-in for both Marcion and Paul. And it's no accident, since they're all three the same person, in one sense or another. Marcion is the fountainhead of the literary Paul; others joined in and wrote Pauline stuff. But he started the ball rolling with parts of Galatians and Ephesians. Then, Simon Magus is the guy we know of as Paul—whether Paul is an actual name or a title, there are several likely possibilities. There's just a lot going on here, and this is a great example. Like, where there's smoke, there's fire.

Well, conventional church history people and New Testament scholars have this idea there may be lots of smoke, but there's no fire; that all of this evidence that doesn't fit into the orthodox paradigm—it's not a sign that anything happened. Since we can't be *sure* what happened, we can just go on assuming nothing happened, and it was all just a Sunday school story.

No, if you try to make sense of all these odd things that survived the purge of Christian literature under Constantine, you get some pretty interesting, viable possibilities. They can never be more, but they are pretty tempting.

MC: You mention a Queen Helene that Paul knew, but doesn't the *Toledot Yeshu* also talk about a Queen Helene that was taken or seduced by the magician Jesus?

RP: The widow of Alexander Jannaeus. There are other Jewish and Jewish/Christian references to Jesus being crucified, along with a lot of Pharisees under Alexander Jannaeus, about 100 b.c.e. She calls in Jesus, who is creating a lot of great controversy among her Jewish subjects. She gives him a listen, and he gives all these prophetic proofs from the Bible that he is the predicted Messiah. And it's interesting, the *Toledot Yeshu* never refutes any of them.

I think Hugh Schonfield was certainly right—that this was based on a Jewish-Christian gospel, because the treatment of Jesus is pretty mild. If this thing is what it's often said to be—just a nasty satire on Christianity—it doesn't read that way. So, he gives his case, and does these miracles, and she's converted. The Jews are now afraid, and they manage to convince her that he's a charlatan. But they bring him back in, and she's convinced again, and so forth. Here is Jesus looking like Simon Magus with a miracle battle, and he's associated with a Queen Helene. Then, the Paul character comes back in some years later in the story.

And this, of course I'm getting from the great Robert Eisenman. In his book, *James, the Brother of Jesus,* one of several cities, called Antioch, was also the one known as Edessa. Right next door was Adiabene, and King Abgarus, of the famous letter to Jesus, who was in some sources, the husband of the Queen of Adiabene, Helene—who is known to this day as a benefactor the Jewish people, and a convert to some sort of baptizing version of Judaism.

Josephus tells us that she sent unnamed delegates to Jerusalem with huge amounts of money for famine relief. And Eisenman shows us how this is tied up in the story of the Ethiopian eunuch in Acts very convincingly. I'd like to see somebody refute it. Not likely. You've got Paul coupled with Queen Helene, and you can't help but think of Simon Magus and Helene, who had been a Queen. It's just a hypothesis, but it might be intriguing.

MC: In our past interviews on Paul, we never really covered the Simonian sect, ostensibly spearheaded by Simon. As you point out, Justin Martyr himself said that the Simonians were entrenched in Samaria and Rome, and weren't going anywhere. Could you tell us a bit about their origins, and how they were tied to Paul?

RP: In my view, if this is even accurate historical material. it sounds a little odd. There's also some anachronism in one of the writings attributed to Justin, and I have to admit I begin to wonder if the guy they say had written them really had written them. But let's assume for the sake of argument he was; that would simply be a reference to the earliest actual Pauline Christians. This may be a title of Paul; so we may have Paulinism already.

As Bauer pointed out, when we have the story of Peter rebuking Simon Magus in Acts at Samaria, everybody's been baptized, including Simon. So now, he's a Christian—he's just converted to Christianity—he comes up to Peter, and he asks to buy the unique privilege of the apostles. He doesn't put it that way, but it's clear, given the rest of the story.

Philip has converted the Samaritans, but that's not good enough. You need the apostolic imprimatur. So, two apostles come from Jerusalem to lay hands on the Samaritan converts, whereupon they receive the Spirit, which they wouldn't have done if it was merely Philip. Simon sees this, and says, "I'll pay you to confer this gift on me." As J. B. Phillips translated, Peter says, "To hell with you, and your money. You thought you could buy the gift of God? You have no part in this word, this ministry." Well, as Bauer said, isn't it obvious that this is the Peter versus Paul encounter that we read about in Galatians?

And the business of Paul seeking apostolic recognition at Jerusalem—they're willing to confer it *if* he will collect money for the Jerusalem church among the Gentiles. And he agrees to do it. Well, that's buying apostleship. Bauer said the author of Acts is trying to reconcile the Pauline faction with the Petrine faction. The story of Peter rebuking and refusing Paul is now unusable as it stands.

The Catholics are trying to say, "To get you Pauline Christians in here, we will admit Paul was a good guy. But what are we going to do with the story? Well let's make it kind of an evil counterpart, an evil twin of Paul; let's change it to Simon." So, Bauer already saw that this was really about Paul and his followers in Samaria. Justin Martyr may be referring to the same thing, that it was a Pauline mission.

To quote Oscar Cullmann slightly out of context, in his book *The Johannine Circle,* he says that, the John 4 thing, where Jesus goes to Samaria, and the Samaritan woman is evangelized in town and they come out believing, and Jesus says, "Look at that. The field is ripe for harvest." Others have done the work, and he's inheriting their harvest. Cullmann says this has got to refer to the same thing as in the Acts 8 story of Peter and Simon Magus. Philip, standing for the Hellenistic Christians, converted the Samaritans. But then the Jerusalem faction, owing allegiance to the figureheads of the twelve, reaped the harvest of it. They kind of usurped it. He says that's certainly what's being referred to. Jesus says to the twelve, "You're going to inherit the fruits of others' labors." Well, that seems to me to be just what is said in Galatians, about Paul founding churches. Also it's in Romans, and First Corinthians, and other people—Jewish Christians coming in on his heels, and converting his converts to their faction. It all seems to me to be not only the same *kind* of thing, but the *same* thing. So, there is evidence that the

Acts story of Simon Magus and Peter in Samaria is another attestation that the earliest Christianity of Samaria was Simonianism.

The thing I try to add here is sociology, or anthropology of religion, with the way sects evolve. They tend to start as radical, ascetic groups—certainly the Encratites and the Gnostics in the ancient church were. And they have these wandering apostles—a great book on this is Stevan Davies' *The Revolt of the Widows: the Social World of the Apocryphal Acts*, where he says there were these wandering brethren or apostles that Matthew 25, and the Didache, and third John talk about. These wandering mendicants who preached Christ are obviously the Gnostic apostles that Schmithals talks about. They were loose cannons; they had left everything behind—which, as Gerard Tyson says, how do we have those things at all, who else would've preserved them but people who left everything behind and followed Jesus? They said, "I did it. See? I'm to be listened to; I'm walking the walk." Well, they garnered people that would leave their families and homes behind. But eventually, a sect begins to re-assimilate the values of the larger society, when some get married, have kids, and have to send them to school.

So, the guys that founded it become more and more alienated. I think this is what happened between Simonianism and Marcionism. Marcionism was ascetic, but it had a two track system: you could wait to get baptized until you were ready to renounce marriage—or sex anyway—because you had to. But you could be a member of the church without doing that.

I think we can interpret, we can discover or peel back layers of the Pauline texts, to see whether they represent radical asceticism—which would come from the original Simonian base—or whether they are dealing with accommodations to that, like in First Corinthians 7. Should you be an ascetic, or should you just set aside times for prayer and celibacy, but have sex the rest of the time? That presupposes this re-assimilation, gradually—with difficulty—to societal norms. And so, that's Marcionism.

Then, we have stuff elsewhere in the Pauline epistles that says marriage is fine, that represents the Catholic overlay. It's like tree rings, and you can use them like stages of evolution of sectarian groups, which use the same path again and again. Not only on this, there are other issues as well, where you can trace the sectarian evolution, I think.

MC: I think your analogy is, the hippies become corporate lawyers. They've got to grow up from these Gnostic Simonians to more respectable Marcionites, and then eventually to Catholics.

RP: Yep, exactly. I see you have the true Gnosis.

MC: [laughs] For the time being. Another thing you point out, we find hints of Simon Magus in the New Testament, in the Gospel of John, with the story of Jesus and the Samaritan woman with the five husbands, and Mary Magdalene and the five demons. Doesn't this symbolize the concept of Simon being the standing one, who's always reincarnated, looking for his divine consort?

RP: Yeah, and that she has been abused as a prostitute and an adulterous in life after life, as Helen of Troy, and then as the prostitute in the brothel, from which Simon is said to have rescued Helen. I can't help thinking of Travis Bickle in *Taxi Driver*. But the succession of husbands, the number of demons—it seems to me those are kind of "garblings", or just exoteric cloaking of the Simonian doctrine.

And the John 4 thing, with the Samaritan woman who represents Helena—that may somehow have to do with Dositheus the Samaritan. Who, we're told, competed with Simon for the leadership of the John the Baptist sect, and Simon won out. But in this, the hint that had something to do with Dositheus is where Jesus said, "If you knew the *Gift of God*, you would have asked *Him* for water." Well, Dositheus means "the gift of God". So, you recognize Dositheus as the standing one.

All of this stuff mixes together. The fact that that story has the woman say, "I know a Messiah is coming"—when it wasn't even a Samaritan idea—shows you that *something* is going on.

MC: And don't you propose that Marcion may have been a disciple of Simon Magus?

RP: Here I owe a bit of the puzzle to my pal Stefan Hermann Huller, who's written all kinds of fascinating books—some on paper, and some on his website. I often don't accept his larger conclusions, but I find everything he writes endlessly fascinating; he has the command of a vast amount of ancient lore. The possibilities he sees in it are just eye-opening.

One of them was that Ireneaus and the heresiologists claimed that Simon Magus had a disciple named Marcos. They called him Marcos the magician. And Stefan says, "Wait a minute. Is Marcos the magician Marcion?" The whole idea, even according to the Orthodox, says the

Gnostics all descended from Simon. Well, that's pretty much a flat-out statement, saying that Marcion was believed to have been a Simonian, just as Jesus is depicted as having been a disciple of John the Baptist, and then striking out on his own. Same with Plato and Socrates.

MC: Moving a little bit to the actual Gnostic literature—probably a lot of listeners don't know this; they assume a lot of the concepts, like the Pleroma and the Kenoma, came from some Platonized Vision Quest by the Valentinians. But wasn't all they were doing was simply reinterpreting the epistles in very radical ways?

RP: Well, there's the chicken and egg problem again. The way I view it, the stuff that sounds Gnostic, like the kenosis thing in Philippians 2— you were talking about the Gnostic man of light exiling himself from the Pleroma, and entering the Kenoma. He emptied himself, kenosis means emptying oneself. As Bauer pointed out, that's very likely a reference to the Kenoma, the void outside of the Pleroma. The exaltation would be the reintegration of the man of light, and so on.

Then, in Colossians we hear the Pleroma of God dwelt in him bodily. That, together with the idea that you have already been raised with Christ. Romans doesn't go that far—it *hopes* for a resurrection in the future—but Philippians does. Colossians sounds pretty darn Gnostic. The idea that the principalities and powers had enslaved the human race, by means of the laws of Judaism? That's just Gnosticism, period.

Does this reflect an earlier phase of Gnosticism than the Valentinians? Were the Valentinians interpreting something that was pre-Valentinian, or is this part due to Valentinians? To me, it doesn't really make any difference. It's hard to know. Are the Valentinians interpreting, or reinterpreting an early proto-Gnosticism? Or did they actually write this part of the epistle?

I think that none of the epistles go back to the time that we say Paul lived. Except possibly Romans, if we think Simon Magus was Paul, and he was that early. He could've been. Even at that, most of this stuff is later—late first century, early second century.

Philippians tells us that there were people who were known as Paulinists, but the writer thinks that they're just making trouble for Paul, saying crazy things so that he'll be blamed for them. We have competing Pauline epistles admittedly, and I think the same is true with each one. They're like the Upanishads—it's difficult to find any coherence in them, because they've been overlaid with scribal interpolations.

MC: On the other side of the aisle, we have the Sethians—and this is a question I wanted to ask you—you have the text the *Hypostasis of the Archons*, which begins with an invocation to the great apostle, and it quotes Ephesians with "wickedness in high places". Do you see the Sethians leaning on Paul and the Simonians, or do you think this was a later redaction?

RP: It's hard to say, but as R. Joseph Hoffmann points out in his great book on Marcion, Ephesians probably was the original Marcionite Epistle to the Laodiceans. And only after a series of interpolations, in which he maps out and explains why he thinks that's what they are, then it becomes the Catholic, sanitized epistle to the Ephesians. Well, the Sethians may have known it in the earlier Marcionite form that they were different from Marcionites.

Just look at the Nag Hammadi library—there's all kinds of flavors and varieties of Gnostic material. They read each other's stuff. So, it could be a quote from the Marcionites' Laodiceans. We don't know who wrote that, but it almost doesn't matter; you've got Valentinian works like the prayer of Paul the apostle—that has plenty of quotes from the Pauline letters.

Yeah, there could be influence, but it's just such a mixed bag and a mess, it's hard to say. Sethianism seems to assume this kind of prophetic succession doctrine that we find so many centuries later, among the Ismailis, the Druze, etc. And in the Qur'an, there was this reincarnating, or prophetic, or messianic divine figure, who came to Earth again and again. The Sethian writings tend to squeeze in Jesus as a reincarnation of Seth and/or Melchizedek. To me, that comes from a more Jewish, Gnostic Christian milieu. But even such people could well have been reading Paul, simply by dint of the fact that we know they were reading him. There are some parts of the Pauline epistles that seemed to be Marcionite, that are against the law, and against Christians that exalt and still use the law.

Lutgert, whom Schmithals quotes quite a bit, says he saw Gnostic Judaism in the opposition to Paul. That could've been the Sethians, but some of them liked him. It was such a ricocheting ping-pong ball back then, as to who influenced whom. The Jewish Christians like Paul, and said as long as we can keep the law, he's okay. Others said he was a false apostle. They could have been influenced by him, they might've just picked up an idea.

MC: Another interesting insight that most don't know about concerning the Pauline literature is that of the *Apocalypse of Paul*—not the Nag Hammadi one, but the later one. Could you briefly tell us about it, Bob?

RP: That appears to be a Catholic work, written by and for monks, though I'd also say that in the Gospel of Thomas, the *monokoi*, the single ones, seem to represent monastic ascetics. But the *Apocalypse of Paul* seems to be Catholic, because of the idea of the ascent to heaven. That could come directly from Gnosticism. On the other hand, it's preserved in the Catholic sanitized Pauline corpus. And I think that's what the *Apocalypse of Paul* would've known, but it's interesting that this apocalypse (which is quite long), does not refer to any of the revelatory material in the Pauline epistles. So, they had some knowledge of a Catholicized Paul, but not the epistles. There's loads of stuff that could've been quoted in the *Apocalypse of Paul*—some is, in the very short Nag Hammadi *Apocalypse of Paul*. But this one, the later one—it looks like somebody didn't know, or didn't like the epistles, but were happy to use Paul's name. I have a section in the book about the acts and apocalypses of Paul, and why there's such a mysterious and conspicuous absence of knowledge of Pauline texts in Catholic-leaning literature.

MC: Alright Bob, I believe that's all the time we have for today. I'd like to thank you very much once again for gracing Aeon Byte in discussing your book, *The Amazing Colossal Apostle*.

RP: And I'd like to thank you for not falling asleep!

MC: [laughs] It's very engaging stuff, and I look forward to having you back on.

RP: That'd be great, thanks for having me.

GARY LACHMAN

In the last decade, Gary Lachman has ascended to become the premiere expert on the Western Esoteric Tradition. Although a nonacademic, Gary considers himself a scholar of consciousness, expanding and evolving the ideas of such occult icons as Carl Jung, Gurdjieff, P. D. Ouspensky, Colin Wilson, and Aleister Crowley.

Our interview dealt with the figure of Hermes Trismegistus, the fabled godman not only of the pagan Gnostics known as the Hermetics but also of the Abrahamic faiths. It was based on his book, *The Quest For Hermes Trismegistus*. Beyond how the inspired works of Hermes Trismegistus expanded the consciousness of Western Civilization—from the science of the Muslim caliphates to the Renaissance movement—Gary also discussed his left-right brain paradigm, and how its imbalance has resulted in this modern world of runaway warfare and materialism. After all, he convincingly argues that the marginalization of Hermes Trismegistus and Hermetic philosophy during the Age of Enlightenment was a possible cause of humanity abandoning its inner, contemplative life (the right brain) and fully embracing a mechanistic worldview (the left brain) that directly leads to 20th century carnage.

Needless to say, the interview is a straddling history of Hermeticism, beginning with ancient Egypt and ending with the possibility of Hermes Trismegistus returning in the 21st century, before it's all too late.

MC: You are known primarily as a scholar of occultism in modern times. What exactly inspired you to write a book on such an ancient figure?

GL: I had written a book called *Politics and the Occult*. Part of that book dealt with understanding some of the political implications of a school of contemporary esoteric or spiritual thought called the Traditionalists—René Guenon and Frithjof Schuon and Julius Evola and some other figures. The theme uniting these different writers and thinkers is that there was some sort of primordial tradition, some primordial knowledge or wisdom or ancient teaching that was revealed to mankind in the dim, dark past. This primordial tradition, which became known as the perennial philosophy or the pristine theology, was this initial primary revelation of the truth, and then in time it later got filtered down and separated into all the different religions that we know: Christianity, Judaism, Buddhism, Hinduism, Islam and so on. But uniting all of them was the idea that there was some sort of ancient teaching which was the central one from which they all came. This idea seems to have originated with the figure called Hermes Trismegistus, Thrice-Greatest Hermes. Hermes Great-Great-Great. (Tony the Tiger used to say that about Frosties Flakes when I was a kid.)

So I just became very interested in this character and this whole idea. Anyone who is interested in the occult and esotericism and the inner tradition of the West and all these teachings, they know who Hermes Trismegistus is. He's the character who is supposed to be one of the great creators of magic and writing and thinking and civilization and so on. I became interested in who this character was, because when you look into it you realize that for a great many centuries he was a revered figure. At certain times he was considered to be an actual real person, at other times a God, at other times a half-human god, a magician, and so on and so on. But in the early 1600s it was found out that actually there was no figure like this at all, he was more like an invention of certain spiritual groups and devotees in the first and second centuries following Christ, who invented this character. So you can see in the history of ideas suddenly he loses credibility and the Hermetic teachings and the Hermetic philosophy and the character of Hermes Trismegistus himself suddenly drops down to be seen as mere superstition. And the whole school of Hermeticism, that for many years has been considered prestigious and up there with Plato and Jesus and Moses and all of the other big hitters of western civilization at the time, he becomes a kind of charlatan figure, this fool, in some ways. His followers are seen to be mere followers of superstition, and that's where the whole esoteric tradition goes underground. So I just became fascinated with the whole shift in our thought. It's almost as if someone like Einstein, let's say, or Stephen Hawking, the smartest man in the world, who can say important things about everything, it's as if 200 years from now people figure out they were completely wrong. Or even decided they didn't exist and suddenly their street cred collapses down to nothing. I just was fascinated with that whole shift because in many ways our modern world, our modern times, begins at the same time that this Hermetic teaching and this figure of Hermes Trismegistus goes into eclipse.

MC: As your book points out, Hermes was respected and at least accepted in early Christendom, in the Byzantine Empire, in medieval times. How exactly does this pagan figure become so much a part of the pantheon with the other luminaries in the Christian dispensation? How did he get away with it?

GL: Well, there were various different thinkers and philosophers and theologians in the Christian tradition, going back to Clement of Alexandria, of the early church father, going up into the Renaissance, people like Marsilio Ficino and Pico della Mirandola and other who wanted to somehow find a place for the Hermetic philosophy within Christianity, within Christian philosophical thinking, and they all wanted to find a place for Plato. So they basically wanted to find a place for the Greek philosophers and what were known at the time as pagan philosophers. When the church, or the church up into the Renaissance, refers to pagans, it's not talking about people here in England who go out into the forest.

MC: [laughs]

GL: I'm not in any way dismissing them, but it's not that kind of wicker man paganism, it's not nature mysticism, it's the Greek neoplatonic philosophy that they considered pagan. And there were many within the church who were very intelligent thinkers, who realized there was much of value in that. People like Plato were seen to be precursors of Christianity. There was no doubt that Christianity and Christ were the culmination, the final product of dialectic, let's say. But earlier than that you have these pagan thinkers who, in abstract terms or logical terms, seem to be saying the same thing. So you find thinkers in this period seeing some of the parallels between the Hermetic, platonic philosophies and some of the things in Christianity. And even at times during the Renaissance when there were Christian thinkers advocating the inclusion of figures like Hermes Trismegistus within the canon as being one of the prophets, let's say, of Christ. So this is to suggest how important this figure of Hermes Trismegistus was, and also how at a certain time in the west, in Christianity, there was a possibility when what we today see as the strange, woo-woo, weird world of the occult, and mysticism and esotericism was actually being promoted as something that could be an active living part of the whole western consciousness.

MC: Yeah, and he even survived the barbed words of Augustine, didn't he?

GL: Yeah, well, Augustine took argument with the Hermetic philosophy and Hermes Trismegistus. He wasn't aware of the Corpus Hermeticum, but he did know of a book called the Asclepius, one of the longer Hermetic books. What Augustine didn't like is that in the Asclepius there's instructions on how to animate statues, this notion of bringing the god down, the god-force down, and fusing it into these figures that were made, and these become animated. This was something that Augustine thought was something that I guess we would consider something like Satanic or black magic. At the same time, he also recognized, even by arguing against, he recognized the importance of this character Hermes Trismegistus, so again you have people like Augustine, Clement of Alexandria and other in the Church recognizing how important this figure is, and then in the early 1600s it becomes clear that actually he's not what everybody thought he was. It would be the equivalent today, let's say somebody figured out the sort of thing that goes on with the *Da Vinci Code*, this whole idea that what we thought the case turned out not to be, and the effect this has on western consciousness in general.

MC: In your research, Gary, and obviously most conservative scholars would say that Hermeticism began around the second century after Christ. What do you think are the historical origins for Hermeticism?

GL: I think that term, Hermeticism, starts up around then or a little bit earlier. In that sense I think that's a correct assessment. But the ideas, the knowledge, the wisdom that is being transmitted in Hermeticism, as you say, probably goes back earlier. One of the things I try to do in the book is answer my own question: What is this Egyptian wisdom? You hear stories of Plato going to school in Egypt, and Pythagoras beforehand, and the whole idea that for everybody back then it had to be part of their curriculum vitae that they went to Egypt and sat at the foot of the priests there and learned something, much like today people go backpacking off into some third world country in search of the indigenous shamans or whatever, or in the 60s or 70s going out to India to meet the gurus there. So there may have been something like that going on then, and it got me thinking: well, what is this Egyptian wisdom you hear so much about in books about magic and the occult and esotericism and so on? And I speculate on a few different things, on what it might be.

I draw on the work of a very brilliant writer names Jeremy Naydler who has this notion of Egyptian shamanism in the ancient Egyptian time, the priests performed rituals or participated in ceremonies that are very much like what we understand shamanistic practices to be, and the central theme around this is that the Egyptians had a very complex notion of the soul, of the human being—its eight parts—and there's something particular that relates to this. It's something called the *akh* and the *akh* is this kind of immortal, immaterial, spiritual undying essence that one can come to awareness of oneself through certain rituals and practices. Naydler presents the idea that the *Egyptian Book of the Dead*, which most mainstream Egyptologists see as basically a funerary text, something to be read over the dead body of the mummy. And Naydler says, yes, it was used like that but it was also equally used as a kind of instruction book, a kind of Rough Guide to experiencing the underworld, what the Egyptians called the *Duat*, while still alive, without having to physically die. This, Naydler argues, is an idea that gets picked up by Plato, or appears in Plato, the whole notion that Socrates argues in the *Phaedo* and also the *Apologia*, the notion that philosophy is a kind of discipline in which you practice dying. You learn how to die to the physical, external world while still alive in order to awaken what the Hermeticists call Nous, Mind, this kind of immortal, immaterial, universal mind that we all participate in.

So looking at some of the things that Naydler talks about, also looking at some of the work of René Schwaller de Lubicz, his ideas about what he called *symbolique*, which was what he thought was happening with Egyptian hieroglyphics, in the sense that the kind of figures that the hieroglyphics are composed of, they serve two purposes: they denoted things, they pointed to things as language does, this particular figure meant that sort of thing, but they also evoked, they triggered this broader consciousness that de Lubicz called the intelligence of the heart, where you have intuitive, participatory experience of what Egyptians called the *neters*. So looking at that, comparing those sorts of ideas with those things that are in the Corpus Hermeticum, this collection of Hermetic writings that more than likely were written in the first few centuries after Christ and later resurfaced a thousand years or so later, in the Renaissance, looking at some of the things that are talked about in there, I see some parallels. So the reason I'm getting into this is to suggest that, yes, even though these texts were written in the first, second, third century after Christ, they seem to look back to or to be informed by metaphysical, psychological, esoteric ideas that go much further back and seem to have an Egyptian origin.

MC: Very interesting Gary, because it was Valentinus who called Gnosis "the knowledge of the heart" and you mentioned that the Egyptians called it the intelligence of the heart. You also call Hermeticism the religion of the mind. You're basically saying that to the Hermetics, who are maybe the closest bridge we have to the really alien consciousness of the Egyptians, which we will probably never be able to understand— and the Greeks wanted to understand—but as a way of completely gaining the access of our lower and higher mind and expanding our consciousness to its extremes, right?

GL: Well, yes, the central idea in Hermeticism is the notion of Gnosis. We know Gnosis is shared with another philosophical-spiritual school of the time called the Gnostics and Gnosticism, but they both were very much centered on this idea, and it's the Greek word for knowledge. For the Hermeticists this Gnosis was the experience of the Nous, the experience of the universal mind, that is the fundamental really real thing in existence is this mind and we participate in it, it's all around us. The Hermeticists have this notion they call the One or the All, which when you think about it makes a lot of sense, because the only one that we could conceive of in the world that we live in would have to be the entire world itself. Within that collection of things, basically everything, there's multiplicity, there's diversity, there's all different sorts of things. So for us to in any way comprehend the one it would have to at the same time mean comprehending the All and for the Hermeticists this is the basic kind of movement or direction for their spiritual practices and for their meditative work.

In the book I try to relate it to this notion that starts up in the early twentieth century called cosmic consciousness. Now we know in the sixties this phrase, cosmic consciousness, got picked up and used for anything that was groovy. In the early 1900s, 1901 I think, a fellow named Richard Maurice Bucke, who was a psychiatrist, a psychologist, in Canada, he wrote a book called *Cosmic Consciousness* in which he argues that the human race was evolving into this wider, deeper, more profound, more expanded form of consciousness, and he traces throughout history different examples of that: Buddha, Christ, lots of other sorts of people that are in there. And he himself talks about an experience he had. Now what struck me about this was the way Bucke described his own experience of cosmic consciousness and the descriptions of it with others, especially people who read Bucke's book, one was William James, who experimented with nitrous oxide and had other mystical experiences, and another was P. D. Ouspensky, who is best known for being Gurdjieff's brightest student but was a very important insightful thinker in his own right. He, having read Bucke and also having read William James' *The Variety of Religious Experience*, he too experimented with nitrous oxide and had very similar experiences. And this cosmic consciousness, the way they all describe it, suddenly they become aware of everything going on around them in very minute and vivid detail. They all describe it as this flood of information.

In some ways there's nothing very mystical about it, it's not this kind of supernatural thing, it's not a visitation by Christ or Buddha or Krishna or anything like that, it's basically becoming aware of a huge amount of facts, of knowledge—too much actually for any of them to handle at any one time. I was struck by the way William James and Ouspensky described their experiences and how it seemed to relate and parallel the way Gnosis is described in the Hermetic books. That was exciting for me because it made me feel that because these guys back in the second, third century talking about their experiences and then you have these modern accounts of the same sort of thing. So I'm always very thrilled when I find parallels and similar accounts about our inner world and our inner experiences coming from different sources because that reaffirms my notion that we're talking about something real. These are from different times in history, different cultures, totally different backgrounds, but the experience is very similar. Again, as you say, it has to do with this notion of the sense of mind.

MC: You give plenty of really great examples. For examples, Herman Hesse and Aldous Huxley. It seems the point is, whatever you need to do to get to that state of consciousness, go ahead and do it. We really don't know what the rituals were of the ancient Hermetics, do we?

GL: No. There's some speculation. It's probably easier for us now, because we can go and get ayahuasca or mescaline. Aldous Huxley took mescaline. Herman Hesse's experience is different in that he's describing the experiences of his character Harry Holler in his novel *Steppenwolf*. Steppenwolf is this middle-aged intellectual who has basically given up on life and the novel is basically him avoiding going home, because if he goes home he's going to slit his throat. So he tries to keep himself away from the razor. But he does have these moments when suddenly this tension that he's living under and this excruciating boredom relaxes and he has experience of being somehow vividly aware of other times in his life. The same sort of thing happens in *Remembrance of Things Past*, the huge novel by Marcel Proust. Famously the character in the novel tastes a bit of biscuit or cake dipped in this tea and it suddenly reminds him of his childhood, and he's thrown back into this other time, and it's not as if he knows, oh yes, I'm here in this place when I was ten years old, it's as if he's there again, it's living, it's alive. It's 3D as, sadly, most movies are today. This relates too to this Hermetic notion of becoming God. To me, one of the most tremendously thrilling passages in the Hermetic books is one in which—usually it's either Nous talking to Hermes, or it's Hermes talking to his disciples, his students—this is one of the early forms of the teacher student, guru-chela structure. He's saying that if you want to experience Gnosis, if you want to know God, if you want to become like God, and that means to exist in all points of your life, at the same time be the foetus in the womb, be rotting in the grave, be the young man, be the mature man, but also be everything else.

There's this tremendous sense of participating in everything, hence this notion of cosmic consciousness. And it's something that Hesse's character Harry Haller and Proust's character in his novel, it's something that they both experience and again it's interesting for me because neither Hesse nor Proust are making any ostensible references to the Hermetic teaching, but the phenomenology of the experience they're describing is similar, if not exactly the same as the kind of thing that the Hermetic books are advising the students to participate.

Again, it's a religion of the mind. It is a kind of religion in that there's a belief in a spiritual reality beyond the material, but it doesn't depend on any particular kind of rites or hierarchy or structure or ritual or whatever. It's basically coming to understand your own mind, the potentials of your own consciousness. This is what excites me about the Hermetic school. And it's one of the differences between the Gnostics and the Hermeticists who were around at the same time. They knew of each other. We know some Hermetic texts were found among the Gnostic texts that were discovered at Nag Hammadi in the 1940s and we know that at least the Gnostics were reading some of the Hermetic stuff as well. The difference between the two is that for the Gnostics there is this kind of paranoia consciousness, there's this kind of conspiracy consciousness, the whole notion of the archons, the whole notion that we live in this false world, we're trapped in this world of matter and space and time that's been created by this idiot demiurge God who in the Bible is Yahweh, and William Blake referred to him as Nobodaddy, and all of this, a dark Phillip K. Dick sense that there are others out there who are controlling everything, like *The Matrix* or something, we have to escape from it. But the Hermeticists don't have that sort of paranoid sensibility about the cosmos. They say, yes, we are sunk into matter.

What we have to do is actualize our own full self, our own full being, our own full consciousness in order to master the world of matter and space and time and reality, and to take our rightful place within it, which is that of the caretaker, this whole notion that's discussed in more than one of the Hermetic books, that's man's place as the cosmic caretaker. We're here to help take care of things, similarly to a notion in Kabbalah of *tikkun*, the whole idea that humanity's job is to repair the mistakes in creation. When God or whoever created the everything, he actually did a sloppy job, and things broke, and things spilled, and so our job was to clean up the mess, and this was something that the Hermeticists shared with the later kabbalist thinkers. There isn't this wanting to escape the cosmos that you get with the Gnostics. The Gnostics are closer to the existentialists, or even to some more modern esoteric schools like Gurdjieff and the Fourth Way, this notion that we're trapped in a prison and we have somehow to find a way to burrow our way out. It's very different with the Hermeticists.

MC: You do mention, Gary, the Goldilocks effect, in which we have to have one foot in the spiritual world and one foot in the material world. And what I also liked, and I often have arguments between people on the difference between Gnosis and mysticism, and you put it very well when you say that part of Gnosis is having that valve, is to be able to control archetypal energies that flow through us, or else we can't go to our jobs. We've got to keep it in control.

GL: Well, yeah, it's great to have these powerful mystical experiences either produced through spiritual practices or taking some psychoactive substance. But Aldous Huxley said, when he was under the influence of mescaline, yes, if everyone took mescaline there would be no wars, but there would be no civilization either. Huxley talked about looking over at a sinkful of dirty dishes—which gives us some idea of how Huxley lived—and thinking, well, they are beautiful. Why would you want to go over and wash them? Thankfully, Huxley was a fairly responsible psychedelic imbiber, but I'm sure we all know from experience that many agreed with him, why go wash those dishes? So in a very practical, simple way, the idea isn't completely to be immersed in this cosmic consciousness all the time, but to draw from the experiences that we do get the knowledge that the universe is much more fascinating and more interesting living place than we generally take it for.

We have to get on in the world and Huxley talks about how mind at large has to be siphoned out to a kind of tiny trickle, but it's just the amount of consciousness we need in the trickle to deal with things. We seem to have two forms of consciousness: one is to deal with things, which we all do, and the other is to appreciate things. Our problem in the modern world is that we're very successful at dealing with things, which is why we're very successful and the most dominant species on the planet and so on and so on, and why we're able to focus our consciousness and our attention onto minute specifics and actually do things that, as far as we can tell, most other living creatures can't do. But the downside of that, that funneling of our attention, is that we lost awareness and consciousness of the rich meaning that saturates the world around us. And this is when Huxley takes mescaline, as he tells us in *The Doors of Perception*, that's more or less what happens, that part of his consciousness, that kind of consciousness that's focused on dealing with the world, was put out of commission, and suddenly the richness, the meaning that's soaking in things became available to him, and he could see it.

MC: You do mention, Gary, the Goldilocks effect, in which we have to have one foot in the spiritual world and one foot in the material world. And what I also liked, and I often have arguments between people on the difference between Gnosis and mysticism, and you put it very well when you say that part of Gnosis is having that valve, is to be able to control archetypal energies that flow through us, or else we can't go to our jobs. We've got to keep it in control.

GL: Well, yeah, it's great to have these powerful mystical experiences either produced through spiritual practices or taking some psychoactive substance. But Aldous Huxley said, when he was under the influence of mescaline, yes, if everyone took mescaline there would be no wars, but there would be no civilization either. Huxley talked about looking over at a sinkful of dirty dishes—which gives us some idea of how Huxley lived—and thinking, well, they are beautiful. Why would you want to go over and wash them? Thankfully, Huxley was a fairly responsible psychedelic imbiber, but I'm sure we all know from experience that many agreed with him, why go wash those dishes? So in a very practical, simple way, the idea isn't completely to be immersed in this cosmic consciousness all the time, but to draw from the experiences that we do get the knowledge that the universe is much more fascinating and more interesting living place than we generally take it for. We have to get on in the world and Huxley talks about how mind at large has to be siphoned out to a kind of tiny trickle, but it's just the amount of consciousness we need in the trickle to deal with things.

We seem to have two forms of consciousness: one is to deal with things, which we all do, and the other is to appreciate things. Our problem in the modern world is that we're very successful at dealing with things, which is why we're very successful and the most dominant species on the planet and so on and so on, and why we're able to focus our consciousness and our attention onto minute specifics and actually do things that, as far as we can tell, most other living creatures can't do. But the downside of that, that funneling of our attention, is that we lost awareness and consciousness of the rich meaning that saturates the world around us. And this is when Huxley takes mescaline, as he tells us in *The Doors of Perception*, that's more or less what happens, that part of his consciousness, that kind of consciousness that's focused on dealing with the world, was put out of commission, and suddenly the richness, the meaning that's soaking in things became available to him, and he could see it.

But, as I said, he had absolutely no inclination to do anything. William James, talking about his experiences with nitrous oxide, when he had this deep conviction of this metaphysical profundity that he perceived, also came to the realization that, after spending some time in this absolute oneness of things, the complete total relation of everything to everything, where everything made sense, there was a sense of indifference, because if everything was one, why do one thing rather than another? Why do this rather than that? So he came, like Huxley, to the conclusion that our consciousness seems to be limited and filtered through necessarily, in order for us to go on. One of the things I propose in the book is this notion that, well, even though most of us tend to enjoy the other form of consciousness, which is why we drink wine or take other sorts of things, to relax or dealing with consciousness in order to sink into the other mode, that we need to find some balance, to open up this reducing valve, and after that we don't think, with so much of modern culture, that so much of life is meaningless and pointless. There isn't anything out there. It's just atoms floating about meaninglessly. But not too much so that we are able to actually function in the world.

The point that I make in the book, getting back to this notion of Gnosis, I think our job is to translate those insights that one gets in those moments of cosmic consciousness into this other form of knowledge which we use another Greek word for, *episteme*, which is the knowledge we can house in books and libraries, on computers, and so on and so on, and it's a knowledge you can pass on to others. I might have this incredibly ecstatic cosmic experience, but if all I can say to somebody is, "Oh wow!" they're not going to get a heck of a lot out of it. But if like Huxley and others, who are able to write clearly and logically about their mystical experiences I can do that, and pass that on, that's how knowledge in the broader, larger sense grows. To me this is one of the important realizations I came to, that the whole idea isn't to go plunging into cosmic consciousness and mystical consciousness and oneness and stay there. It's to dip your head in for a bit and then come back and tell us all about it.

MC: And the other thing about the Gnosis of the Hermetics, and this is probably attractive to many of the medieval thinkers and the renaissance thinkers is the fact that part of it is really maximizing your own mind so that you understand the world. It seems the culmination of this would probably be Giordano Bruno and the way he was drawn to the Hermetic ethos and created these amazing memory techniques. That story of being in front of the pope in that seven year trial and being able to quote the Bible backwards and forwards. So isn't that part of the Hermetic Gnosis—I'm quoting Giordano Bruno, "Be all you can be"—be as smart as you can be?

GL: Well yes, absolutely, at the side of it there are people like Giordano Bruno and others, Pico della Mirandola was another one, who had tremendous powers of memory, something that we rely on memory sticks to do now, or hard drives. They seem to be able to not only house a lot of information but somehow to create this inner space, this inner architecture, that knowledge somehow existed in this form of encompassing the whole universe, and this goes back to the Hermetic notion of as above, so below, the idea that humankind, we are all microcosms of the macrocosm. Within us the entire universe exists, in the sense that it exists outside of us. This is part of this fantastic notion of what being human was, or meant to these Renaissance thinkers. They had come out of a period that we call the middle ages or medieval times, and human beings were pretty much considered these abject creatures, riddled with sin, corrupt, who live in this corrupt world and basically our life is a kind of test and trial to see how we are going to spend eternity. You know the picture when a leaf falls from a tree: why did God do that? What does it mean? Did the devil really do it?

And so you get this sense starting with Marsilio Ficino—I mean, the whole reason we're talking about this is because Ficino, this young Italian scholar of the Greek philosophers, Plato, was in the employ of Cosimo de Medici, the great Florentine powerbroker in the Renaissance and he was translating Plato from Greek into Latin for Cosimo to read, and Cosimo was a big reader, and he had book scouts, out all over the world of the time, and one of them had found this collection of texts in Macedonia and brought it back to Florence, and it turned out to be the Corpus Hermeticum, these books that had been written 100-200 C.E. but had been lost until then. Cosimo is excited about this discovery and he tells Ficino, put Plato on the back burner, give Plato a break, forget that, translate these first. Now Plato was enough of an incredible discovery at the time to have, and he'd been lost for many centuries, but then to have him made second best, he played second fiddle to Hermes Trismegistus, that's how high a street cred Hermes Trismegistus had then.

And then these books are translated. Ficino passes this on to Pico della Mirandola who wrote the *Oration On the Dignity of Man* and argued his case in front of the pope and other church officials. He's basically arguing this Hermetic view, this whole new vision of man that is no longer a medieval vision of us being these abject sinners, but suddenly this notion of being human as being something absolutely unique. Pico says that unlike all the creatures in the universe we have no set place. We are even higher than the angels in the sense that even though they're transcendent, they are a superior, superabundant being above ours, that they have a particular place in the cosmic scheme and they have to stay in it, whereas we can do anything. Man can soar to the heights and sink to the depths. This is unheard of. This is absolutely unheard of before, and humanism comes out of it. Now strangely if you follow the historical path, humanism is something that is actually anti this point of view. "Curb your enthusiasms" becomes its sensibility.

But still, this early humanism, this kind of superhumanism in the way I speak of it in the book, is something that's completely informed by these Hermetic ideas, and it has to do with our own mental capacities, and what is called the art of memory becomes developed then, whereas these Renaissance thinkers were able to create in their own minds these vast cathedrals of space, these imaginary spaces they would walk through, and the idea was that when they orated, when they gave speeches like Pico's *Oration On the Dignity of Man*, in order to remember everything, and to remember the different parts of the speech, and so on, they created this mnemonic system where they would create this inner theater with stage sets and so on, and different symbols that they would visualize would be the triggers for different parts of this speech. So when they were giving a speech, when they were talking, inwardly when they were walking within this inner cathedral of ideas. It just boggles our very tiny minds nowadays as to how they could possibly do this. It's this notion of the macrocosm and the microcosm. We can house the entire universe within our own consciousness. And we're the only beings in creation, outside, I guess, God, who can do that. Sadly, that's something that we don't really think about much these days.

MC: No, not at all, unfortunately. What I found interesting about your book, Gary, I don't know if you caught this, but you write about how you've got Asclepius and he's in a very relaxed state, a trance, maybe his chakras are open, maybe his channels of communication are open, and there comes Hermes and begins to teach him. Then suddenly you're going through history and you're looking at these figures who were influenced by the Hermetic spirit, like Paracelsus or Giordano Bruno and you're going, man, these guys really had some big egos, how did they get relaxed? Did that cross your mind at all?

GL: I guess the whole idea of that is that in our little universes we are supposed to be godlike in order to know God. I guess that could go to many people's heads, and that's something that's a bit of an occupational hazard.

MC: It made a lot of bigheads.

GL: No, you're absolutely right and they were two rather belligerent characters. Paracelsus was famous for getting into tussles with his critics and he was notorious for the kind of language he would use, and he was able to curse people in ways they didn't even know were possible. Giordano Bruno locked horns with papal characters who were equally convinced that they were right and knew everything. So, yeah, you do have that sort of thing. Perhaps there is a dissonance at times between those who know what to do and how things work, and those who are actually able to do it and know it as well, the ones who can actually sink into these mystical states might not be the same ones who can write about them lucidly and clearly. You talked about Hermes Trismegistus and when Nous comes to him he's in this very relaxed calm state, and again this is something that was the same in the later figures, people I talked about before like William James and Ouspensky and R. M. Bucke. Again that suggests to me that we could possible do that too.

We can learn ways in which to relax the tension over everyday consciousness which we have. Most of us aren't aware of this, but I think pretty much all of us exist in a state of hypertension. We have to deal with so many things. We're talking about people who live in 200-300 and the Renaissance, but I think the world we live in today is probably much more hectic than anything they lived in. So we probably live in a state of hypertension where we don't even know it. We just accept it as how things are in order to deal with it. The idea that there's so many different schools and approaches to relaxing or meditating or whatever, going within, now, suggests that there's a whole plethora of variety of different techniques to somehow learn to relax and open up, and all the different ways we talk about it. But you're absolutely right about characters like Paracelsus, Bruno and Pico della Mirandola. But again, because they did that back then, we can learn from them. We don't need to blow our horns quite as loudly as Paracelsus may have, or Pico did. Because they did that we can learn from what they did and build on it.

I myself, I'm thrilled by the vision of humanity that people like Paracelsus and Bruno and Pico had, but I'm not going to start trumpeting it. Nowadays the whole idea of celebrating your humanity, celebrating being human, is politically incorrect. We're supposed to feel mea culpa, we're supposed to feel guilt.

MC: We've gone full circle.

GL: We're supposed to feel how bad we are because we've ruined the environment and we've screwed up the planet and so on and so on, and we've done all these bad things. And rightly so, all these problems exist and we have to deal with them. For myself, I feel we would have more of a chance of dealing with them successfully if we had something more of the sense of confidence that these Renaissance magi had.

MC: The Hermetics have always been associated with alchemy and this grand Egyptian magic. For some reason I'm picturing the cover of an Iron Maiden album or something like that. But there really isn't anything of that in there, is there?

GL: Well, alchemy doesn't turn up in the collection we call the Corpus Hermeticum, or in the Asclepius which is the one Hermetic text that was available during the long stretch of time when the Corpus Hermeticum wasn't. Asclepius was the text that kept Hermes Trismegistus' name alive. The early alchemist Zosimos from Alexandria talks about the Hermetic texts and you can tell from his writings that he must have been aware of them. If there's one text that people associate with Hermes Trismegistus it's what is known as the Emerald Tablet, the Emerald Tablet of Hermes Trismegistus. But there's no mention of that in the Corpus Hermeticum, there's no mention of it in the texts that Ficino translated from Greek into Latin. There's no mention of it in any other of the Hermetic texts that came to light, those discovered with the Nag Hammadi Gnostic texts. As far as we know it doesn't appear until an Arabic version of it in the works of Jabir, who in the west we know as Geber. The word gibberish is said to come from him. The alchemical writings were so obtuse and nobody could make any sense of it so when people got a piece of writings they couldn't understand, they basically said, well you write like Jabir. This was more than a few centuries later than when the Corpus Hermeticum was written. It's interesting the connection between the two. More than likely there was alchemy going on in Alexandria at the time the Hermetic texts were being written and the two groups probably knew of each other, maybe even knew each other, but it isn't something that's part of the Hermetic teaching until later on.

And one of the things I do in the book is devote one chapter to alchemy. But I make a point of saying, well, actually when you look at it, alchemy isn't a part of these early Hermetic texts. The macrocosm-microcosm notion as above, so below, which is the Hermetic or alchemical aphorism that most people know, is part of the Emerald Tablet, but that's the focus really off the Corpus Hermeticum. It's much more this cosmic consciousness focus, this notion of expanding your mind so that you can encompass the All within your mind. So that's the focus rather than the hands-on alchemical work of transmuting the elements. Part of the whole esoteric tradition is this ambiguity that's involved with so many different esoteric writings.

More than likely, the authors of the Hermetic texts, whoever they were—we don't know their names, we have no names that have come down to us of these Alexandrian hermeticists. We have the names of some of the Gnostics from the time, but we don't have the names of any hermeticists. But more than likely they had already heard of Hermes Trismegistus, this notion of the Thrice-Greatest Hermes starts up a bit earlier than that, and we know that the Greek God Hermes was associated with the Egyptian God Thoth and the blend of the two created this figure, Thrice-Greatest Hermes. So the people writing the Hermetic texts used that name for a few different reasons. One was probably to get people to pay attention to them, and if somebody said, oh, here's a piece of writing by Aleister Crowley, you'd read it, just because you knew the name, or if it was by the Buddha or someone. But also in a sign of respect, they're writing not about their own minds, not their own personal ideas. This is the wisdom of the mind, the universal mind, so they use the name of one of the most revered thinkers they could think of as the author. So likewise, whether Jabir, Geber, this alchemist, came up with the emerald tablet or he found some text. There's supposed to be a Greek original but it's never come to light. Whoever wrote it, they too used the name of Hermes Trismegistus, so by that time somebody decided, yeah, we should use Hermes to give alchemy some more street cred because it's a very renowned name, and he's a very revered figure, and we're talking about the highest things here, the transmutation of matter into spirit, and so on, yeah why not, why shouldn't we associate Hermes with this?

MC: And it should be mentioned too, Gary, because you do spend a chapter on it, but Hermes was even popular in the Islamic world.

GL: Yeah, that's one of the things I loved about doing this book, was discovering these things, or rediscovering or understanding more deeply. Certainly, we know a great deal about Hermetic philosophy because when the Arabic Islamic invaders came to Alexandria and that part of the world, they absorbed their philosophers, their thinkers, their mystics, their esotericists. They absorbed the whole Hermetic philosophy and kept it alive during time when in the west Christianity, which it would again do later on, a thousand years or so down the line, was trying to wipe it out.

Alexandria was a remarkable place, a Greek city in Egypt, that developed this really unique atmosphere, this milieu of philosophical, scientific, spiritual and esoteric study and knowledge and blending. It's very much what we'd like things to be like today, a multicultural, multi-faith combination of things, and that was going on then. Over time as history progressed, Christianity rose to power and it became more and more the dominant force in Alexandria until finally it was completely in power and, as it did in other places, it started to wipe out its rivals or its predecessors. And it did that to Hermeticism and the pagan philosophies. And it was later when the Arabic powers invaded and conquered Egypt and Alexandria that the Hermetic thought was transmitted into the wider world. One of the places it went to was this remarkable place called Harran in northern Turkey that actually was a Hermetic city for a time. Hermes Trismegistus and Hermetic books were more or less the official religion, or official sacred book of the city. This is one of the things I found fascinating when I was doing this book, which was to see the collision between the spiritual energy of these texts and writings and thoughts and ideas of the different people who carry the ideas on, with historical forces, mostly of conquest and war. Much like today you have refugees from different areas, and in that part of the world, having to flee different cities and different countries because of the wars and conquests going on.

Among the other things that were transported during these chaotic times were the fragile pages of the Corpus Hermeticum. This is very encouraging to me. You have these tremendous forces, these historical forces, at work—wars, fire, burning, destruction—and these tiny fragile leaves of whatever these things were written on managed to survive. They sunk, they went out of view, they went underground, but they surfaced again. And it's very encouraging to recognize that the mind can survive in these very difficult times. They moved from Harran to Baghdad, Baghdad to Constantinople, and then Constantinople to

Macedonia and Macedonia to Florence. From there they re-entered the mainstream of western culture. So certainly Arab Islamic thinkers of the time kept the whole Hermetic philosophy alive, and we have to thank them very much for that.

MC: Well, I was going to end by asking you how the Hermetic sensibility can help our modern days, Gary, but you've given a lot of hints and your whole book is full of gems about how Hermes can help us get back on track, especially in this era which has become the realized eschatology of Jean Baudrillard or Marshall McLuhan, where we're just in this cul-de-sac or this desert of the real, and we are stormed by social media and technology and everything, but I'm presuming the answer could be as simple as the Blake attitude of "A universe in a grain of sand and heaven in a wild flower." and "My business is to create." Is that the attitude you think we need to get back to?

GL: Well yes, I think more or less something along those lines. There's quite a few things we can learn from the Hermetic books. I mentioned earlier this notion of us being caretakers of the cosmos. Certainly we are animals, but we're not only animals. We're animals-plus which sounds like a vitamin of some kind, but it's actually I think a very important thing to recognize To recognize that isn't to pat ourselves on the back and trumpet our superiority. It is to accept and embrace the obligations and responsibilities we have for doing that. We're the only creatures on the planet who can be concerned about the environment. We're the only ones who can worry about nature and how it's being upset, and all that. And the reason we can do that is that we're something more than the environment, more than nature. There's a part of us that stands above it, and that's the mind. Whatever you want to call it, you want to call it the spirit, the soul, whatever, the Hermeticists called it Nous, they called it the mind.

I think you're absolutely right, it behooves us to try and understand and experience and live and make a practical application of this notion that you said of Blake, that infinity is in the palm of our hand and eternity in an hour, whatever. We have the capacity to do that. I give different examples in the book of that, and one is directly related to the Hermetic teaching, from the Hermetic books itself, others as I said from people like William James, Ouspensky and R. M. Bucke and later on examples that turn up in literature that ostensibly may not have anything to do with Hermeticism, but describe the kinds of consciousness that are associated with it. And to me I think are much more available to us than we realize. I think one of the things that confronts many people who get interested in different spiritual and esoteric disciplines and practices, this idea that it's an incredibly hard, difficult sort of thing and you have to sacrifice everything for it. And yes, of course you have to commit and, yes, of course one shouldn't be complacent, yet at the same time think we experience more of these things than we actually realize.

One of the things I try to do in the book is point to some of these experiences that we have and also to suggest that there might be a new way to look at things and the world and the chaotic mess we seem to exist in right now, not so much from wanting to retreat from it into some earlier primal, more certain form of thought, which I think both the traditionalist school that I mentioned earlier and forms of fundamentalism, whether Christian or Islamic or whatever, do, or throw ourselves into some strange future world of transhuman, or somehow blending with machines, or something like that. But it's to understand more fully what our humanness is, and I think that's what the Hermetic books are about. You mentioned earlier that they were at the core or beginning of humanism and that humanism somehow turned into something smaller than what it started out as, and that's why you talk about a kind of superhumanism. I just use that as a way to look at it, because I'm not thinking of any kind of ubermensch elite character, but really just becoming more and more fully human, and I think that's really what the Hermetic things are about. If we can do that I think it would if not solve, it would certainly throw a lot of light on many problems today.

MC: I think that's all the time we have. Gary, I'd like to thank you very much for coming on Aeon Byte and giving us a very stimulating and edifying conversation based on your book *The Quest for Hermes Trismegistus from Ancient Egypt to the Modern World*.

GL: Well, as I said it's absolutely my pleasure, and thank you very much for having me.

TOBIAS CHURTON

Tobias Churton is a scholar of Rosicrucianism, Freemasonry, Gnosticism and other esoteric movements. He is lecturer at Exeter University and author of *Gnostic Philosophy*, *Freemasonry*, *Gnostic Mysteries of Sex* and *The Mysteries of John the Baptist* and other books.

It would be hard to name any nonacademic who has promoted and crystallized Gnostic studies more than Tobias Churton. His 1987 drama-documentary, *The Gnostics*, remains a mainstay in modern Gnostic circles, as does his 2003 book, *Gnostic Philosophy*. Outside of his focus on historical and cultural Gnosticism, Tobias has published several well-received books on the occult and secret societies.

Churton's strength beyond his excellent research lies in his ability to venture into topics that are largely disregarded by mainstream scholarship. For example, his recent book, *Gnostic Mysteries of Sex*, deeply delves into the often ignored possibilities that Alexandrian Gnostics practiced sexual magical rites. Also, he has tirelessly explored the Gnostic influence on Secret Societies and modern pop culture, as seen in *Gnostic Philosophy*, never shying away from provocative ideas but always proposing sober theories.

Tobias did the same with John the Baptist in *The Mysteries of John the Baptist*. John the Baptist does make appearances in the Nag Hammadi library and other apocrypha. However, scant is the scholarship on his role or impact on classic Gnosticism—at least not in the same depth as Mary Magdalene, Judas Iscariot, Simon Magus, and other Gnostic exemplars. As always, Tobias expanded his scholarship to offer how John the Baptist influenced esoteric spiritualities and philosophies, even to the present.

That was the topic of our interview. John the Baptist, according to Tobias, was no mere country clodhopper with a brief role of ushering in a messiah. He was perhaps the epitome of esoteric spirituality and lofty Jewish philosophy. Regardless, John the Baptist's role in religious history seems as marginalized as that of the classic Gnostics, and they both make very good bedfellows in heresy.

MC: How are you doing, Tobias?

TC: I'm doing very well, thanks Miguel, very good to speak to you again.

MC: Likewise, great to having you on back. When the mainstream world envisions John the Baptist, it's the image of a Charleston Heston or Michael York: an aging hippie dressed in furs and eating insects. What exactly is wrong with this image, Tobias?

TC: Well it came from a cross between Hollywood and the Old Testament. I don't think the real John the Baptist did look like somebody out of 1,000,000 years B.C.E.. I think he was a very very modern character; but the thing is that his garb has been turned into that of Elijah. It was believed in the first century, and stated plainly in the book of Malachi, that Elijah will precede the arrival of the messiah. Now when they looked in First Kings for what Elijah wore, they found he was rough-clad for outdoor wear. Basically I think they've dressed him as they thought Elijah would be dressed. But I think the real John was a very different character. I strongly suspect he wore fine raiment that would have probably looked like a priest or possibly an Essene, and probably dressed in white with a girdle, I would imagine. That's what I strongly suspect.

But the image is very powerful when you see it in films. It's a bit like the history of mankind. Then, out of the water comes a new era where all the attention then goes onto Jesus, who comes out so sparkling. John is supposed to be quietly forgotten. He's supposed to exit at this stage, his part is played. John's whole image has been manicured, and prepared for consumption by the later Christian church—as one might suspect.

MC: And Tobias, before we go further into the history of John the Baptist, how exactly did you decide to write this book? In the occult and alternative Christianities, nobody touches John the Baptist. How did you meet him again?

TC: Well isn't that funny? It's a strange path that lead me to write about John the Baptist, and it's more valuable because of it. I was invited by the master of the Alexandria Lodge 22. That was George Washington's Lodge in Washington DC. They meet at the Washington Memorial, which is this huge phallus of Alexandria. They invited me to address their John the Baptist Festival. Now in England, in Masonry, there is no John the Baptist Festival. So I was already intrigued. Why do some

American Freemasons have a John the Baptist Festival? I said, I like the sound of that. You know there are no Christian saints celebrated at any point in English Masonry? So I was already intrigued by that; and they said come and speak to us, and I thought what am I going to speak about? I thought, what else but John the Baptist! What's the connection? How is it that John the Baptist is Freemasonry? That was the starting point. So I started doing an original talk. I uncovered a few things that fascinated me and I thought would interest others.

Later, over the year and a half following that, the subject wouldn't leave me alone; and I thought there's a book. There was a book sort of in rebellion popping out of me somewhere on this. It wanted to be written, and I didn't want to write it. I knew it was going to be a bit of a tough experience because, probably like you and most people, I'd never really considered John the Baptist very much really. I mean he pops up here and there.

Then, suddenly, I felt the moment I got to write. I just sat down, and I got going, and it was an amazing experience to write. I very often was led. I'd be woken up very early—at four o'clock in the morning, three o'clock in the morning—and I just had to write. There was something very high going on. There was a higher light switching on parts of it. I mean odd things. I'd be following a thought, and I thought is there anything on this in the Old Testament or something. I'd open the book; and there: I'd be on the page with the quote I needed. So, it was really quite a magical experience.

I felt the book was given to me: first by the invitation from Washington to cross the seas, and secondly the content itself seemed to be given to me to a large degree. I wouldn't say I was just the scribe; but everything I'd learned up to that date sudden started to coalesce and I was able to use my knowledge in a way I almost never expected. It was a remarkable experience.

MC: But Tobias, this would beg the question: why is John the Baptist important in Freemasonry? You write in your book the 24th of June is the feast day of John the Baptist, but it's also an important day in Freemasonry, right?

TC: Yes! I don't speculate and create fanciful ideas. I try to deal with the facts, and the facts are these, that: the very first meeting of a Grand Lodge for a feast in the records of the Reverend James Anderson for 1717, when they meet for this feast at a pub in Covent Garden, it's on

John the Baptist's Day 24th of June which is the date of midsummer's solstice, and no explanation is given. But, what we do know is that between 1717 and 1738 the existing Masonic organization in London removed bit by bit the emphasis on St John the Baptist; until by 1738, the date had become irrelevant. All that mattered is what's good for the craft. Which means the Hanoverian Aristocrats, who are now running the show. So, 24th June is maintained as a time to choose Grand Masters. Saint's days are no longer important. I've the feeling that Issac Newton's hand had been in there somewhere, or his side-kick Desaguliers who believed that all Catholicism had corrupted the ancient science and primordial wisdom. So John the Baptist is dropped.

Now the next thing we know is that between 1748 and mid 1770s in London, six times a year men had to pay a special fee to go to a registered lodge affiliated with a new order. They paid a fee and they had to sign themselves as St. John's Men.

So you have this intersection with a preexisting Masonry who valued St John, and then a post-organized Masonry that want to drop it and start confusing John the Baptist with John the Evangelist. So you have the tension of the two Johns that has never been explained or resolved. Now that set me a-thinking. What was it about St John that made older Masons feel it was an identity focus? Why did they want to be known as St. John the Mason? That lead me to look into the mythology around the mid-summer festival which existed in medieval England: things like poppets being put outside being decked with foliage. All sorts of rites were conducted all over Europe in the name of John the Baptist, to do with fertility and harvest, all these ideas of rebirth. John the Baptist is linked with a happy time. It's very unusual. John the Baptist's day is the day of his death, which most Saint's days is their death day. It's the official birthday of the summer solstice. So, he is the lord of the harvest, lord of midsummer. He's the saint that presides over your summer festivals or feasts; and that seemed to have been important to the old Masons and that came to America.

There was a split in Masonry. An organization that called themselves the Ancients were saying the old traditions were lost. It had a strong Irish influence. Laurence Dermott led it. It was very popular with sailors and military people. It went off with the army to New England and to what later would become the United States. The Ancients' Lodges were in the colonies, and for that reason the Festival of John the Baptist has survived in the United States. But, again, for reasons nobody really understands.

So I went back. That was strong part of it. So I explored the mytho-logical John, and what he would have meant to these old Masons in the middle ages. What sort of ideas were there? Some of which were mysterious. We know songs like "John Barleycorn Must Die," which is an old broadside song, which talks about the beheading or the flaying or otherwise the torture of the barleycorn who has got to be cut for the harvest. So you have that idea as well linked to John the happy lord of midsummer, and you can see it: the tendrils and the idea of the green man coming through here as well. I think the fact that John's head is traditionally severed and his blood a fit sacrifice, and in some way that's coming through there as well. But, then I decided: I took the story further, and then tried to understand what had happened in the New Testament about John. Why is he famous at beginning and then drops out, all too conveniently?

MC: And also isn't John the Baptist paralleled by, or is a sort of a Hermes, a messenger of the Gods, a herald of the one true God in the Renaissance and afterward?

TC: Yes! Yes, I think that's a vital thing: the *kyros*, which is the Greek for herald. He is traditionally, in Christianity, the herald of the messiah. Again, the Elijah role: he comes first, and then the messiah comes. Or, rather, in the older prophecies, first comes the herald then comes the Lord God. There's no obvious messiah in the original prophecies, but this is built of over 700 years. You get a build up of ideas of the end times. One of the staples that goes right through is that there is a her-ald. Now the Greek *kyros* is a herald at a feast; and Hermes, the Greek god Hermes or the Greco-Egyptian deity Thoth/Thoth-Hermes, also presided over feasts. He is the messenger from above who brings the message of the one giving the feast. So you have that idea of Hermes; but you've also got Hermes as the mystagogue, the one who leads the soul across the waters. So we hit this idea of baptism. We have it in alchemy, associated with Hermes, in the Corpus Hermeticum, the her-metic writings, the fourth treatise on the birth. You actually have a figure called the herald, who's not named, who brings down a bowl of *Nous*—that is divine mind, the faculty for receiving higher knowledge—and he presents this to mankind. He says "He who is dipped in this bowl of Nous shall be dipped"—the word is baptized, *baptiza*—"He will receive gnosis". He will receive the liberating knowledge, and the herald invites people unto this baptism. So that is an idea which you get in the third century: an Alchemical term for a hermetic baptismal figure.

My favorite Da Vinci painting bears this androgynous figure, called John, pointing at the dark. I think that that is the idea of one who baptizes, who tears across, into another It says that John is baptizing at Abara, which as far as I can see seems to mean a ford or crossing place on the Jordan River; and I think that's symbolic. I think we have the idea here of one who takes the soul across. So his baptism is also spiritual baptism. It could be interpreted that way anyway. He's like the Green Man almost who takes the soul from this world to the next world.

So you've got all this cross-fertilized symbolism going on around the figure of John over a very, very long period. It's not particularly integrated, because in the Christian church of course you couldn't venerate John too much even though several cathedrals claimed to have his skull. At the city of Aleppo, today in Syria which is being bombed as we speak by government forces the head of John the Baptist is probably in Aleppo. It used to be in Damascus. It was thought to be an inspirational power even after the Islamic conquest. It's been venerated by Muslims as *Yahya*, that's the Muslim name for John. So even in Islam, John comes over as a powerful source of new life and inspiration.

MC: In your book, Tobias, you present a fascinating overview of the political and religious tempests surrounding John the Baptist. Were you astounded by what you saw not only in John but everything around him?

TC: I looked at John on several levels: the mythological level, theological level, and the historical level. When I embraced the historical level, I was truly astonished by what is known about John the Baptist which you don't find in the New Testament. That was a revelation to me. I could say I was just too ignorant to know about it, but it was an amazing discovery to find that John was a politically significant figure in the late thirties in the Palestinian Jewish history.

It is quite exceptional. He really was an Elijah! He did what Elijah did in the book of Kings where he confronts the king, Ahab. The real John actually confronted Herod Antipas, the ruler of Galilee, the son of Herod the Great, the massacrer of the Innocents. He confronted him and said: you are marrying your brother's wife, it's forbidden by our laws, you'll be punished.

An element of this occurs in the New Testament because he's sent to Machaerus and executed. But if you read Josephus, the Jewish historian—who's not a Christian writer—just writing history, who was born in about the time that all this was going on. He was just a toddler really at the time of the Crucifixion. Josephus gives us a much plainer political picture. That, in fact, Herod Antipas is fighting a war with King Aretas the IV of Nabataea in the south. This is going on in biblical New Testament times. When Herod Antipas lost this war, Josephus said the people believed he lost the war because he's responsible for the executing John. That is the main story of John in Josephus the historian. Now, we hardly get a fragment of this in the New Testament, but of course it opens the whole thing up.

John is a political figure. He's obviously of service to a Nabataean King. Why? Because King Aretas IV's daughter, Phasaelis, was married to Herod Antipas; and she was the woman being divorced. That is why Aretas decides to fight what, in fact, was effectively a scion of Roman power. By fighting Herod Antipas, he was taking on the Roman Empire.

This is Nabataea. You've probably seen films like Indiana Jones and the Holy Grail. There's a scene at the end at this rock temple, it's very famous, at Petra. That was built by Aretas the IV, who in Arabic would be called Hareths. Aretas is the Greek form. He was an Arabic King of Petra; and Petra was where Phasaelis, Herod Antipas' wife, escapes to. And where does she escape from, to get back to her father? She escapes from Machaerus, the place that even the bible tells us is where John the Baptist was incarcerated, just across the Dead Sea from Qumran in fact, not very far from where the Dead Sea scrolls were discovered.

MC: It wasn't just a prison, but you say it was a jail for bankers or white collared people.

TC: Machaerus, again contrary to myth, was not a prison. Archeology has shown it was a palace. It was a place to get away from it all. So Phasealis had gone to ease out and cool off. It was a very secure palace on a mountain. Effectively, it was a well appointed castle. If it had a dungeon, it had a dungeon. My suspicion is that John would originally have been put under some sort of house arrest, shall we say a pressured invitation to be there. Herod was loath to kill him. We do have that sense he doesn't want to get rid of him but he thinks it's politics. Of course it would be politics because if John is supporting the case of

Phasealis the Nabatean wife of Herod Antipas, he's effectively operating politically in favor of King Aretas.

Then after Aretas defeats Herod Antipas in late 36 or possibly early 37 c.e., the emperor Tiberius says "I want the head of Aretas"—ha ha, very interesting. Robert Eisenman thinks that becomes the head story of John the Baptist, that it got inverted but Emperor Tiberius calls for the head Aretas, the head of John the Baptist presumably perhaps even having been severed. But he's a major political figure. He challenges the Herodian dynasty. John has this role.

Now the role allotted to him in Christian tradition is entirely, I'm sure we can say, messianic. His job is to announce the messiah and then quietly please disappear. And it is convenient that he's later arrested. How that story is handled is different in all the gospels as I show in the book. We get the feeling that John was, in fact, an embarrassment for the Christian church, especially after the Jewish revolt of 66 to 73.

After that time, the Christian church was just spread to largely gentile places in Asia. The Jewish setting is consistently diminished. We could say the edges are smoothed because the Jews were suspected by Roman authority after that revolt for all being messianic hoodlums and dissenters and causers of rebellion. The gospels, which are written after that revolt, are careful to show the strictly Jewish aspects of the history.

Frankly, they're distorted. Either their knowledge is suppressed, like the knowledge of John the Baptist, or the Jews are presented in a hostile like as "the Jews", that's a phrase we get in John's gospel, or the *Ioudaios*, the Judeans. Even Jesus talks about "the Judeans" it's very odd, he was a Judean himself—ha-ha! So the Jews are kinda slapped all kinds of literary pitch. That anti-Jewishness is right through the New Testament, oddly promulgated by Paul himself who tells the Jews proudly that many of their traditions are weak and of no use, and that the Jews must accept that a new covenant has come down. Which makes me wonder just how Jewish Paul was. One thing we do know about Paul is that he was an opponent of John's baptism. That is clear from the account of him in the Acts of the Apostles, and also from his Letter to the Galatians where he condemns the baptism of John as an inadequate dispensation, which is certainly not clear at all if we say that Jesus wanted to be baptized, and it even says that the holy spirit came upon him, that is the understood view. It is clear this baptism of John is not without significance. At one point in the gospels Jesus asks the temple Sadducee "is John's baptism from heaven or is it of men?" It is clear from the answer that it is considered a heavenly baptism. But John had his own followers that clearly didn't follow Jesus, and this is the embarrassment. In fact John still has followers today that still do not follow Jesus so you've got that going on as well.

You know, it is amazing how all of this stuff floating around unconnected and all I tried to do was to put the parts together, not in some kind of "I want to create a speculative picture" but you could actually see how they joined. It was a bit like how you could look at the Tectonic plates and how the body of the continent of the Americas was once joined to Africa. They had become separated, but you could see from the coast lines that the plates once matched. It's a bit like that. You see this evidence. You could see the elements of the evidence had been torn asunder by time and deliberate interference with tradition; but they're still there. You can find it. You've got to ask the right question.

The question I ask is at one point is what would have happened if John had not been arrested? What would have happened if Herod Antipas had said "Well, I can live with a troublesome prophet, because he's got a lot of support and it might make me popular if I appear to support him." It would have been a political decision he would have had to make. What if he had done that? Well the entire structure of the Gospels breaks apart. Jesus doesn't start to preach repentance, which by the way is John's message. "Repent ye, the Kingdom of Heaven is at hand, the kingdom of God is at hand." That is John's message, and it is taken on wholesale by Jesus who when he hears of John's arrest. He then goes to Galilee, and starts preaching the gospel of repentance: John's gospel, in fact. That whole concept of Jesus' operation falls apart had John not disappeared.

The whole thing is manipulated to make it appear that Jesus came after John, first the herald then Jesus. But according to Luke's account John is born before Jesus. They would have known each other if Luke's account is historical. They were cousins. They were related. How could they not have known each other? They had almost identical interests; they both grew up among temple priests, temple (girls? gold?). It was a fairly small world. To me it's obvious the two of them were involved in the same movement.

MC: Yes Tobias, and it seems one of the key elements or something that really stands out has to do with where Jesus is allegedly born, Nazareth. But when we find out Jesus is being called Jesus the Nazarene, that really gives an insight as you find in your book or as you present in your book.

TC: One of the many discoveries that occurred to me over the last few years is the origin of this word "Nazarene" which is the earliest name given to Christians—a word which apparently later emerged in Antioch, which is a Greek word, obviously. *Christos*, anointed ones, followers of the anointed, you know it just means messianic. But the original word given for them is Nazarenes and the Greek is *Nazaraion*. I am absolutely convinced that this is a straightforward translation of *Natzarim* which is Hebrew and means the watchers or the keepers or the guardians.

It occurs as that word in Jeremiah chapter 4, and it talks about the *Natzarim* who will come from a far off country and preach judgment on Judea which has been badly run. It's the prophecy of Jeremiah. You have here the keepers, the watchers, the guardians. What are they keeping, watching, and guarding? The will of God, the law, the holiness tradition, and this is announced in Dan. Anyway, once you've made this connection, of course you can hardly avoid that this term. *Natzarim*, watchers is a very key one in the esoteric tradition of the first century B.C.E., and the first centuries of the so called Christian era or the common era, C.E., A.D. Anno Domini.

This is encapsulated in a work which has come down to us called the Book of Enoch which was really kind of hip book in the first century for seriously devoted Jews. More than an average number of copies have been found in fragments in the Qumran Dead Sea Scrolls material. The Book of Enoch is the key. It tells the story of how another set of watchers—if you like, the evil watchers—the evil watchers had come down to earth. It's all in Genesis 6, it's kind of an esoteric commentary on Genesis 6. Watchers come down to earth, lust after the women of earth, and produce a race of giants: the Nephilim. Some how through this the Earth is corrupted by these fallen angels or lights. We must think of the watchers originally as images of stars, or reflected to earth as stars, who fall to earth and corrupt.

This is the explanation of the corruption of human existence in the book of the Enoch, which passes straight into the New Testament period. It's there. It's not trumpeted. You can find it in the Epistle of Judas, commonly called Jude but if you look at the Greek it's Judas, it's Jesus' brother, I'm completely sure of that. You have references to the Book of Enoch, and the Watchers, and the judgment from the Watchers.

All this business of Jesus exorcising people of devils, this messianic exorcism is exactly what we'd expect when the judgment against the evil watchers is announced in the Book of Enoch. Where is this judgment announced? It's announced as it is in Jeremiah: at Dan. Where is Dan? Dan is in the very north of Israel right by Mount Hermon. What do we know it as in the New Testament? Well, it was called Caesarea Philippi. It was a new city being built there by Herod Antipas' brother Phillip, in fact, in honor of Caesar. Caesarea Philippi is the biblical Dan and it is right by a place now called Paneas, or the Muslims call it Banias, which is the ancient source supposed of the Jordan. That is where the judgment is published against the evil Watchers. Where does Jesus take his followers and ask them "who do the men say that I am?" It's at Caesarea Philippi. It's at Dan.

But all the detail is lost in the New Testament. Why Caesarea Philippi? If you read it, it just sounds like the shores of Galilee and other places. But, it's a highly significant place that he goes to. Peter famously rebukes that. He attacks Jesus, "What's all this stuff about the messiah dying? No, totally unacceptable, not gonna happen." So, it's a place where the messianic message is revealed to the disciples.

Again, it was astonishing to find this in relation to the John story, because I think this is the original movement we're talking about that John and Jesus were a part of. They are the *Natzarim*, the guardians of the uncorrupted faith of Israel. Who's corrupted it? Well it's especially obvious who was corrupting it in the first century. It was the Sadducees, and high class richer priests in the temple, and of course the fact that the country was being ruled by a combination of half-Arab princelings backed by the Roman Empire. Herod built the temple. When he put a Roman eagle on it, there was a massive riot and demonstration. Many, many, many people were killed and priests were slaughtered in the temple, and this is all going on at the "childhood of Jesus" period. So there was nothing bucolic. You wouldn't have had much time to enjoy the lilies of the field oryou would very soon be trampled by Roman soldiers or soldiers of the Herodian dynasty. So the movement of the *Natzarim* is a nostalgic movement. It's looking back to the great days of David and well beyond that: to the primal creation, the unspoiled creation.

MC: And what's fascinating, Tobias, is that don't the Mandaeans the famous "John the Baptist Christians", they call themselves Nazarenes too?

TC: That's right, the priests are called Naṣuraiia. That's exactly right. So that word has come down in their tradition. Careful what we say when we say "John's Christians", this was a name that the Jesuits gave to the Mandaeans in the 17ᵗʰ century. The Mandaeans at that point were quite happy to be called that because Christians were accepted in the Qur'an as people of the book and they didn't want to make a case that they were that different. But, in fact, there's no place for Jesus as a figure in the Mandaean tradition. *Manda* means knowledge; and they believe this knowledge goes back to Adam, and their great prophet is John. I don't see any great objections to the fact that what we have with the Mandaeans of Northern Iraq and now dispersed around the world we have a genuine survival of the John church, if you use that phrase "church", or the John community: those who revered John and regarded him as the great prophet of a redeemed life and a spiritual existence. It's quite possible that the knights in the crusades came across these people amongst the many other interesting groups that in the Middle East at that time; and it may be the origin of the Baphomet, the head the Templars were accused of worshiping. I have a strong suspicion the head had some link perhaps to John, but it's a fertility link.

MC: Yes, you give a very fascinating theory how the Baphomet is a corruption of Greek for Mithra the baptizer, and Mithra is of course a Persian redeemer.

TC: It may be so. Aleister Crowley thought that's what it was, it was a Mithraic baptismal figure. But, I wouldn't come down strongly on that. It's interesting. I don't know how you get from "Baphe Metous" to Baphomet, really. I mean: OK, just put it down to scribal error. Some people say Baphomet is just a sort of swear word. We don't know, is the real answer. Some say it's actually just Mohammed mis-written. So we don't know.

Anyway, we do know there was a head worshiped; and we do know the skull of John was respected and adored in Aleppo, in Damascus, and also in several European Cathedrals. So, you have the head link. It's just one of those interesting things you can speculate on and build traditions on if you're very romantic. I find you get to much more interesting results if you keep romanticism to a minimum. I think we're all spurred by a romantic urge for the truth and beauty and integration and all of that. But, when it comes to "well, what happened?", you've got to take the romantic hat off it and deal with such facts we can discover. That's the approach of the book; and it yields far better results frankly than all of books that have speculated about the Templars and all of that.

MC: Yes, it's a very sober and good book. Tobias, what role does John the Baptist have in Gnosticism? He doesn't appear in many of the texts. I think he's mentioned in the Gospel of Thomas and a few others. Aren't there some early church writings that say that John the Baptist appointed the "father of all heresy", the "father of gnosticism", Simon Magus, as his successor?

TC: One of the most remarkable things—and, you know, one would love to get to the bottom of this—is the tradition that Simon Magus, the arch heresiarch according to church tradition. Epiphanius. I can't recall if Irenaeus blames Simon Magus, I think he did.

MC: I think they all do, sooner or later.

TC: Simon Magus is the author of all the heresies, that's the view. And, we have a kind of walk-on part for Simon in the Acts of the Apostles where he tries to buy the secrets of the Holy Spirit and does tricks. There's a peculiar film made of this in about 1953, Paul Newman's first film, *The Silver Chalice*, Which, I got a hold of recently, to see Jack Palance playing a very good Simon Magus. Anyway, many legends were told of this character. Sober scholars are of the view that whoever Simon was, he wasn't simply a malevolent demon mucking around in the New Testament trying to rob the apostles of their proper role.

But he was a religious preacher, a Samaritan, in his own right and contemporary with Jesus. I think the way movies are made and the way we're taught in churches, we tend to separate the apostolic period from Jesus' ministry by a mental leap. It's almost like: after Jesus we don't know, and then Paul appears, and then Simon Magus appears, and the Christians appear and they're being persecuted. You've got to look at the time scale. It's very important. One of the things I do in the book is I've re-dated, I think historically accurate, the crucifixion to where it fits perfectly with the historical process. I don't think has been systematically in a book before. You never know if somebody's walked the trail, but it's new to me. It's remarkable. When you put the crucifixion at March, 37 c.e., suddenly, the whole thing rings right. All these characters we have from the early traditions, we see they are contemporaries.

Paul could very easily have been involved in the arrest, accusation, and crucifixion of Jesus; as, I suspect he was involved in the arrest of John. He says himself in Galatians he "wasted" the church. He wasted, but he never apologizes: "I was doing the will of God and then the will of God tells me go the other way, and I went the other way, and I've been zealous in all." He's been a zealous persecutor. He's now a zealous prophet of the Christ cult that he developed, once he combined the ideas of atonement with mystery ideas of being baptized and Jesus resurrected with him and all of that. That, we get in his letters, which is so is difficult for many Christians to understand. There was a leap between Jesus' teaching as we find in the gospel and then what Paul makes of it in these letters.

I go into that in the book, what is it in Paul that makes him do this? Why does he set himself up against John? Why does he have so little interest in the Jesus that we get from the parables and many of the sayings and his observations. Gentle Jesus meek and mild is very hard to find in any part of the New Testament. But, there are hints of a more human character in the death sentence of the gospels, whereas, in Paul, we get "The Christ". He's more interested in "The Christ" than a man. That would appear to be the case then. Paul sets himself as the number one interpreter of the whole thing. I can imagine the effect of that.

Now, sorry, to answer your question. Simon Magus is described in the Clementine Homilies which, admittedly, are romantic fiction in the fourth century. But, based on what traditions? It appears to be based on Jewish Christian tradition. Simon Magus is a disciple of John, and would have replaced John as leader of the church had he not been in Alexandria when John was arrested. I mean, this is an amazing little titbit. What are we to make of this? There is the suggestion that John had his own mystical organization going, and that this had been deemed irrelevant by mainstream orthodoxy, the Pauline tradition, and is somehow absorbed into Syrian gnosticism.

So there is the possibility that John was not only a Jewish prophet in the Elijah sense, but he was more of an Essene. Josephus the Jewish historian says the Essenes more or less followed a kind of Pythagorean cosmology and spirituality. Meaning that, coming in to the body, the body is a temporary garment at best, at worst it's a tomb which encases the spirit. The release of the spirit back to its spiritual home, this is what it's all about. This is why the Essenes could embrace death. They showed immense courage when they were tortured by the Romans, presumably being asked "where are you hiding people, are you hiding zealots, are you hiding bandits?" They are remarkable.

I find it very hard to think of the Essenes and not think of John.

I think he's something to do with the Essenes. And, I can't help but think that the *Natzarim* of Jesus and his family, his brothers, are also connected intimately with the Essene tradition, because we have the bizarre mystery that the word "Essene" doesn't occur anywhere in the New Testament. This is so ridiculous. It doesn't make any sense of the real picture of religious life in the first century. Josephus refers to the Essenes. Pliny refers to the Essenes. Philo of Alexandria refers to the Essenes. They are there. But no, no, in the bible we only have Jesus in contradistinction to the Herodian people, the Sadducees, the Pharisees, the people who were to do with the running of official religion in Jerusalem, and scribes. But the Essenes aren't there at all. They don't exist.

So it wouldn't be unnatural to think that in fact your proto-Christian church or original Christian church has some connection with them. Especially when we read the doctrines of the Essenes—which tie in perfectly with traditions about John—saying if a man asks for your coat you must give it to him, how you treat strangers: this spiritual pacifism we find in Josephus' presentation. Josephus himself may have been trained by an Essene. Did the Essenes write the Dead Sea Scrolls? Well we can argue about this. A lot of people say "well, we can call them Essenes"; but we don't really know the origin of the word "Essenes". But, there is a mystical proto-gnostic movement.

Now I would say also that the whole mythology of the archons which you have in a more developed second-century century Gnosticism, the evil angels who keep man in the thrall of his body, denying him his spiritual home, we find this I'm am sure that the root of this belief in the archons and the demiurge is our old friend Enoch again, the Book of Enoch. These watchers, these stellar angels who have come and become the geniuses of the nations dividing mankind from itself, giving them forbidden knowledge, tempting them into immoralities, these fallen watchers must be the origin of your archons, the demonic angels and later or course in the catholic tradition the just become Satan and all his horde. But, I think this is your origin. So I do think the authentic Gospel of John is proto-gnostic and was probably heading for development of that kind.

Very odd. If you ever see the film *The Greatest Story Ever Told*—a very good, interesting movie made by George Stevens in 1965, which is basically the Gospel of John shot in Arizona I think with Max Von Sydow as a very interesting Christ figure, a big big production—the John the Baptist stuff is dealt with in a very mature way. Charleton Heston plays John, and he has arguments with Herod Antipas at his castle Machaerus. He says, "I'm going to have to kill you John", and John says "You'll be freeing me!" I mean you couldn't put the gnostic point of view more bluntly than that, and clearly the script writers I think had known a bit about the Dead Sea Scrolls and looked in to this tradition. So, yes, I think John is a Gnostic hero.

I'm also interested we have in the gnostic tradition and also the fringe Masonic tradition of this whole thing of the Johannite tradition. But it's normally associated with John the Evangelist but I contend in my book that in fact the Gospel of John was called the Gospel of John because in the first few chapters you keep getting this stuff about, "and I John testified". If you read the first few chapters of John, it's John's testimony that is being put forward that he's not the messiah and all this. And you would call this the Gospel of John. That would be the natural name to call the book. So the idea of the beloved disciple who testifies is another thing; but I think it was originally called the Gospel of John because we're talking about John the Baptist. I think, the elevation of John the Elder, or John of Patmos, or John the Apostle: there were admittedly a lot of Johns. John is even mentioned in the prologue of John's Gospel which is magnificent. "In the beginning was the Word, and the Word was with God, and the word was God, and without him nothing was made" and so on and so on. You even got a reverse of that that refers specifically to John, "There was a man who came, but he was not that light." He was not that light, but he was pretty important. He was important enough.

Jesus himself describes John as the greatest man born of woman, for goodness sake. Well you'd think there would be a few biographies of this man. The greatest man every born of woman? That's Jesus' endorsement of John; and that's my defence to anyone that says "You've raised John and you're playing the heretic's game." I'm doing what I hope Jesus would regard as a worthwhile project, which is to give proper reference and honest appraisal to the man he thought was the greatest man ever born from woman. And if you think Jesus' opinion on this is of little significance, that's up to you. I'll take that endorsement as having quite a lot of significance for a theologian and historian.

MC: In the Gospel of Luke, it seems John has doubts that Jesus is even the one to take over the movement. Do you see that as just an interpolation?

TC: No. I think Luke is well known to be a Pauline disciple. The Luke gospel, whether a "Luke" wrote it or it's come partly from testimony of a Luke mentioned with regard to Paul's doctor and all that—whatever—OK "Luke", somebody, a Greek doctor possibly, wrote this gospel "Luke". But who ever wrote it has quite clearly accepted hook line and sinker the Paul version of the messianic faith; and the Paul version of messianic faith consistently underplays the significance of John.

So, for example in Luke, he doesn't mention that John ate wild herbs. Why? I think it's perfectly obvious. Paul in his letters makes a very strong case that the eating of the vegetarian diet for religious reasons is a sign of weakness. Now this vegetarian diet has been followed by Judas Maccabees, the great Jewish military and religious hero. It was the diet associated with the holy men of Israel. But Paul says, "No, no, no. This is totally unnecessary. We can join in with the meat feasts of the pagans. We can eat their meat because we know their pagan gods are worthless and meat is meat, and it all comes from God." You have that whole Pauline thing about the dietary considerations of pious Jews. So, John in Luke doesn't eat this wilderness diet which is associated with the great holy men of Israel. So he just doesn't eat it.

There's the constant Pauline thing. John is put in the role of somebody who doesn't understand what's going on. He doesn't really understand it. If you read the account of the Baptism in Luke, you'll find that in fact John is separated from the baptism itself. The wording is quite extraordinary. You have the sense that John is doing baptism but Jesus himself is somehow baptized slightly apart from that. Read the wording and compare it with the other Gospels and you'll see for yourself if you care to.

John's agency as a transmitter of Holy Spirit must be denied in the Pauline tradition because Paul said his baptism was the true spiritual baptism. I mean he argues the case in Corinthians that, "I actually didn't come to baptize." and he's comparing his baptism to Apollos another follow of John who interestingly also came from Alexandria. He says "Apollos' baptism is just with water, mine gives you the spirit. Which one is going to be the baptism which holds you when the judgment comes?" Well if I may say so, the entire basis of the baptism of John, even in the gospels with Luke very weak on this, is that to be baptized to repent is the only way to survive the judgment. Then Paul says no, this water baptism isn't good enough. I think he's using an old Builder's Law tradition of the two creations which require two pillars. Anyway it's also a Masonic mythology of the pillars which will survive the end of the world, the second flood of water and fire. Paul is using that, and he's saying: "Will your baptism withstand the fire because you need to withstand the fire conflagration which is going to wipe out mankind or judge or purify or purge mankind. You have to have the fire baptism." You have this distinction again in the New Testament of "I baptize in water, but one will come who will baptize with fire." I think this is Pauline.

What's the point of a deficient baptism? Anyway, it wasn't deficient to Jesus. When Jesus was baptized by John, he received the spirit that comes on his head in the form of a dove and almighty God said "This is my beloved son in whom I am well pleased." That's pretty good for a water baptism, and that was John's. Now the baptism of John, historically, Josephus says was a sign of purification, that they had turned again to God. It is the turning again to God that is going to save the soul from the judgment and the end of the material existence which we'll face in our own lives whether once at our death or an end of the scroll of time and space collectively.

So yes, we have this thing in England for playing-field reasons: "Fair Play". I don't think John has received fair play. I don't anyone who gets in the way of orthodoxy Christianity ever gets fair play. Unless it's a Newtonian theologian. Then that's called Liberal Christianity which all the evangelicals are deeply hostile to. "Why are you giving fair to play to Satan. How Dare you." Fair play just stops at John and John has been treated atrociously and he's very important.

The feeling I got when I finally had the opportunity to have the book in front of me and I read it was first of all, "I wrote this? What?" I had a feeling of spiritual thrill. My God, you know my being was being opened by things in this book, so it was reminding me. That's what the book is: a reminder. This whole Gnostic thing about waking you up and remembering: "Remember, I'm the remembrance of the pronoia. I'm the remembrance of providence. God has found a way for us." John has that capacity still I believe to wake us up, and give us a good douche you know, and take us to the other side.

MC: Your book certain does justice to John, but I think that's all the time that we have.

ERIC G. WILSON

Eric G. Wilson is the author of *The Mercy of Eternity*, *Against Happiness*, *Gnostic Cinema*, *Everyone Loves a Train Wreck*, and *My Business is to Create: Blake's Infinite Writing*, as well as Professor of English at Wake Forest University.

Many in both scholarly and occult circles view William Blake as a sort of latter day Gnostic saint. I include myself in that camp. Thus, it made sense to invite one of the world's leading authorities on England's Poet to discuss his Gnostic (and esoteric) leanings.

That is Eric Wilson, also a bestselling author (*Against Happiness*) and a friend of Gnostic philosophy (*Gnostic Cinema*). From that first interview, Eric would return to Aeon Byte Gnostic Radio to expand on William Blake and other Gnostic-minded artists of modernity. As Stephan Hoeller once said, "Every artist is already half a Gnostic." By that, he means those who create art usually understand the falseness of reality and discover the beauty of the journey of self-knowledge.

With William Blake, we get the full Gnostic, though, as the poet was personally gripped throughout his life by the mystic visions and keen cynicism the classic Gnostics were infamous for. And as well as their intense sensitivity to the plight of humanity. Consequently, Blake's painting and art are suffused with Gnostic cosmology and theology, and again, Eric was my first and only choice on this topic.

MC: How are you doing today Eric? Always great to have you here in the kingdom of heresy.

EW: Well, Blake is certainly the king of heretics.

MC: You've taught Blake for many years, and, like you, he has definitely changed my life, transformed my life since I was a kid. I remember the first time reading "Tyger" and I think I was seven years old in a British school in Mexico and walking out and I never saw reality the same again. It both like terrified me and beguiled me at the same time. What was your experience with Blake?

EW: Well, I, I came to Blake a little later than you. My first taste of Blake didn't really come until I was in college and I got to Blake by way of Allen Ginsberg. I was nineteen, I was going through an early stage of rebellion, I was reading the Beats, in particular Ginsberg's "Howl" and in my reading about Ginsberg came across that really surreal moment that he himself writes about of being in a Harlem apartment in the late forties. Ginsberg being very ill at ease, spending a lot of time masturbating and reading William Blake and he tells the story of how, after reaching climax after having read Blake while masturbating, he hears this disembodied voice reciting the poem "Ah, Sunflower," and of course Ginsberg said, "Well this is William Blake himself," and he saw this as a major moment in his own poetic development. He called it his Blake vision.

So I immediately went to Blake and read first of all his poem "The Marriage of Heaven and Hell," you know this wonderfully iconoclastic, satirical rebellious prose poem tractate, essay: it's a very strange work. And I found myself in the next few days copying out "Sayings From the Devil" and cutting them out and pasting them all around my room. Like, "The tigers of wrath are wiser than the horses of destruction," ah, "The fool who persists in his folly will become wise," and then of course later on in the poem the wonderful one that has of course become so famous in the counter-culture: "When the doors of perception are cleansed the world will appear as it is, infinite." So that was really my awakening to Blake and he's really informed me probably more deeply than any other writer since that time. He's really got into the fiber of my being and is really, I guess, a soul doctor for me to this very day.

MC: I would agree with you definitely on that. So of all the ways you could have approached Blake, why did you decide to write this book in this way?

EW: Well, I was fortunate enough to be contacted by the University of Iowa Press. The editors there at the press wanted to put together a new series of books called The Muse Series, books that would address issues of creativity and writing primarily but also in art or music through the eyes of one particular writer. So he asked me if I'd be willing to contribute to this series. He said I could choose whatever writer I wanted, so I immediately chose William Blake who not only really is a poet and an artist but also someone who really emphasized artistic creativity as really the core value of existence.

From a very young age Blake felt called to be an artist. He tells the story of being four years old and a spirit appearing before him and saying, "Blake, be an artist, in this there is felicity," and that was one of many such visions he had before the age of ten years old. From angels, from God, from other artists like Raphael basically saying to him, be an artist. So as Blake developed over time becoming a skilled book engraver and a skilled poet, he more and more thought that when we are most human we are most imaginative. The height of the spiritual life in other words is to be an artist and he saw Jesus himself as the consummate poet, the consummate artist, and came to the conclusion that the path to wisdom, the path to life is an artistic path and he didn't mean by that that one had to be necessarily a great painter but that life itself could become a kind of art. So it just made perfect sense to me on so many levels to use Blake as the subject of my book on creativity.

MC: It's very interesting because in your book Blake didn't see art as something that you know you sat down with your cup of tea and the muse came down to him, but you write that he saw art as warfare. What was he going to war against?

EW: Blake hated oppression in any form and he was very wise to realize that the most pernicious and powerful forms of oppression are mental forms of oppression. He talked in one of his poems about the "mind forged manacles" and he came to the conclusion that most of us when we experience the world around us aren't really having a unique, personal experience of the world; we're seeing the world through the ideas, the abstractions, the concepts that have been inculcated into us from our culture, from the religion of our culture, from the political systems of our culture. So for him the primary way to break out of these tyrannical forms that society imposes upon is to learn to value your own particular, unique experience, trying to shatter those manacles of the mind and experience the world as only you can experience in your own unique, idiosyncratic way.

For him this is the beginning of all art. He says to generalize is to be an idiot and the particular alone is the foundation of the sublime. So first and foremost for Blake the artistic life is a way of seeing, it's a way of experiencing the richness, the texture, the strangeness of the world, denuded of overly cumbersome abstractions. And then after having these experiences of the world, we want to express our joy at such experiences, and certainly one can learn to paint, one can learn to write but also one can just learn to take joy in life, seeing life aesthetically, selling life as a series of opportunities to enjoy the beautiful and the sublime.

MC: It seems our, or my, exegesis. Obviously I'm going to be looking at things through the Gnostic point of view, which is not very hard because we are talking about William Blake, and the classic Gnostics would agree, okay, we are here because of the force of the stars; the rulers. Eric, Miguel and William Blake are thrown into these Caucasian bodies, into this Christian milieu, and instead of running away to some island in Taiwan and becoming a Zen Buddhist and that sort of rebellion, it seems like the Blakean attitude is, "No, I am going to face this mythology in this world and I'm basically going to reinterpret it the way I want it, recreate it and find the beauty in it." Am I close?

EW: You're exactly right. For Blake, Eden is not resting in a nice enclosed garden feeling no pain. For Blake Eden is, to go back to your earlier point, mental warfare. For Blake, for the mind always to be questioning, seeking, creating, destroying, acting, this is Eden for Blake because it is the highest manifestation of human potential. Our minds at work questioning and creating.

Blake was extremely Gnostic in his disposition. Even though he wouldn't necessarily say that he was influenced profoundly by one Gnostic or another. Blake's greatest enemy, and this is using his vocabulary was what he called the Ratio. This is Blake's word for the overly rational systematic view of the world, and he would attribute this, he would call this I guess the view of the demiurge or Yaldabaoth. And here's what he means by Ratio, I think it's important we get this. For him Ratio is a lowest common denominator of perception.

What does that mean? If you and I, Miguel, and maybe two or three of our friends, were sitting in a room and I put a plant in the middle and I said let's each describe this plant in language and we all described it, and I took all those descriptions and I collated them, and I found five adjectives that we all agreed describe this plant, and I said, okay, this plant equals these five adjectives and any observation you can make about this plant that doesn't fit within those five adjectives is inaccurate or even shows that you have no sense of reality.

For Blake this is how the abstractions that inform our perceptions work. They are ratios. So when we look at the sun we say, "Oh, that's what looks like a coin in the sky," and if I say, "It's a fiery ball in which angels are singing holy, holy, holy," I'm deemed crazy, right? So Blake was very much aware of how basically any given society downloads, as it were, abstractions in our head that try to make us conform our perceptions to mainstream ideas of what things are. So for instance if I see a feathery blackish, reddish creature, I immediately try to plug it into some preconceived abstraction like "robin, oh, that's a robin." So I'm really not seeing that robin, I'm seeing that as an example of this concept in my mind. That's Ratio for Blake. That is Blake's demiurge, that is Blake's Yaldabaoth. So the mind endlessly has to push against those easy, easy perceptions, those easy conclusions and really try to get at the strangeness, the weirdness of the world, that ultimately is too rich, complicated and intricate to ever be corralled into easy concepts.

MC: It seems he's very anti-Newton but it's almost ironic because Newton himself was a pretty much a magician and pretty much into the occult, so I always found that ironic.

EW: It's true. I don't think Blake knew about Newton's alchemical studies. For Blake, Newton was the scientist who tried to reduce the great qualities of the world to quantity. He tried to reuse the universe to number and tried to see matter as indifferent bits moving at mathematically predictable ways, that's Blake's Newton and it is an unfair reading of Newton, but again Newton the alchemist was fairly hidden back in those days.

MC: He seems to have a very almost Kant/Hume view of reality doesn't it? He feels like you and reality have to interact, in order to find some meaning or truth.

EW: That's exactly it. Blake's was very much against Lockean empiricism which as we all know assumes that the mind is this blank slate on which sensory data write. So Locke basically says we are subjects standing over against separate objects, these objects emanate data which then becomes imprinted onto our minds. So basically we are shaped by our environment, we are shaped by our experience. There isn't much room for agency, creativity, imagination, at least that's the way Blake read Locke. So Blake basically believed that to be is to be perceived. There's no such thing as an objective reality outside of our minds.

This is where the Kantian flavor comes in as you correctly say. For Blake we do have innate ideas, we are born, our minds are like gardens already sown with seeds and it's our job to cultivate those seeds. So for Blake our minds shape experience. The way we perceive the world is never objective. It's always based on who we are, our disposition, our choices as he says elsewhere: "as a man is, so he sees." In other instance he talks about how a miser will look at a tree one way and an artist will look at a tree another way. So given this, for Blake the idea was well, why don't I live a life and choose a perspective, choose a worldview that makes the world appear to me in as rich, full and beautiful a way as possible, as opposed to seeing the world as a Newtonian or a Lockean would as just distant matter that moves in mathematically predictable ways through empty space.

MC: And speaking of Blake, not speaking of Blake, we are speaking of Blake, and this is a pet theory of mine. I've had Lance Owens on, who's the creator of gnosis.org, and he discussed and also Stephan Hoeller and he discussed, how Carl Jung and Tolkien were very much into what he called the active imagination. They believed that that realms that they went to, the unconscious for Jung and the fairy realm of Tolkien, were actually very real and were places where they could bring out great truths and express it through them. Would you say and am I wrong to say that Blake might have been the first person to equate imagination with Gnosis?

EW: I don't know that he would be the first. I mean I think there are some Neoplatonists who probably had ideas somewhat like this, but I think Blake was the first really formally to articulate the idea that imagination is not simply some mental faculty that allows us to create unreal worlds, but to perceive the world imaginatively is to gain the richest, fullest knowledge that we possibly can. And to use Jung's example, to delve into the collective unconscious as Jung did, and to sense there all these energies and potentialities and then to try to find a way to manifest them through imagining them in one way or another—through painting or through writing, as Jung did in his red notebook, or through building an actual tower as he did in Bollingen. This would be a way of saying that to imagine one's experiences of the world in harmonious, beautiful ways allows one to know oneself more deeply, and also allows one to connect to the world around one in a more, in a richer way. That's Jungian, and I think Blake would say the same thing.

Blake constantly talks about it; he says exuberance is beauty. I mean there's a real sense for Blake that we are cauldrons of creative energy. He didn't have the word unconscious but he might use such a word if he'd lived after Jung and the goal in life is to figure out a way to express those deep full potentialities of our being which are not necessarily rational at all, and this is what the artist does and this is what each of us can do in our one way. The more deeply we delve into the mysteries of self, the stranger it becomes, the more in need of enlightening aesthetic expression we are. So I would say for Blake; yes, to imagine the world fully, not only your own personal experience but your perception of the world outside of you is a way of knowing as well as a way of creating.

MC: In your book you simply say Blake saw imagination as a vision.

EW: That's exactly what he said so to put it another way, when we are experiencing the world, not as an example of s certain idea, not as an example of a certain theory, but actually experiencing the world as it is in all of its irreducible particularity this is a vision, this is an imaginative vision, this is a sense of the world as infinite. Now what do I mean by that? In my book I talk about this, this really cool short film that maybe you or some of your listeners saw in Junior High called Powers of Ten. Well, this is an old school film, I think it was made in the early seventies. I'll be brief about it because I think it really gets at this idea of imagination of vision as knowledge.

In this little film you see a couple sitting in a park and then suddenly the camera zooms into the ground where they are sitting. Then the camera zooms down under the ground, down to the dirt and the earthworms. Then it zooms in again, going into the cells of the earthworms, then it zooms in again, more deeply each time, magnified by the power of ten. So eventually as this camera penetrates very deep into the very fabric of matter itself, it's gone down ten to the powers of ten in magnification. And by that time you're at the very atom itself and you see this empty space through which these particles are constantly whirling and then suddenly the camera zooms back out to the couple sitting in the park, and then it starts going the other direction into space, ten to the powers of ten. And then we finally get to the outer reaches of the known universe, and we see images that look very similar to those that we saw at the very heart of matter itself. Now I think this is a wonderfully Blakean film.

So when Blake says that when we perceive the world as it is that it will become infinite, and when we see the world as it is, it will be through seeing the unique particular, I think he has something like this in mind. In other words, the more closely and intensely we observe the world around us, the more complicated, heterogeneous, intricate it becomes. It becomes infinite in its possibilities, infinite in its relationships. So for Blake this is seeing the world imaginatively. This is connecting to the very fabric of existence, infinity, and this is also knowing the true nature of existence. It is infinite. So to put it another way, Blake was not some misty eyed mystic. I mean he was an artist first and foremost. He was very interested in the visible world.

MC: It should be mentioned again, some of us might have this, for lack of a better word, romantic idea that he sat down and the energy just flowed through him. But he worked very hard and that's important advice for any artist.

EW: I think Blake really understood the mystery of artistic creation. Sometimes we do actually have what's called inspiration, and he talked about how on one occasion a fairy came and sat on his desk and dictated to him a poem. On another occasion he said in writing a long poem, "I just transcribed what the eternals told me to write." So Blake did have these moments where suddenly the idea, the work, came to him almost like a gift given down from heaven. But these were rare moments as they are for all of us. Blake also understood that the artist's life is the life or work. Blake probably worked every single day of his adult life on his art. Now it's important to know that Blake lived a very poverty-stricken life. I mean early in his life he got some money for engraving books, illustrating books but as he over time developed into a poet and an original artist on his own, mainstream publishers wanted nothing to do with this because it was simply too strange. Well, Blake didn't stop. He continued creating these poems no one would read, creating these images no one would look at everyday, ten hours a day, twelve hours a day and this was not easy labor. He developed an engraving process that allowed him to publish his works on his own. And if I can just briefly talk about this just to give you the sense of the gruelling nature of his life; he would get a copper plate and he would get a paintbrush, and he would put some kind of oil onto this copper plate. He would write his poems backwards and then he would paint beside the poem whatever image he wanted, still in this brush dipped in oil. And then he would put some kind of acid onto the copper that would eat away the parts not covered by the oil, take the oil off and you would have this plate. He would put black ink on the plate, he would press it onto the page and now the words would appear in the right direction for writing and then onto this black outline he would paint.

So each Blake book is actually unique, painted freshly. Now this process would take hours and it was really dirty work. He's inhaling these fumes. In fact, scholars speculate that he died of a liver disease caused by him inhaling these fumes all day, so he literally died for his art. So Blake understood both sides of the creative process. In a way you're only going to have that vision and that fairy visit you and that muse sit on your shoulder after you've worked, worked, worked for year after year. It's very much like an athlete, right? You can only be graceful on the basketball or the tennis ball court and do those magical leaps and dives like Michael Jordan if you've practiced and sweated year after year after year.

MC: Eric, you also write which is also very interesting and this would definitely break away from the Gnostics, or perhaps not, that Blake did not see the Bible as allegory. I mean even Augustine and St. Ambrose saw the Bible as allegory, so what did he see it as?

EW: Well, he made this distinction talking about the Bible, between allegory and vision. For him the Bible was not simply some visible narrative rendering of some sort of heavenly narrative. For him the Bible was an original, unique, artistic vision of the prophets who wrote the biblical book. So for Blake, Isaiah, Ezekiel, Jeremiah were poets. They were artists pure and simple and they were trying to express in powerful, highly imagistic language their own experience of the divine. Jesus was doing the same thing. So for Blake the goal of the spiritual life was not simply to imitate let's say Jesus or Ezekiel, to try to model your behavior on their behavior, quite the contrary. It was to find the same energy that inspired them and then find your own unique expression for that energy. So someone like Jesus for Blake is not someone to imitate but a spur or impulse or prod to create in your own way.

Now I think of someone like Whitman here who says that, you know he says, I'm the teacher of athletes, he who most honors my style destroys the teacher. So that is the teaching that Blake got from Jesus, just as Jesus in a way destroyed the Old Testament prophets by creating his own unique vision, so Blake would destroy as it were Jesus by creating his own unique vision. Blake understood this at a very early age I should add. Blake was brought up in a lower middle class milieu of very radical Protestant thought. So he had no formal schooling. In fact, his parents very much encouraged him to read the Bible on his own, to think about the Bible on his own, to come up with his own personal interpretation of the Bible with no need to conform to any doctrine whatsoever. So from a very early age for Blake the Bible was a poem, pure and simple and as such an inspiration to him to write his own poems. So in a way Blake was Gnostic, you know just as the early Gnostics were constantly reading against the grain of the book of Genesis and coming up with their own creation myths, in a way Blake throughout his life was trying to write his own Bible.

MC: Blake reminds me very much of people like Lewis Carroll or John Lennon. People who just decided they were going to invent their own vocabulary, their own context, in addition to their own worlds and their message seems to be: you are welcome to come into my world and figure things out but don't expect me to give you a dictionary or a map of what's going on.

EW: That's exactly it. It's almost like Blake wrote in such a way that his language constantly pushes against any conclusive interpretation. Blake does later in life in his great prophetic poems like Milton or Jerusalem create his own personal mythology. Now this doesn't mean that it's just nonsense. I mean, he creates these mythological figures that bear a slight resemblance to mainstream mythological figures. For instance he has a figure that runs throughout his later poems named Urizen which reminds us of Jehovah or Yahweh, which remind Gnostics of Yaldabaoth, an overly tyrannical God who is associated with reason, Ur-reason, Urizen and also associated with limitation, horizon.

So when you come across Blake's mythology it's both strange and familiar at the same time; it's a very strange reading experience. It's almost like you've entered into someone else's dream and you realize that you might have had this dream before yourself a long time ago and this is a very unsettling experience, but I think Blake wrote in this way again to keep readers from being overly systematic in reducing his works to easy interpretations.

It's almost like each time you read Blake it undercuts your expectations and keeps his language fresh and new and interesting. And I think that's what art does. Shelley says that poetry rips away the veil of familiarity from the world and suddenly makes it seem strange and fresh and wonderful in ways that it usually doesn't seem when we just go through the world with habit and we numb ourselves to what's there. So reading a Blake poem intensely, energetically, really does cleanse the doors of our own reading perception and opens us up to the mystery of his work. The goal in other words is not simply to understand what it means but to have it open you up to imagine your own artistic visions. To read Blake well in a way you have to be Blake.

MC: Which is almost impossible. In your book you quote Walter Benjamin who basically says Kafka and Blake, "took precautions against interpretations of their writing".

EW: It's true and that's so frustrating to so many readers of Blake, especially undergraduate students who are dying to know what does this mean? What should I write on my paper, what should I write on my exam? And I certainly understand their dilemma. So I really try to open them up to the fact that we should see Blake's text and this is true of most any great literary texts or work of art in general, as a place that defamiliarizes our habitual relationship to the world. That shocks us out of our perceptual and interpretive complacency. I mean I talk in my book about this really great essay by Walker Percy, who's most famous for being a novelist, a Southern novelist in the middle part of the twentieth century. But Walker Percy has this great essay called "The Loss of Creature" where he says that so much of our education now is too theoretical. In other words in a Biology class we might dissect a frog, not because we care about this particular frog with this particular brownish, greenish skin, but see this frog as an example of certain anatomical theories and the same way in an English class you might look at a Shakespeare sonnet not to pay attention to this particular sonnet but as an example of the sonnet as a certain poetic form, so Percy says in this way we've lost creature. We've lost a sense of the texture and the reality of the world because we've turned everything into a cipher of an idea.

So Percy says that Biology teachers should come to class with sonnets on some days and English teachers should come to class with frogs some days, just to shock us out of that complacency and, boy, you're really going to see a frog if you're expecting a sonnet, and you're really going to see a sonnet if you're expecting a frog. This is what Blake's poetry does. I think it's possibly one way of working to undercut these expectations and in doing so it unsettles us but also it refreshes our connection to the world.

MC: So when your students and other scholars might come up with some very wild or not so wild interpretations of Blake and we've both read them—you know, Blake was a Neoplatonist. Blake was an alchemist, Blake was a revolutionary, Blake was a kabbalist. You don't have problems with that Eric?

EW: Blake was these things, but so much more. I mean no, I certainly can say; no, Blake had Gnostic tendencies, that is the case. Blake had radical political tendencies, that is the case. He had Neo-Platonic tendencies, that is the case. These are useful maps. These are useful maps for negotiating the wilderness that is the textural world of William Blake but I'm constantly reminding my students that the map is not the territory. We use maps to help us negotiate strange landscapes but if we spend too much time looking at the map we won't see the landscape.

So I think at a certain point the map takes you deep into the terra incognita, the unknown land and then at a certain point that map no longer is useful and what do you do then? You have to start making your own map. And that's where the imagination comes in. I can treat Blake as a Neoplatonist, but that's only going to take me so far, and then I know I have to come up with my own way of connecting to the poetry of William Blake. And, yes, that's hard work but as I tell my students, it will reward you, it will nourish you. Again by giving you the gift of refreshing your relationship to the world around you, because it has hopefully shocked you out of your habitual ways of relating to the world or at the very least unsettled you a little bit.

MC: What's great about Blake and I'm sure you'd agree is he's someone you and I both know we will take our last breath and we will never have figured him out, or probably no scholar will ever have figured him out.

EW: No, that's true and again that's not to say there aren't some really scholarly books on William Blake that I drew on myself in writing this book. But you're exactly right that we will never figure Blake out once and for all, and again I think this is true of all of great literature, this is part of what makes literature literature, as opposed to say journalism or history. Literature, basically turns language in such a way that words become less signs of only one meaning but sites of potentiality and possibility. Emily Dickinson said; "I dwell in possibility, a fairer house than prose. " Poetry does exactly this; it's almost like poems wrench the words away from their original definitions and employ them in new ways so we can come up with different ways to make the words mean something. Dickinson also says in a letter: "My business is circumference. " I think this is a very Blakean utterance, it suggests that if I have an object that I'm paying attention to I can endlessly circle around it like a circumference and at each point in the circle I'm seeing the object from a slightly different perspective so at each point in the circle I am seeing something new. I think this is another way to think about Blake's way of seeing, getting attuned to the fact that each moment is something new and fresh and shocking if only we are attuned to it.

Now. again, most of us want certainty, conclusiveness, completeness. That's a very understandable human desire. I want it too but I think this is why we need art and I think this is what Blake knew about art. Science is all well and good, History is all well and good but we need sometimes to be pushed back into potentiality. Our minds need to be freed from actuality, freed from certainty, freed from security and put back in Eden, as Blake saw it. Eden as a place of endless intellectual play. Sort of rough and tumble play. In hopes of coming up with new ideas and new ways of seeing. That's Eden.

MC: Yeah, that's Blake's warfare and, for the reader, Eric definitely has some very good prose of his own, very inspirational prose in My Business Is To Create. For example you write, "Commemorate and negate. Elevate to erase. Thus double vision is essential for revisionary irony. Accept your past but know it hinders you." Again, that's right into the Gnostic ethos right there.

EW: That's totally it, I'm so glad you bought that up. This is another way of talking about how Blake relates to traditions, be they Neoplatonism be they Christianity, and that is: look, we're all shaped by a certain past, you and I were brought up in a certain place, we were brought up with a certain set of ideas and we can't escape that, we're shaped by that but we can question that past. We can both embrace that past and negate that past at the same time. For Blake this is what Jesus did. Jesus looked at the laws of the prophets and said, "I embrace these ten commandments, they're valuable, powerful codes of conduct, but I want to go further by looking within and saying; it's not enough to not commit adultery in action you can't really commit adultery in thought either, this internalization." This is Jesus commemorating and negating and I call it irony because it puts you in a duplicitous position where you both affirm the past which has value but also question that past and devalue it at the same time. So Blake is constantly moving back and forth between tradition and innovation, what he calls the daughters of memory and the daughters of innovation. He knew this.

I think some people misunderstand Blake and creativity in general when they say, "Oh it's all about being innovative, it's all about creating something new, it's all about being totally spontaneous." Well, Blake would say you can never be totally innovative, totally new, totally spontaneous because the reality is we're shaped by certain pasts, by certain environments, by certain ideas that we can never transcend once and for all, so we have to think about these limiting factors in new ways. And when we think about them in these ways that both commemorate and negate we can move beyond them by taking what is best from them and deploying what is best in new contexts. New wine skins for new wine would be another way of putting it.

MC: But you mention Harold Bloom. What do you think about his advice? He says most poets—and I'm sure this goes for artists and their respective fields—but a poet might be threatened by Shakespeare or Milton, but Blake just actually misread these poets and show that they have something lacking and the poet doesn't. Is this advice or is this Bloom giving you a confidence boost before you even write something down, you know?

EW: I think that's a great way of putting it; Harold Bloom giving a confidence boost. It's a really provocative theory. Bloom says, look, if you're a poet writing after Shakespeare and Milton, if you're William Blake, if you're William Wordsworth and you read Shakespeare and Milton you think, "Damn, they've done it all, there's nothing left to write, there's nothing left to do," so for Bloom, a really strong poet (that's his language) will find a way to read those poets of the past in such a way that the poets of the past seems somehow lacking, seem as if they need a completion to their vision and that creates a space in with one can create. One can push against what Bloom calls the anxiety of influence.

Blake does exactly that. In his poem Milton, John Milton is the main character and he imagines John Milton up in a heaven of his own imagining. John Milton in the heaven he imagined in *Paradise Lost*. And he's up there and he realizes that he was wrong. That because he denied the feminine energy, because he overvalued reason and devalued emotion, that his vision was incomplete. So the poem Milton, Blake's poem Milton is about Milton coming down from the heaven he imagined, trying to reclaim his feminine energy or reclaim his emotional life and make himself whole again. This is a perfect example of Blake reading Milton in such a way that he can see himself, Blake, as completing Milton's vision in the same way that Jesus related to, say, Ezekiel or Isaiah.

It's a really provocative way to think about how really powerful writers relate to the past, but I think it's advice for all of us if we feel overpowered by a certain thinker, it's okay to be influenced by that thinker but you need to create your own space where you can take those ideas in directions you want to take them in. I think that's quite Gnostic too. If you think of the early Gnostics, clearly they find the book of Genesis to be a fascinating, powerful book but it needs revision. It needs to be rewritten in such a way to show that Jehovah isn't the true and only God but a second-rate God. So I think that's another way of thinking about the Gnosticism of Blake.

MC: How do you think Blake saw nature? It's almost like contradictory because it seems like he's extolling us, or extolling nature and inviting us to see nature in a new way but at the same time for example Crabb Robinson's letter where he says; "Nature is the work of the devil," and goes as far as calling Wordsworth an atheist. It seems that and then there's another of his poems where he says that nature deadens him or deadens his senses. How did Blake see nature?

EW: In a very complicated way. On the one hand Blake thought, yes, that if a poet thinks that nature is all there is, if a poet thinks that we are shaped entirely by the physical world, if our minds are subservient to the physical world, this will be an extremely limited poet and in fact will be a poet who's worshipping something that Blake would call satanic. Really for Blake Satan is not some horned creature in a fiery hell. For Blake Satan is Isaac Newton, essentially. Satan is that part of our mind that embraces limitation and subverts mind to environment. That's Blake's Satan and what see how he takes all these terms and employs them in his own way? So he saw Wordsworth as someone who was satanic in that way because he worshipped nature and didn't emphasize mind enough. Now I think this is probably a misreading of Wordsworth. Wordsworth certainly was just as interested in mind as nature. So this is why Blake would say negative things about the natural world, thinking that if we overemphasize our natural being we dehumanize ourselves. Think of it: the great human virtues like charity, mercy, unselfishness, these things do not take place in nature. You don't see animals behaving charitably and mercifully. So for Blake we need to emphasize what in us is most human and again what in us is most human are those virtues that transcend nature, some Darwinian nature struggle for existence, red in tooth and claw.

I would say this about Blake: Blake as an artist really valued the texture and the beauty of the physical world, but he also valued the power of the mind to shape experiences of the physical world into aesthetic or artistic powers. So he certainly wasn't an anti-naturalist, he certainly wasn't a dualist, but he was just always cautioning don't put too much emphasis on the body, don't put too much emphasis on nature because it could dehumanize you. And if you look at Blake's art, his drawings of animals are really quite bad, I would say, but his drawings of humans are wonderful. I mean he was just really fascinated by human form. So I would say that for Blake the true ideal of the artist is the garden or the city, both of which are patterns where humans take natural resources and transform them into structures that satisfy human aesthetic desire. So a garden uses nature but humanizes nature. A city humanizes the natural world as well. So someone like Rousseau or someone like Wordsworth who is more pastoral, more back to nature, that would be problematic for Blake.

MC: Eric, why was Blake so concerned with the concept of innocence?

EW: There's this great story that, one of Blake's friends came to visit him and his wife Katherine at a certain point in one of their London houses. He knocks on the door and no one answers. He opens the door, yells, "Mr Blake! Mr Blake," and he hears the voice from the distance, Oh, we're back in the garden come back here," and so the friend walks back through the house, goes back into the garden and sees William Blake and his wife Katherine sitting naked, reading passages of *Paradise Lost* to one another and Blake says, "Oh, come on back, it's just Adam and Eve you know." There are many such stories that I talk about in the book. These wonderful examples of Blake living his ideas.

So what is innocence for Blake? One of Blake's earliest books, and really his most popular book and the book that was most popular during his lifetime, was Songs of Innocence and Experience and in this he really tries to get at the psychology of what it means to be innocent and what it means to be experienced. And the subtitle of this book is "Showing Two Contrary States of the Soul," which suggests that for Blake both innocence and experience need one another to be valuable. Here's an example: if I'm innocent I'm childlike, I'm playful, I'm open, I'm trusting and I have a really immediate spontaneous response to the world. And that's wonderful, but at the same time I'm very limited because I don't know what evil is, I don't understand that the world is a place of deception as much as it is of honesty. I don't understand sex. I don't understand death. So for Blake, to fall into the experienced world is to gain a really dynamic knowledge of sex, of death, of complexity, but of course experience is severely limited too because you can fall into depression, you can fall into melancholy, you're sick, you decay, you become skeptical and cynical.

Ultimately, I think Blake had this vision of the artist as someone who is able to synthesize innocence and experience. Someone who as an adult, who understands the fallen nature of the world, who understands oppression and tyranny and injustice. Who has knowledge of these tragic elements of existence but yet can somehow return through his imagination to that playfulness and spontaneity and childlikeness of innocence, and use that as the seed from which his creative artistic work can emerge, artistic works that hopefully enlighten his readers about the nature of injustice and tyranny and hopefully make the world a better place.

MC: And a passage that really struck me in your book—well, a lot of passages struck me, for the readers it's a wonderful book you should own if you're an artist or a fan of Blake or Gnosticism—but you talk about this word (and I know I'm going to mispronounce it because I usually do) this German word called *Sehnsucht.*

EW: Ah, *Sehnsucht.* this is a German word that really is not quite translatable into good English. I mean it's often translated as "longing" but in German it really captures something much different; a deep, deep longing for something ungraspable that is in a way pleasurable because in the longing for it you're constantly thinking about what is ungraspable that you really, really want. So it's contradictory and we all feel that way sometimes. If you feel really nostalgic for a memory, you feel a kind of pain because that memory can never come back again, but also there's a kind of pleasure in reliving that memory. That would be sehnsucht. It's a deep, deep longing that even though it's empty it's also strangely full, right? So near the end of my book I talk about *sehnsucht*—and by the way it's a term that C. S. Lewis uses quite a bit in his own work. He talks about *Sehnsucht* in his memoir *Surprised by Joy* as the faculty of his soul that opened him to God. I mean he realized that this world, the physical world around him, simply could not fulfill his longing for meaning and he felt, well, only something beyond this world can fulfill that. And that's when he started thinking about God and became a Christian.

But I think for the artist, for all artists, there has to be some yearning for, there has to be some sense that we are always, wherever we are, incomplete. We are always wherever we are limited and finite. We never write the perfect poem. We never paint the perfect picture. We never know the world completely and that's painful to us because we probably long for the perfect poem, the perfect painting, perfect knowledge. But I think in that longing for perfection, in that longing for an ideal is precisely an endless inspiration to keep thinking more widely, meditating more deeply, creating more intensely. So I think to me this idea of *Sehnsucht* fits perfectly what I think the proper artistic sensibility should be, a feeling of constant incompleteness that spurs you to quest after a completeness that you can never attain and if we have this sensibility we'll never rest with our one particular poem or painting but we'll endlessly create. We'll endlessly think, we'll endlessly explore and realize it's precisely this process which nourishes us, which gives us life, which keeps us from ever becoming complacent, too imbued by habit, resting on our laurels and also keeps us open to the joy of revision and really understanding the value of revision. You constantly have to remake yourself with each new work of art or you become stagnant. In a way, you're only as good as your last sentence.

This is the very hard wisdom I think that Blake or any artist sends us. To embrace insecurity, to embrace incompleteness. That is sehnsucht.

MC: To end, we can go to the beginning of your book and this definitely summarizes what you were just talking about. Even in the end of his life, Blake was still doing his business. He was creating right?

EW: An extremely wonderful touching moment: Blake one Saturday was profoundly ill. He's suffering liver disease, he knew he had very little time left. He was bed-ridden, very weak. But still he was doing illustrations for an edition of Dante's *Divine Comedy*. He was illustrating someone else's edition of Dante's *Divine Comedy*. So imagine old, run down, decaying, sickly William Blake, still with his sketch pad in his hand, drawing shapes that bring to life Dante's great vision of heaven, hell and purgatory.

At a certain point midway through the day he just felt his energy flagging entirely and he set his things aside and basically prepared to die and this would be last thing he would create. But then out of the corner of his eye he saw his wife Kate there sitting beside him and he said to her: "Kate, you have ever been an angel to me. Bring me my things." So he revived just in that moment, seeing his wife, feeling that affection for her. She brought him his notebook, his pencil and he quickly did a sketch of her, the last thing he ever drew and then he finally set that aside and prepared to die. But he went out singing. He started singing hymns of his own making and died in this joyous, blissful state of creating, making music and right after he died—this is all reported by the way.

Some say it's not true but I choose to believe it is. Right after he fades away, apparently his wife Kate showed no grief whatsoever and I say in my book; one can see why. Kate once said "I have very little of Mr. Blake's company, he is always in Paradise. " So in some easy for Blake to die was not really for him to go away from her but simply to go where he had been most of his life anyway: Paradise.

STEPHAN HOELLER

Stephan Hoeller is an author and scholar of Gnosticism and Jungian psychology, as well as the Regionary Bishop of Ecclesia Gnostica. His books include the The Gnostic Jung and the *Seven Sermons to the Dead*, Jung and the Lost Gospels and Gnosticism: New Light on the Ancient Tradition of Inner Knowing.

Few figures have promoted the Gnostic worldview more than Stephan Hoeller in the last generation. His life seems to parallel the typology of the ancient Gnostic narrative: a Hungarian native oppressed by the archontic powers of the Nazis and Communists, causing his exile and subsequent flight to the Hermetic lands of the United States to find the Gnosis of freedom and the American Dream. Hoeller is both a scholar and a theologian, in his aspect as the Bishop of the Ecclessia Gnostica. From his fabled online lectures to such books as The Gnostic Jung and the *Seven Sermons to the Dead*, his work has truly brought the ancient mysteries of the Gnostics to a modern understanding and even approachable, reconstructions of ancient rituals rituals.

Hoeller is also an avid disciple of Carl Jung, which brings us to the interview. The publication of Jung's *The Red Book* in 2009 caused a huge stir in both psychological and spiritual circles around the globe. *The Red Book* allegedly is the foundation for Jung's depth psychological ideas, as well as an intimate spiritual diary or even a map into the imaginal realms. Perhaps it is more, but Hoeller came on Aeon Byte Gnostic Radio to explain the content and chronicles of Jung's mysterious tome. As always, Hoeller balanced the scholarly with the mystic, which in the end is always the prudent way to address the "Swiss Magician."

MC: Before we delve into the actual contents of *The Red Book*, could you tell us when Jung wrote it and why did it take so long for this fabled book to become available to the general public?

SH: Well, the first question is rather easy to answer: he began writing it, or writing the material that came to be incorporated into it on the evening of the 12th of November 1913 and he kept it up at various intervals for about five years. The main material was pretty much done by the end of 1916. So that's the chronology of the writing. As to why it had taken until 2009 to publish it, that's actually more a matter of guesswork than anything else, but what we know fairly well is that he agonized over it during his lifetime, particularly the earlier period, as to whether he should publish it in some fashion, and then decided against it. And then really what he did almost, you might say, instead of that, he utilized a great deal of the information and inspiration that he received during the period of time indicated, in which he wrote into *The Red Book* and funnelled it into his other psychological books.

So that it's really very fascinating to me at the present time, after having studied and lectures on *The Red Book*, to go back to his psychological works, or at least many of them, and to discover the material in a slightly transformed manner, of *The Red Book*. So *The Red Book* was the inspiration or the source of a tremendous amount fo his subsequent writings, but he felt that there would be very little comprehension and very little appreciation for *The Red Book* itself at that time of his life. Then he died, of course, in 1961, and the family, primarily the head of the family his son Franz Jung, with whom I had some correspondence and he was very gracious to me, as I will mention later on in another context, the family felt that it should not be published, that their father's idea was the right one, and they kept it in seclusion. And it wasn't really until about 15 years ago that a historian of psychology Dr Sumu Shamdasani developed a great interest in the material and he befriended the family and with a great deal of difficulty persuaded the family to allow him to work with the material, to edit it, and to prepare it for publication. So finally last October the book was published.

MC: I've heard that one of the reasons Dr Shamdasani used was he told the family there were actual partial copies of *The Red Book* out there and they could be mistranslated or misinterpreted, especially at the time there was an American psychologist named Richard Noll who was painting Jung as an Aryan cult leader or something.

SH: Yes, Richard Noll who wrote two very hostile and in part inaccurate books about Jung, and Shamdasani defended Jung very cogently at that time on the Internet and elsewhere, so he adhered himself to the family. By this time the Jung family consists really of the grandchildren and the great grandchildren of Jung. Franz Jung, the son, had died a few years ago and I think one or two of the daughters are still alive, but it really was the latest generation who were much more open to this. Dr Shamdasani also said to us—we met several times here in Los Angeles—he felt that really since/between the time of Jung's life and now so many things have happened, there has been such a change in much of the consciousness of at least certain strata of the population, that the possible acceptance level has really risen tremendously. Because we went through the sixties, we went through many things and it is now possible for this work to be appreciated by a much larger number. And certainly the reception that it is receiving seems to bear that out.

MC: It seems that the Jungian community had some resistance towards this publication. Have you seen any damage done to them?

SH: It's still pretty early, but if there are people in the Jungian community who are unhappy over the book and its content, they have not said so thus far. But we are not just dealing with the Jungian community here, we are really dealing with the general public, which has responded to the publication of the book and the availability of the book tremendously. There is an exhibit of *The Red Book* that is touring the United States at the present time. It has been for several months in New York City. It has been in Los Angeles and just left and it is now in the Library of Congress in Washington DC. In each and every case the public response was overwhelming. The various museums where it has been exhibited expected a certain number of people and the visitors and the attendees, their number has vastly outstripped all of the expectations. So the response is really tremendous. And I think to a certain extent unexpected.

MC: And, Dr Hoeller, what really compelled Jung to write *The Red Book*? It seems a short answer is he needed to go on a voyage, basically to find his own soul, his own individuation, or perhaps the map of individuation itself.

SH: Yes, that's certainly how the book stands. But actually Dr Shamdasani's introductory material and his footnoting is very informative concerning many of these issues, so I would advise anyone who has access to the book to really not just read the text itself but read these explanatory materials as well. But Jung had outgrown psychology as it existed at that particular time. He had outgrown Freudian psychology and he had left the Freudian school and he was on his own, and many feel now it was really the kind of experiences that went into *The Red Book* that made him break with Freud rather than the other way around.

So Jung had lost faith in many of the underpinnings of the psycho-analytic discipline as it existed at that time. And it would seem that this opened him up to certain deeper influences and deeper insights, and these started pouring in, beginning as I mentioned in November 19 13 and continued from thereon. So I think it was largely internal psychic pressure, or forces that were within him, or that he had access to, that drove him into these experiences and into keeping notes of the experi-ences and writing them down, which subsequently went into the book.

MC: And what he basically did, he went deep into the unconscious knowing that there was a risk. He was travelling the borderland where lunatics and great artists go to. But at the same time he dared this ex-periment so he could record it.

SH: Like so often, the people of religious or spiritual inspiration really don't have much of a choice once the forces begin to move, you have to move with them. But it is risky to exist and it is risky to go along with this, both. But Jung was a very remarkable man who managed to handle this immense internal transformational journey in a very sane manner. He wrote mostly at night. He still kept a full practice of patients. He met with fellow analysts, so during the day—and he had a growing family already, he had a nice house in Zurich, and his wife and his chil-dren, so he took care of all his normal responsibilities and then did his journey in the inner world so to say in addition, and at a different time of the day. The way in which he handled this, and the way in which he kept one foot in the physical world, so to say, I think was to his very great advantage and he thereby avoided some of the difficulties that often have arisen in connection with visionary people who then just fall into the internal abyss and haver a really hard time coming back from there, or maybe don't come back from there at all. And then psychoses and various things of that sort obtain.

MC: Didn't he use something called the active imagination? What is the active imagination?

SH: The active imagination was the term or the concept that Jung developed in the wake of *The Red Book*. This was particularly what he felt he was doing while having these visions and commenting on them. Because if you look at any chapter of the book you will find that there is a description of a visionary experience or experiences, and then there are Jung's evaluations of the experience and commentaries upon them, in every chapter. Which is also very unusual with visionary literature. Because what you get with visionary people is usually that they are so over-awed by their experience that they don't feel that they can really comment on it at all. Sometimes they are forced to comment on it later. But Jung did it simultaneously, practically. So when you look at that you see it there. The active imagination is actually the process whereby he obtained these experiences. He subsequently named it active imagination.

In fact, the first thing that he wrote after he finished *The Red Book* was a longish essay which deals with the active imagination. At that time and for a number of years thereafter he advised his students and his patients to engage in this active imagination, which they often referred to in an abbreviated word as "visioning". And it is still a practice that exists in Jungian circles but for a variety of reasons which I'm not really aware of it has been lacking in emphasis for quite a number of years. But active imagination was the practice, the technique, whereby he acquired these visions so he felt that other people, those who were psychologically ready for it, could really do the same thing. Because it's important also to keep in mind that he insists that the experiences in *The Red Book* are his experiences. They are not the experiences that would come in the same manner to anyone else. They are personal to himself, and that people would have to get their own experiences of the deep psyche in their own way. He merely could show them the way and indicate a certain way in which this could be done. But the active imagination was really the way in which he obtained the material that went into *The Red Book*.

MC: I see it as a series of initiatory journeys. Probably the most important one is he goes down into the cave, into the underworld of the unconscious, into the world of archetypes and mythology. There he meets Elijah and Salome. Salome seems to me to be one of the most important gatekeepers because it seems to me she represents wisdom in a sense.

SH: It's probably largely up to the interpreter to explain these things, because Jung doesn't explain them that much, but Salome is, I would say, primarily a wisdom figure that is very highly conjoined with feeling and with love. So initially Elijah stands for the much more mental and less emotionally involved approach to the wisdom, who he actually states at one point in the book is really only interested in prophecy. Elijah is only interested in what is going to happen in the future. But Salome is interested in love and in the manner in which the power of love and feeling and love and emotion and so forth worlds into the transformation. Elijah and Salome, important as they are in the book, are not the main instructors. They definitely act as imitators, and there is a particular big symbolic initiation described there, which somehow Richard Noll had gotten hold of, some part of that description I think in some private seminar that Jung had given and he recounted some of these experiences. And that is where Jung finds himself tied to a cross and then it is the serpent who crawls up on the cross and he has the face of a lion, and Elijah and Salome are standing by, and that is one of his truly big initiations in the book. But it's not the only one. It's probably the first one as you go on in the book that really has a tremendous amount of affect, a tremendous amount of drama with it.

But after that the big hierarchic figure, the big initiator and teacher, is another figure altogether who is called Philemon. Philemon stays with him and continues to teach him right up to the very end of the book, even into the portions that he did not put into the book. The so-called Scrutines which Dr Shamdasani then included at the end of the book. That is, I think, a very interesting figure—, probably in the long run more portentous even than Elijah and Salome. But they are all important because they all indicate phases in the transformation of Jung's psyche.

MC: Yeah, because Philemon also has a wife, Baucis, and they are taken from the Roman writer Ovid, the myth of Philemon and Baucis.

SH: Yes, there is a story of Philemon and Baucis, which was quite a popular one and, in fact, a portion of it was incorporated in Goethe's Faust, which of course all the German-speaking people, including Freud and Jung, were very familiar with. Freud never travelled anywhere without a copy of Faust. He would always have it on his bedside. So the figure of Philemon and Baucis in the ancient form was undoubtedly present, but this Philemon has the name, and possibly there is some association, like he would be a later embodiment of the Philmon of Greco-Roman lore, but it's really a more complex and much richer figure. Philemon then really becomes the instructor, becomes the teacher. And Jung's relationship to Philemon changes in the course of *The Red Book*. Initially he is suspicious of him and he thinks he is only a magician, but then as there is more and more interaction between Philemon and Jung, Jung begins to recognize that this is really a tremendously important figure.

MC: Could you compare Philemon to his Socratic daemon? His Manichaean divine twin? Is that what Philemon ultimately was?

SH: Well, possibly. I think, at least as far as the results of my studies are concerned, I think that all previous analogies break down. All those that you mentioned are present. They are aspects of the situation. But it seems to be yet more than that. And as the figure of Philemon really grows throughout the book, until at the conclusion of Scrutines, which is the third part of *The Red Book*, which Jung did not actually write calligraphically into the book himself, but it remained in manuscript form and then Dr Shamdasani included it, but by that tie Philemon is practically a saviour figure. Very, very numinous being.

MC: I don't know if it's in *The Red Book* or in the Black Book, but isn't there a part where Philemon tells Jung in the garden that he's actually Simon Magus?

SH: Yes, it's in the present format of *The Red Book*. It is in Scrutines. In the garden there is a conversation between Jesus and Philemon. Jesus appears as a blue shade, and Philemon addresses him very reverently and addresses him as lord and Jesus looks at Philemon and sayd, "What are you calling yourself now, Simon?" and then Simon tells him that Helena, who was Simon's consort in biblical times, NT times, that Helena is now called Baucis. Interestingly enough, Baucis never appears in *The Red Book*. Unless I've misses something, and don't think I have, Philemon talks about Baucis and she is around—but she is by no means as active in the situation as, for instance, Salome is in connection with Elijah. And Elijah kind of fades into he background as time goes on. He's sort of left behind because he's the Old Testament prophet who just wants to prophesy in the future and isn't interested in anything else. While Salome is the love figure.

It's also interesting to know that initially Salome is blind. She walks around with Elijah but she is blind. And when Jung undergoes that big initiatory experience, which was I think one of the experiences that Richard Noll became so excited about in a negative way, then as Jung is tied up on the cross and the snake coils itself around him and he undergoes a kind of shamanic death, and the he looks down and Salome is down at the base of the cross and she has recovered her sight. So Jung's experience restores Salome's sight, which I think is also a very interesting element. Because it shows how there is a give and take, a back and forth relations between the envisioned figures and Jung himself. It's not all a one-sided business like a biblical prophet where God speaks and the prophet listens and writes it down and that's it. But here there is always a back and forth. There are dialogues and conversations and interactions. But certainly Philemon is of tremendous importance.

MC: But Elijah also serves as the archetype of the human who reaches the divine while still alive, like the Gospel of Philip. "Become Christ while in the flesh."

SH: Yes, biblically and Kabalistically certainly, he's one of the deathless ones. He has gone to heaven without dying, such figures being rare, shall we say? I can't think of anyone that I have met so far. You see really that as time goes on Philemon begins to take the place of Elijah. What started out as Elijah continues with Philemon.

I'll tell you a little story about that that was a big revelation to me. There is one painting that Jung did of Philemon in *The Red Book*, and it's at the conclusion of the chapter where Philemon first appears, at least I think it's after the first appearance. It's really a large initial of a new page, it's vaguely "P" shaped and there is Philemon bearing the wings of the kingfisher, and the snake at his feet and various things that Jung had written next to the picture of Philemon. Interestingly enough, one of them being a quotation—now get this, and if you haven't yet —a quotation from the Bhagavad Gita in English. The only thing in English that is in the original calligraphic text of *The Red Book*. It's a quotation from the Bhagavad Gita where Krishna says that whenever unrighteousness increases in the world I come back to enlighten the people and to restore righteousness and to restore the law. And that's written right next to Philemon. It's quite an obvious question, why would Jung select that passage? And he apparently had only access at that point to an English translation of the Bhagavad Gita. And he wrote it there, because he looks upon Philemon as an avatar. In some ways an equivalent to Krishna and other avataric figure.

And then in the later part of the book in Scrutines it's evident that Philemon becomes a sort of successor to Jesus. But here is my own personal little story: that picture of Philemon had been available before the publication of *The Red Book*. They allowed it to be published just by itself in some books, for instance there is a coffee table book called C. G. Jung Word and Image, and that has the full page from *The Red Book* with Philemon's picture on it. So I have looked at that picture for many years until a friend of mine who helps me with audio and visual activities, Mr Brian Campbell, a very wonderful helper, I'm so grateful for his presence, he photographed some of these pictures and then we projected them in a very enlarged fashion during one of my lectures. Then I saw that way up on top of the picture in very small letters there is a Greek inscription. So I studied that and, since I had a few semesters of Greek in my youth I was able to decipher it. And it says in Greek, "father of the prophets, beloved Philemon." So obviously the truly numinous importance of this figure goes all through the book.

There is another interesting thing that no one really so far has commented upon, I think not even Dr Shamdasani, that right from the opposing page from *The Red Book*, on the left side as you look at *The Red Book* is the picture of Philemon, on the right side is a full-page picture of a feminine figure, a huge feminine figure with a partially veiled face, who stands in a temple-like structure with a whole bunch of people— the temple is full of people who are looking every which way, and two angelic figures up on top, and then Jung has an inscription, mostly in Latin, on the border running on all four sides, and the inscription says "The wisdom of God" sapientia in Latin which is the same as Sophia, "the wisdom of God who long ago had unaccountably gone away." And that is the feminine figure there. There is no reference to her in the text, but that huge figure is there, facing the picture of Philemon. So there is So there is Sophia, it quite obviously can't be anyone else, given a Latin name as has often been done, and the implication is that she had gone away. But she's coming back. And that is the picture of her coming back. She appears in that temple, and there are all kinds of people, there and Jung did this a few times in *The Red Book*, which is kind of humorous, he would draw a picture with a lot of face on it, and many of those faces are the faces of actual people. There is the face of Sigmund Freud, who undoubtedly was on his mind!

MC: Not in a good way, though.

SH: Not in a good way, no. Sigmund Freud, Albert Einstein, a number of people. Some of them are looking at the feminine figure, the goddess figure, Sophia, that has appeared, and others are looking away. Thereby he symbolically indicates that when she comes some people will look at her, some people will accept her, and some people will not. Needless to say, Sigmund Freud looks away.

MC: That's very powerful imagery. It reminds me of other gnostic sages like William Blake warning people, don't go too much towards scientism or rationality. Or Philip K. Dick telling people in Valis, Sophia is returning.

SH: All good visionary writing has certain things in common. The ones that you mentioned, in fact Dr Shamdasani frequently mentions in his comments and his lectures that he was given the similarity between the prophetic writings of Blake and *The Red Book* of Jung. So there is a distinct similarity. The illustrations, as they may be called, the pictures which Jung all painted himself—this guy was a terrific artist—there are some paintings of his that don't pertain to *The Red Book*, which eh just painted. Landscapes, this and that, and some of these are exhibited in the exhibition at various museums. And he was a very fine artist with very little or no training. So he employed his artistry in *The Red Book* and there a lot of pictures in *The Red Book* which are actual illustrations of the text. They are usually small and they are usually at the beginning of a chapter, like a medieval initial worked into a letter with which the chapter begins.

But then there are whole other bunch of pictures, many of them full page pictures, which are not demonstrably related to the text at all. There is no reference to them in the text. Many of these are mandalas, gorgeous powerful pictures. And this Sophia picture is one of them. So he is teaching or he is giving us information in the pictures. Often information that is not in the text, or is only implied very slightly in the text. One of them is the feminine wisdom Sophia that is returning, along with in association with Philemon. So that is also present there, so this is a subtle message which is there in addition to Salome and some of the other figures that appear.

MC: Dr Hoeller, did *Seven Sermons to the Dead* come out of this period?

SH: It most definitely did. In fact, now we know something that we did not know before. As you may be aware I was one of the few people who walked in where angels fear to tread, and I did a translation and a commentary of *Seven Sermons to the Dead* back in the 1960s, and that's my book The Gnostic Jung and the *Seven Sermons to the Dead*, which incidentally was very favourably commented upon Jung's son Franz, who sent me then in appreciation for my translation when the German translation came out, an original copy of *Seven Sermons to the Dead*, with a handwritten letter which I have under glass here. It's my most prized possession bar none. The Seven Sermons are present in the third portion, in Scrutines, of *The Red Book*. They are in there and Jung extracted them from there, changed them around very slightly, and allowed them to be privately published in the 1920s, and that's the Seven Sermons that we are aware of.

But in *The Red Book* it is not Basilides or Jung who talks to the dead, and to whom the dead talk, but it is Philemon. Philemon then makes comments on the Sermons. The text of the Sermons is not appreciably changed, so it is the same one we had before. But it now comes in a new context. I still think my interpretation was on the whole quite okay and quite useful. There are a few parts now, however, where we can see what Jung really meant because there are interpretations there. So the Seven Sermons was part of the latter portion of *The Red Book*, and then Jung extracted it from there and then published it for a few of his friends, and that was therefore the original privately published edition, in German with Latin titles, Septem Sermonem ad Mortes. Then it wasn't really published again. I think there was another translation after Jung's death.

MC: And then he was scolded by Martin Buber for it.

SH: The Martin Buber affair occurred early, on the basis of the privately published copy. Somehow a copy reached Buber. I am sure that Jung didn't send him one. He had more sense than irritating the lion. But some mutual acquaintance who did receive a copy from Jung, passed it on to Buber, and then Buber really blew his stack, as he was wont to do.

MC: A silly notion of Gnosticism being anti-Semitic.

SH: One of the scholars, Dr Brasshe, who was the assistant to Dr Jim Robinson, in Claremont years ago, we knew him quite well, and as Dr Brasshe once answered at a lecture at our society here, when somebody asked about whether the Gnostics were anti-Semitic. He said, no, the Gnostics were not anti-Semitic. In fact, many of them were Jewish themselves. They just didn't much like the biblical Jewish God. He said, you know, I can't really blame them that much for that.

MC: They didn't agree, they thought Moses got it wrong.

SH: They thought Moses might have gotten it wrong, yeah. That is a silly notion that has now pretty well gone out of the picture.

MC: Dr Hoeller, someone said that Jung's visions and torments through *The Red Book* were sort of a prophecy to World War One. Is that just folklore, or is there any truth to it?

SH: It's like this. Before he started writing *The Red Book*, in October 1913, the same year but earlier, he started having some very impressive visions, which had to do with things like a tremendous flood of blood covering Europe, and so forth. He had several of these. In fact, he was in the Swiss Army part of the time, because in Switzerland everybody has to serve a period of time in the armed forces, and he was a doctor in in the medical corps.

Anyway, he was having these visions which were very, very ominous—blood and fire, things like that—and he couldn't quite figure out what they referred to, and then the whole World War One broke out. Then he said, aha, I know what they were about. But they were not part of *The Red Book*. They came before. And in fact, him having discovered that he had actually had a precognitive vision, sort of reinforced his confidence in his own visionary abilities and he no longer felt that he had to worry that these ominous visions may have had something to do with him having a nervous breakdown. They actually predicted the war. And then he went into the visions of *The Red Book*.

MC: Another thing, and again I'm going by the Black Book, but he writes that he was called upon by the master, perhaps Philemon, and he was told, you are being inspired, just as Buddha, Mani and Christ and others, to commune with the divine. But it seems that Jung is having an argument with himself, with his soul. In the end, doesn't he refuse to be one of those and decide that he is going to be a therapist who records the process?

SH: Well, it's not entirely clear. I am aware of the sentence you are talking about but I would have to look it up and I am almost certain that the sentence you are quoting about Jesus and Mani and Muhammad and so forth was really a sentence that was written by someone else, by a disciple of Jung whom he allowed to read portions of *The Red Book*, or maybe all of it, and that she said that. And he did not disagree, except that the implication is that, while he may be inspired in a similar way, he is handling it differently from the others who have come before. That much I can be certain about, but I don't think that he ever wrote about himself that he was exactly of the same order as these previous messengers of light. But someone else said it and he didn't disagree.

MC: If his final message, or Jung's impetus, wasn't, "I am an apostle of light," but I am going to show everybody how to become an apostle of light.

SH: Absolutely. But he was prophesying and there are specific prophecies in the book and among these are what is coming, what is happening is three stages of development of the consciousness of humanity and they are war, magic, and religion. The implications of them being the war, which was probably the two world wars, and then magic being—oh, I don't know, I think that may be the computer technology, magic—at least it's magic to me!

And then a religious, a spiritual dispensation would come which is mainly centered around the fact that there is a God, there is a portion of God within the human and the human has to discover that, and has to work with that. And that's where historical Christianity went wrong, that it just concentrated on the external saviour and didn't really address itself to the God within, the Christ within, the hope of glory, and then he also mentioned in *The Red Book* that what will come in our time will not be an individual saviour like Jesus, in fact I have the exact quotation: "The anointed of our time will be born in the spirit not in the flesh." The anointed of course is the Christ, it's the messiah.

MC: Very powerful words. I'm assuming that the hermeneutics on *The Red Book* have only just begun. We still have a long way to go. Like the Nag Hammadi library, we've just begin on all of this.

SH: Absolutely. After all, the publication has only been recent, it was only by the end of last October that we got the book and we should have various people working on it. I am being bombarded here and there by my publishers to do something myself. I have mainly concentrated on the hermeneutics of lecturing so far. I did 13 lectures on *The Red Book*, going through the book from beginning to end, which are available now, and I have since then given lectures on tracing the influence of *The Red Book* in Jung's works on alchemy and in various other works of Jung including particularly *Aion* and *Answer to Job*. So that has been my hermeneutics so far. But maybe at some point with some help I might be able to combine them into book form.

MC: We look forward to it.

SH: Try to keep cool in Chicagoland.

ERIK DAVIS

Erik Davis is an author and counterculture journalist. His books include *Techgnosis: Myth, Magic and Mysticism in the Age of Information* and *Nomad Codes*.

The 21st century saw the primordial, arcane writings of two modern Gnostics come to public light. One was Carl Jung's *The Red Book* in 2009. The other was Philip K. Dick's *The Exegesis* of Philip K. Dick in 2011. Both works served as the foundational playbook for the ideas of these thinkers, and were only published generation or more after their passing.

Needless to say, it was quite an honor to have a member of the editorial team of *The Exegesis* of Philip K. Dick as a guest. Erik has long been an American expert on Philip K. Dick and modern manifestations of the Gnostic ethos. In our interview, these two streams of contemporary Gnosticism met as we attempted to gain the Gnosis on a large tome that, unlike *The Red Book*, was an unorganized mess of Dick's speculations, visions, and sometimes idle fantasies. As always, Erik provided keen insights with humor and a spanning sense of perspective—in a way that would probably have made Dick himself proud.

As with *The Red Book*, much research needs to be done in deciphering and unpacking *The Exegesis*. But from the initial interpretations, it seems Dick was a far deeper thinker than ever imagined, and an even a more authentic Gnostic than ever believed.

MC: This is the Aeon Byte interview. And today, we definitely have the pleasure of having back Eric Davis, who was part of the editorial team of Philip K. Dick's *Exegesis*. How are you doing, Eric?

ED: I'm doing excellent.

MC: Thanks again for coming on. I have to ask quickly. Can you tell us how you became a part of this project, and do you still have a woody?

ED: [laughs] Yeah, this was really, as they say, a dream come true. I first read Dick when I was nineteen, and I wrote my senior thesis on him when I was twenty years old or so. I was a total fan boy. If you had told me back then that I would be able to work with this document, I just wouldn't have believed you. So, I was definitely a happy, scholar-geek fan boy with this gig. I knew Jonathan Lethem, and I was friends with a number of people who knew Pam Jackson, who is the editor. So, I have a feeling when they were looking for someone to do the work of the annotations, and getting annotators to read it and offer comments, my name must've just popped up.

It ended up working out pretty well, because I helped Pam do some of the support stuff. I just did a very small amount of really grindy stuff; this woman basically read the whole thing. She had this room full of these Xeroxes, all these sticky notes and piles of paper—and somehow, she had this ten-thousand-page document mapped out in her head. Luckily, I didn't have to do anything as gruesome as that. But I did some transcription, and it was an interesting project on a logistical level. In some ways, it was disappointing, in that we were all part of a commercial process. This was part of a big package deal with the publisher, HMH. And part of their deal was *The Exegesis*, which was sort of their leadoff book to their re-issuing of his whole back catalogue.

MC: Before we go on Eric, why did the Dick family change their mind? Were they jealous of Jung and *The Red Book*?

ED: That's a very good question. Obviously, there is an interesting parallel with *The Red Book*. It's a sort of secret document that the family, in a way, has tossed this hot potato, and what are you going to do with it? I'm sure that in their discussions, *The Red Book* came up, but I don't ascribe a desire for a megahit necessarily on the part of the daughters and the estate. In terms of this decision, I think that they'd been getting steady pressure for quite a while to reveal it. Not just from fans, but also from scholars—and I know Jonathan always thought it was a really good idea. I think it just kind of made sense, once they were talking about this whole new publishing deal. I'm not exactly sure how it came up in the course of those conversations about reissuing the back catalog.

But because it was a commercial operation, there were certain re-straints. They had a certain amount of money for it, and most impor-tantly, they had a certain amount of time. So, ideally, this would've been a very well supported scholarly endeavor, where you were able to have the entire thing transcribed. Then, it would have to be checked (and probably rechecked), in order to catch as many errors as you could. Then, you would go through and edit it.

That's the ideal version, which we could not do; it was just not gonna happen that way. The transcription was partial; you had different people reading different folders, pulling out sections that they thought would be good, and transcribing them. They would go back to Pam, and they would edit it together. It was a very hairy, difficult process, and one that inevitably has mistakes and things that were missed. And there're prob-ably some mis-transcriptions.

It was difficult, because it's a very ornery object. I mean, you can't even really call it document, or a text—it's these crazy folders that aren't numbered in chronological order, and some chunks have differ-ent numbering systems.

MC: Are they all handwritten?

ED: Mostly handwritten. The first chunk of *The Exegesis* is all letters, so they're typed. Clearly, he was writing to people about his 2-3-74 mysti-cal experience. And at some point, he just said, "Okay, I'm going to start this Exegesis thing, or I'm gonna keep these letters separately," as part of a process that was for him—not as part of a publication—that we can tell. He continued to write some entries, and to type some entries in '74 and '75. And after that, it's mostly handwritten. But again, it's got different numbering systems, and just to try to put the whole thing in chronological order is a very hairy task that Pam did an excellent job of. The robot historians of the future will have plenty of work to do on this document!

MC: Yeah, it's only begun. It's a living thing, a holy virus, which will of course, expand. Yeah, it's funny, because I remember when I interviewed Tessa Dick, she said that Phil wouldn't let her near *The Exegesis*. He started to wonder if she was a spy and an alien, and all that. It was very important to him.

ED: Yeah, it comes through, and you can tell that he didn't think about it as something that would be published. Whether he thought of it as something that would be read later is hard to tell. I mean, he was messianic in some ways. And in other ways, he was kind of a broken and depressive person. It's not as if he was like, "Someday people will know I was right about the structure of time!" You get that voice once in a while, but usually you get a much more obsessive, philosophical, trying to get down to the kernel of the universe.

And one sign of this is the tractatus that comes at the end of Valis, when he publishes his fictionalized version of his 2-3-74 experience. He includes in the end a sort of appendix that's kind of scripture that draws very heavily from themes, language, and ideas that are in *The Exegesis*. But the text itself is different, so when he came to write something that would be published that was very much exegesis-like material, he consciously rewrote it—and in a public frame, a literary frame. He even quotes the published tractates in *The Exegesis* a few times. He was very aware of the difference between what he was doing, and what would appear in his published work.

MC: What I like is, although publicly he always said he was a Christian and an Episcopalian, he does say at one point that "I feel validated." He says, "I am a Gnostic," and he sounds terrified about it. He knows he's a knower of the unknown, and it's a great responsibility. Then of course, I get romantic and I go, "You know, once you find out, you don't have a long time to live."

ED: Yeah. For me, that was one of the most meaningful passages of all that I read. It comes very late, and there is a sense—partly because we know what's going to happen—of an ending in the last folders of *The Exegesis*. And it's funny, because the way he uses the term there, it's not about having a Gnostic myth, or a Gnostic model of the universe. It's more about having a sensibility, where you're constantly pulling the rug out from under every scenario, every model, every ideology, every mask that you confront in your search.

MC: But classic Gnostic scholars are finding out they were the skeptics, when it comes down to it. They did not trust reality, like Philip K. Dick.

ED: Absolutely, and it's not just that they didn't trust reality; if you look at the Nag Hammadi text, and you pull out the *Apocryphon of John*, clearly this text represents a great distrust of the powers that determine ordinary reality—you know, the world as we know it. It's something we find—in all sorts of ways—throughout antiquity. But in the old days, scholars would go, "That's because these guys were Sethians. They believed this. This is their system, and they wrote text based on this system." And you know, that's probably true for some of these guys. But increasingly, these guys are interested in multiple versions of reality.

We don't know who put together the Nag Hammadi Library. Was it one sect that was collecting everybody else's texts too? Or one monastery that wanted to have a record of all this crazy heresy? I'm just as likely to believe it was a person or group, who were interested—people like Phil Dick, or you and me, or most of the people who listen to your show—in very different views of what might be going on, and who believed that the search was more important than any particular text.

So, even that multiple perspective thing that you find so obsessively with Dick in his approach to philosophical and mystical themes, it's arguable that there was a whole culture of similarly driven people in antiquity. They knew something was up; they were very skeptical and suspicious about things. But they didn't even think these revelations were necessarily pure answers.

MC: Can you tell us some things in *The Exegesis* that really blew you away, or strengthened a view you had, or changed a view you had on Dick?

ED: That's very good one. The way in which he is a Christian has become more complex and rich for me. But not so much because he says he believes in Jesus. There are occasionally parts of it where you get some of the nasty, judgmental Christian voice, that God will come with His army, and destroy all the unbelievers –

MC: He liked Yahweh.

ED: Yeah, he could hang with the judgmental Yahweh, for sure. But in a way, it's almost a more interesting question, for two reasons. One, to look at it in terms of ancient Gnosticism, the whole question of how you categorize Gnosticism versus categorizing early Christianity is, of course, incredibly complicated. And the answer is, that it's sort of both; that you can't say, "Here are the Christians over here, and the Gnostics are over there." It's much more complicated. And in a way—his own ambivalence, his multiple positions—kind of re-create the matrix of that late antiquity, early Christianity mode. Wherein positions that we would think of as orthodox Christianity, and positions that we would think of as very radical Gnostic dualism, or Hermeticism, are all part of this matrix. And it's really the matrix that's being communicated. So, I think that's very interesting.

But it also reflects something about our own moments, where even in our very relativistic age, where we're used to having people with multiple perspectives. It's still very important to us whether we consider ourselves Christian or not. There's not usually a category of, "Well, he's sort of Christian," or, "She sort of believes that Jesus Christ died for our sins, and sort of doesn't." We don't really do that very much; individuals don't do that very much. It's very important, if you say somebody has Christian elements in their work, you're like, "Yeah, but were they Christian?" Did they really believe? And he does not let you answer that, one way or the other. There were tons of stuff that was great to come across, but that was one part.

Also, you've got to acknowledge that a lot of it was just really tedious and sad, and repetitive, and mind-numbing, and dull. And there're passages like this in the published version. So by and large, the editors decided to get to "the pearls", as it were. There are some parts that are in there intentionally, to kind of give a flavor to what a lot of the text is like. Some of it is kind of interesting to think about: what does it mean to say someone's crazy, or paranoid? And there parts of it that are just flamingly paranoid.

But what's more moving and difficult about it is the feelings in it, the affect—you know, there are places where you sense this very profound despair. And then, this very exuberant mania for the new idea, or the turn in his thought. It's sort of exciting, but after a while, kind of difficult in its own way. He had a very tortured emotional life, and that emotional life—even though most of *The Exegesis* is very abstract—you know, it's idea, idea, idea, reference, reference, reference. Building a concept, building a system. But beneath it, there's this very powerful and difficult kind of emotional thing that's going on. And within the midst of that, there are clearings of extraordinary beauty and spiritual serenity, and of profound insight. So, it really rewards the long haul, because you really get an amazing sense of the different positions he had. And I look forward to the point—and it's probably not get a happen for a while yet—you know, the book came out in November—where people really sit down and read the whole thing, and they read it carefully, and they think about it. And then the questions people ask, the reactions they're going to have I think, are going to be really interesting.

MC: So, these are not all of his notes?

ED: No, no. The published abridgment in November is approximately one tenth of *The Exegesis*.

MC: Oh my God.

ED: A thousand-page volume is one tenth of what he did. Initially, we had this fantasy of a ten volume set, or whatever. But it's never going to come out in a book form like that. We've spoken to the daughters and Jonathan about it—that we make it available online. And if you can imagine that we have all of these texts just there, somehow transcribed, and we just let it loose, and people somehow find their way through it, and create their own pathways, their own sets of readings. In a way, that's the ideal form for the text.

MC: Eric, did Dick have any new prophecies in *The Exegesis*?

ED: There was nothing on the order of the whole Tagore event that happens towards the end of his life, where he becomes convinced that there is this savior in Sri Lanka, and then he gets inspired by Benjamin Krim's movement, and he becomes kind of overtly prophetic. He has a vision of the ecosystem as a kind of wounded, Christ-like being, which is very interesting; he had a very Gaian development towards the end that's pretty powerful in a general, prophetic sense.

What do we mean by prophecy? There is a specific, prophetic claim about what's around the corner, on the other side of the historical horizon, or there's sort of a general sense of prophecy, meaning a kind of deployment of the imagination in a quasi-historical way that sort of calls to task the current moment in history. And he very much does that at a number of points.

Probably the most interesting thing along these lines, though, is one thing we learn from *The Exegesis* is that *The Divine Invasion*—the second to last novel that he published—it emerges from a dream. Throughout *The Exegesis*, he records his dreams; I think nearly all of them are in the abridged edition. Pam was very much looking for what's going to be the juiciest stuff for people—the dreams, and the voice in his head that he heard at 4 o'clock in the morning, which he sometimes called the AI voice.

So, he has this dream about the church being taken over by Satan. It's a very Christian, paranoid, kind of dream. And he starts to unpack that, and as he unpacks that, you can tell he's starting to lay the mythological groundwork for *The Divine Invasion*. Which is a remarkable book in some ways, and is very flawed in other ways, and is not necessarily a satisfying read as a novel. But it has some great stuff in it, and reading what's going on in the back drop kind of intensifies its prophetic character.

MC: Did Dick go back to his other works, looking for clues, and say, "Aha! I just predicted myself again!"?

ED: Yeah, that's one of the most interesting things about it, especially from a literary perspective. I'm not really aware of any author who generated as much self-exegesis as Dick did. He wrote extensively about his earlier works, a concept for what the Valis was, or what happened to him on 2-3-74.

So, on the one hand, you have this very peculiar process of someone looking back at their rather significant corpus, and kind of weaving it together for their own reasons at that point in life, which is interesting in itself. But then, he's reading them generally in what you might think of as a kind of decoding manner. You know, all these beautiful ideas, these aesthetic ideas, these philosophical ideas that are in his novels, that's not generally what he was doing. He's generally like, "This book was the anticipation of the nature of reality," which is this construct that's run in God's mind, or it's a machine, or whatever his vision is. He sort of reduces, in a lot of ways, the complexity and richness of his own fiction. Especially the kind of emotional, personal, interpersonal, sociological—all the richness that's in his fiction, along with the crazy ideas and the absurd philosophical scenarios. In a way, you kind of lose that, and what they become is texts to be decoded, in order to support his latest vision of how reality might be taken together. It's not always like that.

To me, one of the most powerful and beautiful parts of *The Exegesis* occurs towards the very end, where he has this almost poetic meditation, once again on the fish symbol that initially triggered this whole series of experiences. Although, in some ways, reading *The Exegesis*, it's not always clear how much Dick was narrating and building a story about his own experiences. That aside, he meditates on the fish, on the pink light, and there's just a few phrases, it's almost a kind of poetic evocation of this event. And then, immediately after that, he mentions two things in the same citation.

He mentions Tagomi, the Japanese bureaucrat who has this moment when he's in the park in San Francisco, and he looks at the small piece of jewelry (like the fish jewelry), and he looks at the way it glints, and catches the light, and then he's transported into an alternate world, which is our world. So, he remembers this other moment that was in his own fiction, of another kind of object reflecting light, and inspiring a mystical state.

And then he mentions Jacob Boehme, who is of course, this foundational theosophical thinker of early modernity. Boehme had tremendous influence that's really only being acknowledged now on the course of Western philosophy. His basic, triadic, dialectical mode directly inspired Hegel, and Hegel's dialectic. So, there's some very powerful ways that Boehme influenced not just esotericism in the modern world, but also philosophy. The myth about Boehme, about his great mystical experience—once again, it was a humble object, a pewter dish that reflected light—that inspired or triggered his experience. So, here at the end of *The Exegesis*, Dick reflects on his own story of the mystical object that triggered his experience. And then he reflects on it in both the fiction that he produced, that in some ways set him in motion, and this kind of myth in the real history of esotericism. If you could reflect the light between all three of those objects, you would get to the truth of the matter.

MC: You would also have to describe somebody's breasts. That's always in any book that he writes.

ED: It's funny you should say that my friend, because I mention the great origin story of 2-3-74 that's repeated in every popular account of Dick's fiction. Writing about Phil Dick in the mainstream is also about writing about his life, writing about his experiences. The two are necessarily intertwined in a way. So, he tells that story a couple of times—I mean, he refers to the fish many times. And it's pretty clear the first time he describes it. My sense of it is the first time he tells the story, it's not like, "I was transfixed by the fish, and it compelled me to explore the visionary realm." He was like, "This chick is hot. I'm looking at her chest. I gotta say something. What am I going to say? I'll ask her about the fish." And I really think that's what was going on, but it's also appropriate, kind of perfect.

MC: What I find interesting beyond prophecy is, I don't think that Dick has caught up to our world, because of his popularity, but I think our world has caught up to the Dick mentality. I mean, don't you think that in this day and age, you're nobody unless you have your own pet conspiracy theory, like chemtrails, and we live in different realities, and stalking is not bad, and paranoia is not bad? It seems we are more and more like Dick. Do you agree with this?

ED: Yeah, I very much believe in that. One of my challenges as an intellectual scholar guy writing about this stuff is, I can analyze it, I can talk about literary history, and I can talk about psychology and cognitive psychology, and the history of religion. But on another level, I remain fascinated with his work because I think that it is actually prophetic. I don't know what that means. And I don't just mean that he, in a literalistic way, predicted our future. You know, in a lot of science fiction. Who predicted the Internet? Well, nobody did.

MC: Was it William Gibson?

ED: He kind of mapped it. But you know, at that point, it was already sort of on the horizon. Even there, you don't get anything like the cultural implosion factor of this thing. But that's another topic. In any case, you could say Arthur C Clarke had satellites. It's not really on that level; it's much more that he anticipated the kind of existential fabric of our experience. In that way, it's prophetic—not in a predictive, futurist way, a literalistic way—but more in an old school, biblical way. What a prophet did was not like, "Okay, this is exactly what's going to go down." There's some of that, but it's also the depiction of the visionary world. The depiction of the trauma of history that's just around the bend is a way of calling people out of their ordinary ways of going through the world, and confronting the deeper implications of what's going down. I think that's the way that he's a prophet. So, including the paranoia, including the breakdown, including the multiplicity of views, including the mixture of humor and despair and lust and nobility, and just really capturing the sort of fabric, there are these distinct moments of, "Is he looking through a crystal ball or something?"

There's one part of *The Galactic Pot Healer*, which is one of those non-top ten (for a lot of people) books that I think is really great, even though it falls apart, is the most Jungian of his novels, but it starts out with a guy in a cubicle. But he's at an office, and they have these pneumatic tubes, through which they are communicating. So, he's all alone in his cubicle, communicating with the world through these pneumatic tubes. Instead of doing his job, he's playing a game. And he's playing a game with someone else, who is somewhere else, by sending these messages back and forth through these pneumatic tubes. And they play this game of translating the name of a novel into another language, and then translating it back into English, and trying to figure out what the actual name is, which is so Internet. This is so much more Internet than William Gibson's Cyberspace.

And the Penfield mood organ in *Do Androids Dream Of Electric Sheep?* Now, we don't have a mood organ sitting at the breakfast table to dial up our sensibility, our attitude toward the day, but if you look at the way that people use food, music, iPhones, psychoactive drugs, meditation. The way people think about their own moods is increasingly instrumental in the way that he was describing. So when you see that, it's like a fantastic allegory for a very real condition that we' re experiencing in a way that I think is more true today in many ways. And often, it's unfortunate. Phil Dick didn't want to live in a Phil Dick universe; it's a rough ride!

MC: Another thing is, he and the Gnostics were skeptics about everything. And we live in the most skeptical times, don't you think? We don't trust anybody—not even our own minds anymore.

ED: I was thinking about that the other day. We were talking about civic religion, and how it wasn't that long ago that lots of people in the United States had this conscious or unconscious sense of this sort of identity of the nation as being this light unto the world. And that's just gone. And it's not just gone amongst liberal progressive people who mistrust—understandably—patriotism. Even among the patriots, they're just paranoid. They're crazy. They don't buy it, either.

MC: Paranoia is almost considered a good quality in people now.

ED: It's a badge of honor. And this one, I have to say, I saw coming. I did a piece about television in the early 90s. I had gotten online, and I was interested in the Internet. I was writing a television column for the *Village Voice*, and I was just thinking, "What's going to happen here?" Cable TV already had its many channels. So, I just started riffing on what was going to happen with the many channels. And, it was very clear to me back then: there is not going to be a mainstream. There was not going to be a sort of commonality that broadcast television produced in the collective psyche of the nation, that we could refer to the same dumb TV shows and the same news broadcasts; that that was just going to go away. And when it went away, you were going to get tons of reality tunnels, to use Robert Anton Wilson's phrase. You were going to get tons of conspiracies, of self-confirming feedback loops, that draw people in. And the more people they draw in, the more real it is, and that actually becomes an active program of reality. It's not even a reflection, or a story, or a myth—it's an actual running machine of information, concept, language, data feedback. And that's a pretty freaky situation.

MC: Yeah, it's a freaky world. Dick would be right at home.

ED: I think acquainting yourself with his work is a way of initiating yourself more deeply into the conundrum, which may or may not be something you want to do.

MC: It's a path that, when you are called, you know you are going to your own Golgotha. Either take heed, or don't.

ED: I've been thinking a lot in terms of the Gnostic stuff that you cover so thoroughly on your show. The kind of resonance between Dick and that the late antiquity moment—you know, one of his famous visions is that he looks out onto Orange County, and he sees Rome. Rome is superimposed on Southern California, circa nineteen seventy-four. And he didn't live that far away from Disneyland, so it was somewhere there in his geographical imagination. Yet he sees himself in Rome, and he has this sense that he's in communication with this second century Christian named Thomas, who actually takes him over, and drives the car for him. Some of it is very multiple personality stuff.

But I keep coming back to this: why Rome? Why this moment? Why the obsession with the time of Acts? Because, of course, that's also what he does. He thinks his most important reading of his earlier work of *Flow My Tears, The Policeman Said* takes place in the world of Acts; the book in the New Testament that follows the four Gospels, and that tells the story of the apostles after Christ is taken by the Galactic space shuttle back into heaven. So, there was something about this period that really resonated with him.

And the more I learn about that period, the more interesting the resonances become. If you think about very simple religions that we associate with hunter-gatherer civilizations, there is a sense of the cosmos as being a meaningful place. A place where you have your place, that the birds have their role, the stars have their role, and that in some sense, it all fits together. And the job of the priest, or the job of the shaman is to make sure that human culture and civilization reflects and tunes itself to the larger world. But somewhere, you find the sense that the cosmos is a big drag—and that sense of holistic, you know, everything has its place—is a trap, or a prison, or a wheel—a grinding wheel of punishment. You can talk about this in terms of Indian stuff too, but I'll leave that aside.

This great sense of suspicion, of skepticism. In a way, it's an experience that's rooted in the human mind. We can understand why any individual existentially would finally go, "Uh-uh. I'm not buying this!" At the same time, it also is very much about a certain phase of society, a certain phase of culture, a certain phase of looking at the world.

In a lot of ways, I think what happened to Dick, for whatever reason, his reading was not that deep in this material. He read the *Encyclopedia Britannica*. He read the *Encyclopedia of Philosophy*. He read Hans Jonas, and he knew some things, and he read the Bible. It's hard to know exactly what he had his hands on, or not. But it's not like he was a scholar, digging into the nitty-gritty of Clement's comments on the heretics. And yet, somehow he was able to boot up the same Gnostic computer, where you're recoding all the elements that you encounter in these counter normative myths.

MC: Like William Blake, or Grant Morrison.

ED: Exactly. There's this way in which he was really at home in that moment of late antique paranoia, where you want to escape. And I think a lot of it has to do with the way in which he understood fate, and understood determinism. Of course, that's the big question—not just in Gnosticism, not just in Christianity, but in a way, it's the thing that everybody's thinking about in the last few centuries of Rome. What's the nature of fate, and can you escape? What is the nature of necessity? Is necessity all? And if it's not, how do you avoid it?

Whether it's conceived of as astrological determinism, where the stars are controlling everything, and the predictions based on astrology are totally true, and there's nothing you can do about it, or whether the world itself is just a kind of an organic machine, that free will doesn't really exist, or is there some gap, some crack in the cosmos that lets some kind of freedom back in? For a lot of those thinkers, this was a mythological problem almost more than a philosophical one. But it hits people much more on an emotional level of myth, of story. In a way, Dick's stories and his thinking kind of "reboot" that problem, almost in those terms. He saw it as this black iron prison, or as a kind of cybernetic machine. There are some very frightening parts of *The Exegesis*, where his description of the trap is so insidious and psychologically real, that it's disturbing. You start getting the sense that once you step away from the surface reality of our world, all bets are off. Where do you actually stop and find the true story behind the mask? And once you see that's kind of an abyss, then it's a very difficult place to be. Sometimes he was in that place, and articulating it very well.

So, it makes those Christian stories, those Gnostic stories, those Jewish apocalyptic stories, the stories about the Torah—they're all very relevant, they're all very resonant. And for me, those things are just as much a part of our moment as biotechnology and the Internet, and all these postmodern, onward singularity kinds of technological, cultural environments. That moment of late antiquity is still very much with us.

MC: I was talking to Jeff Kripal, your boss, and I said, "Jeff, Dick never figured out 2-3-74 in his Exegesis, so it seems like it was a waste of time. It seems like all he did was go on a loop." And Jeff said, "Well, maybe he did figure it out. Maybe the reality is, we are all in a loop for eternity, and you have to accept it." You know, Joseph Campbell said, "There is no meaning to life; why should there be meaning?" In Eastern traditions, and the Greeks, the universe was eternal, and just recycled itself. But that's something our Western minds reject passionately. So, I like Jeff's idea, synthesis, antithesis, and thesis. Or do you have another take? Do you think Dick figured it out?

ED: No, I don't think he figured it out. I think he suffered the conundrum. In the last eight years of his life, he didn't publish as much fiction or essays as he did in the 60s, when he was incredibly prolific, until he started thinking about *The Exegesis*. This guy was clearly staying up all night, may any nights in a row, scribbling, scribbling, scribbling, in this obsessive manner. there might even be hypergraphia.

People of a more reductionist frame of mind say that what happened to Dick was a temporal lobe epilepsy, and it's clear that the temporal lobe epilepsy does have relationships in some cases with hyper religiosity, and particularly hypergraphia, where you write all the time, like a maniac. So, you can even mythologize him, and it fits into a category in our reductionist spaces. Clearly, there is some sort of pathological aspect with him going around and around and around.

And it's not repetitive in the sense he's repeating the same thing over and over. It's repetitive in the sense that he's algorithmically running through possibilities. He'll run through something, and he'll get to a kind of end, or a defeat, or a double bind, and he can't get out of it. And you could just see him go, "But here's the idea!" He does that over and over and over again. And you're like, "What do you mean? You've been doing this for years, man! You should know now that you don't have it, and you're not going to have it. You just keep running this machine over and over again, with variation. Sometimes it goes to interesting places, sometimes it goes to paranoid places, sometimes it goes to very depressing places, and a lot of times it's very repetitive." But it always starts out the same way: "Now I have it! Here's the idea!" And he rolls, and you can see it, and he has a big exclamation point.

So, there's this sense that the repetition is very much iterative, it's like a machine that keeps going over and over again; in a way, paranoia is kind of a machine, it's an engine for making connections, and for building stories on top of these connections that you've made. So, it's a connection machine, in a way. And in a way, you start going, this is it; he's actually modeling this looping process, this is eternal return that we're stuck in.

MC: Sometimes, I think they're right: Around and around we go.

ED: Sometimes I think they are right, as well. There's a sort of bleak Gnosis that I occasionally contemplate. There is a kind of freedom, but the freedom comes only in this profound acceptance, not only in the determined course through linear history, but in the Nietzschean sense, that it's just like this again. All you get is a certain kind of spiritual acceptance, or some kind of affirmation. That's what Nietzsche was on about. Your only way out is to just radically affirm your life, in all of its mess, and all of its confusion, and all of its fear towards mortality, and all the same mistakes you've made over and over again in your struggle. In a way, that's the ethic you get out of reading Phil Dick. You don't get a sense of triumphalism. You don't get a sense of utter disaster, even though there are often nightmarish worlds. They usually end with a sense of people kind of like, "Well, we're all made of dust, but we're not doing so bad after all," to paraphrase. And you know, there's a sense that's very valuable, although it is a little bit challenging.

MC: I'm going to stick to my paranoid conspiracy theory that the demiurge took him out because he was getting too close to the secrets of the universe. But Eric, I think that's all the time we have today. I'd like to thank you very much for coming again to Aeon Byte, and giving us a lot of Dick.

ED: [laughs] Yeah, there's no way to avoid it; I embrace the jokes. Hey, it was great to be here.

39265574R00158

Made in the USA
Lexington, KY
16 May 2019